Theories of Chromatic and Enharmonic Music in Late 16th Century Italy

Studies in Musicology, No. 10

George Buelow, Series Editor
Professor of Musicology
Indiana University

Other Titles in This Series

Theories of Chromatic and Enharmonic Music in Late 16th Century Italy

by
Karol Berger

umi
RESEARCH PRESS

Produced and distributed by
UMI Research Press
an imprint of
University Microfilms International
Ann Arbor, Michigan 48106

Library of Congress Cataloging in Publication Data

Berger, Karol, 1947-
   Theories of chromatic and enharmonic music in
late sixteenth century Italy.

   (Studies in musicology ; no. 10)
   Bibliography: p.
   Includes index.
   1. Music—Italy—History and criticism. 2. Music—Theory
—16th-17th centuries. 3. Chromatic alteration (Music)
I. Title. II. Series.

ML290.2.B47   780'.945   79-24734
ISBN 0-8357-1065-3

Contents

Acknowledgments

I should like to express my deep gratitude to Professor Claude V. Palisca, the adviser for this study, who in addition to his sober and informed guidance generously put at my disposal many of his microfilms and transcriptions of documents.

I received helpful suggestions from Professor Allen Forte and a transcription of Ghiselin Danckert's treatise from Miss Heather G. Anderson; their help is gratefully acknowledged. My appreciation for technical assistance goes to the staffs of the John Herrick Jackson Music Library, Sterling Memorial Library, and Beinecke Rare Book and Manuscript Library at Yale University, and for financial assistance to Yale University.

Introduction

Italian chromaticism of the second half of the sixteenth century continues to be an object of vital interest for modern musicologists at least since the publication of Theodor Kroyer's pioneering study, *Die Anfänge der Chromatik im italienischen Madrigal des XVI. Jahrhunderts*.[1] The great expansion of musicological research since Kroyer's time has considerably increased our familiarity with the chromatic repertory and with the late sixteenth-century Italian music in general, as well as our insight into the technical and aesthetic principles governing this music. Yet, in spite of these great advances, or perhaps because of them, musicologists have not been able to create a commonly acceptable theory explaining the late Renaissance chromaticism, and even a cursory glance at recent literature dealing with the problem reveals that the repertory in question is at least as controversial and baffling today as it was at the time of its creation.[2]

Let it be said at once that the present study does not undertake to resolve these controversies. Its much more modest aim is to gain an insight into the nature of late Renaissance Italian chromaticism through careful reading and interpretation of theoretical treatises written at approximately the same time and at the same places where the repertory which interests us was created. The same basic questions will be examined: a) what is the nature of chromatic musical structures, and how does what is chromatic differ from what is not chromatic; b) in what ways is chromatic music practiced, and how should it or should it not be practiced; and c) why it is, should, or should not be practiced in these ways. Thus we shall learn the opinions of some sixteenth-century theorists on what chromatic music is, how is it made, and why.

It can be reasonably expected that knowledge of such opinions will help us to understand the artistic and intellectual climate in which chromatic pieces were written, to reconstruct the aesthetic and possibly even philosophical beliefs which motivated their creation. It is not at all clear, however, in what sense sixteenth-century theorists may help us to understand the music itself, to grasp its technical principles, especially if what we are aiming at is more than just a reconstruction of the manner in which musicians themselves consciously thought about their music. It is not necessary, after all, that they understood music written at their time any better than twentieth-century musicologists might. It is possible that the theorists shared the unconscious ways of experiencing this music with other musicians and cultivated listeners of their time, but it does not follow that they were able to make these ways of experiencing conscious and to conceptualize them successfully. History of musical thought provides many examples of theoretical concepts formulated a long time after the practical use of musical procedures and forms which these concepts were meant to explain. Consequently, I do not think that we have to imitate sixteenth-century theoretical concepts and to refrain from introducing our own when trying to explain sixteenth-century music. Our musical, historical, and theoretical experience far exceeds those of a Renaissance theorist and our theoretical concepts might penetrate old music deeper than his. It does not follow, however, that we may disregard old theorists completely and to create totally arbitrary and anachronistic theories of our own. A historian's task should be to recreate as much as possible the unconscious manner in which the music of a given era was experienced by the community which produced it. When explaining this music he does not necessarily have to use the concepts of old theorists, since these concepts may describe the musical experience inadequately, but he has to study old theoretical treatises very carefully, because more than any other type of documents they can reveal to him the historical modes of hearing and experiencing music. When describing these modes of hearing, he will use old theoretical concepts if he deems them adequate, or he will create his own. In this last case he will create tools for understanding old music more powerful than those available at the time of its creation, but he will escape the danger of subjecting this music to an arbitrary and ahistorical manner of explanation. Whatever theory will be created on the basis of an analysis of old treatises, it will have to be treated just as a hypothesis to be tested, and if necessary modified, in analyses of music itself.

The first aim of the following study is to create such an explanatory hypothesis for late sixteenth-century chromaticism. The analytical testing of the hypothesis lies beyond the scope of this study, although I certainly hope to undertake such testing in the future. In the process of creating the hypothesis I shall also describe the divergent manners in which the sixteenth-century theorists themselves understood contemporary chromatic music. And finally, I shall try to extract from the analyzed treatises whatever information I can on the beliefs that motivated sixteenth-century musicians to cultivate this type of composition.

The final aim is to understand chromatic music and, as I have explained, to incorporate in this understanding the mode of hearing and experiencing this music by its contemporaries, although it may transcend their manners of making this mode conscious, of transforming experience into understanding. To understand a musical work in this sense means to show that a particular group of auditory stimuli is organized in such a way that they can be grasped as a coherent whole and to demonstrate the principles of this organization. There can be little doubt that the organization of a sixteenth-century work is primarily tonal, that it is the organization of various pitches in certain specific ways, whereas organization of other values (temporal, timbral, dynamic) is of secondary importance. Chromaticism is an aspect of tonal organization. We shall not understand the role of chromaticism before we know the basic principles of tonal organization in the sixteenth century.

I shall call these basic principles of a tonal organization a tonal system. A tonal system comprises the material of all steps and intervals available to a composer and the way in which this material is organized before any actual composition takes place. My reading of the sixteenth-century treatises will be directed primarily at discovering the tonal systems they propose and establishing the role of chromaticism within them. However, since the standard terms of music theory are often quite ambiguous, it might be useful to precede the investigation with a short clarification of the exact sense in which some basic terms will be used:

a) *Step*. The Renaissance theorists did not know an absolute pitch standard.[3] When they talked about a definite step (e.g., a′) it was not an absolutely determined point in the pitch-continuum that they had in mind (i.e., a point which could be unambiguously defined as to its physical properties; e.g., a′ = 440 cps), but rather a point which is relative to all other points of the gamut and which is defined by those relations (e.g., a′ is a perfect fifth higher than d′ and a perfect fourth lower than d′′, etc.). Owing to the introduction of pitch standard modern usage is more confused, and today relative and absolute definitions of a step exist side by side. I shall imitate here the Renaissance theorists and define steps not in relation to a pitch standard but only by their intervallic relations to one another.

b) *Interval*. Since steps are defined by means of intervals and not the reverse, it follows that intervals are logically prior to steps and that the sixteenth-century tonal system should be described in terms of intervallic material available to a composer and its pre-compositional organization. The octave is the absolute reference point of the whole intervallic system. The primacy of the octave derives from the practice of treating two notes one or more octaves apart as if they were unisons with respect to computing intervals as consonances or dissonances. As the result, two intervals distant by an octave are equivalent and two steps distant by an octave are equivalent. Late-Renaissance counterpoint shows no difference in the way in which intervals distant by an octave are used. The rules of counterpoint that may be derived from analysis of sixteenth-century compositions show that the way in which an interval is used depends primarily on whether it belongs to perfect consonances (with certain exceptions concerning the use of the fourth), imperfect consonances, or dissonances. The octave is the only interval which added to any perfect consonance produces a perfect consonance, added to any imperfect consonance produces an imperfect consonance, and added to any dissonance produces a dissonance.

c) *Gamut* is the set of all intervals in a given tonal system. The Renaissance theories discussed below almost universally imply the organization of the gamut on two levels:

d) *Generic level of organization.* The theorists' understanding of the term "genus" (usually qualified with the adjective "diatonic," "chromatic," or "enharmonic") stands for obvious reasons at the center of our interest, and it will be discussed later in detail. For now it will suffice to indicate that genus is one of the two principles of gamut organization. It implies the arrangement of some intervals of the gamut into a series which may be defined by the sizes of its consecutive intervals and by their relative positions. For example, the diatonic series may be defined as consisting of whole tones and semitones placed so that semitones are separated from each other alternately by two and by three consecutive whole tones.

e) *The octave-species level of organization.* The second principle of gamut organization is the octave-species. It arranges some intervals of the gamut into a series which may be defined by the sizes of its consecutive intervals and by their absolute positions. Note that the definition of the absolute position implies necessarily the definition of the relative positions as well. Thus, species is defined in exactly the same way as genus with the additional clause of absolute positions. For example, the species of the Dorian mode may be described as consisting of whole tones and semitones placed so that semitones are separated from each other alternately by two and by three consecutive whole tones and that the first two semitones occupy the second and the sixth positions. It might be said figuratively that genus is a "circular" series with no beginning nor end, whereas species is a "linear" series with a fixed starting and terminating point.

I

Nicola Vicentino
and Ghiselin Danckerts

Nicola Vicentino was one of the few musicians of his era to devote his life almost exclusively to the advocacy of non-diatonicism and the first writer in the Renaissance to discuss all aspects of chromatic music at great length. His writings expressed characteristic attitudes and tendencies among musicians of his generation and of several generations to come. Thus it is appropriate to start with an examination of his theory.

Nicola Vicentino was born in 1511 in Vicenza near Venice, and it was in Venice that he received his musical education as a student of the famous composer Adrian Willaert.[1] Willaert assumed the position of *maestro di cappella* of St. Mark's on December 12, 1527[2], and it is possible that Vicentino became his student in the late 1520s or early 1530s. Willaert's interest in the chromatic and enharmonic genera is well documented,[3] and it is likely that Vicentino developed his own interest under his teacher's influence. According to one contemporary observer, Vicentino's experiments in the practical use of the non-diatonic genera date approximately since at least 1534.[4]

In 1549 he went to Rome accompanying Cardinal Ippolito d'Este of Ferrara as a household musician. It is not known when he entered the Cardinal's service, but it is known that he had previously given instruction in non-diatonic music to several members of the d'Este family, notably to Duke's Ercole II son, Prince Alfonso. In Rome he was reluctant to make his secret knowledge public, since—according to an unsympathetic observer—he wanted to obtain an adequate position (for instance, in the Papal chapel) first.[5] Finally, on October 25, 1549 he agreed to instruct several persons of Cardinal Ridolfi's household in non-diatonic genera, after they had promised not to reveal his secrets for ten years.

In mid-1551, after a musical performance at a private academy in Rome, Vicentino asserted that no composer of his time knew the true genus of any commonly sung contemporary composition, provoking the opposition of the Portuguese musician Vicente Lusitano. The famous public dispute ensued.[6] After several meetings, held between June 2 and 7, 1551, the judges, two singers in the Papal chapel, Bartolomeo Escobedo and Ghiselin Danckerts, gave the unanimous verdict in favor of Lusitano.

Very little is known about one of the protagonists in the dispute, the

Portuguese musician Vicente Lusitano.[7] His position in the controversy is known from the documents gathered by Danckerts and Vicentino. His little treatise, *Introduttione facilissima et novissima*. . . , published for the first time after the controversy, does not add anything of interest as far as his views on chromaticism are concerned.[8] It was one of the judges, Ghiselin Danckerts, the Flemish composer and member of the Papal chapel from 1538 to 1565, who gradually emerged as the true opponent of Vicentino in the eyes of historians, thanks to his treatise which, like Vicentino's own, was devoted to the vindication of its author's position in the controversy. His *Trattato sopra una differentia musicale*, several handwritten versions of which, written during the decade that followed the debate, are preserved in the Roman Biblioteca Vallicelliana, Ms. R 56, describes the controversy and presents the appropriate documents (Part I), explains the author's views on various theoretical topics, in particular that of the genera (Part II), and sets forth his conservative point of view on chromaticism and other ''abuses'' of contemporary practice (Part III).[9]

Not long after the dispute the Cardinal and Vicentino left Rome, to return only in 1555. In this year Vicentino's systematic defense of the position he took during the famous dispute of 1551 and presentation of his theoretical views in general appeared under the title *L'antica musica ridotta alla moderna prattica*.

According to Vincenzo Galilei, around 1560 Vicentino organized public concerts of his chromatic and enharmonic music in principal cities of Italy.[10] In 1561 he published a broadsheet in Venice, advertising a diatonic-chromatic -enharmonic instrument of his construction, an *arciorgano*.[11] By 1563 he left the Cardinal and became the chapel master at the Cathedral of Vicenza, where he stayed for two years. He spent his final years in Milan and died there around 1576, according to Ercole Bottrigari's testimony.[12]

I shall discuss Vicentino's thought by beginning with his tonal system and related topics, continuing with his theory of composition and performance, and concluding with aesthetics.[13] My investigation will be directed at three questions: 1) What is the complete set of intervals postulated by the theorist for use in musical practice and what is the internal structure of this set, that is, the tonal system? 2) How is this tonal system to be used in composition and in performance? 3) Why was this particular tonal system chosen and why were certain practical applications proposed? I hope by this discussion to throw some light on these fundamental problems: the theorist's understanding of what is diatonic and what is not, his ideas concerning the possibility of transcending pure diatonicism in practice, and his reasons for advocating non-diatonicism.

I. THEORY: THE TONAL SYSTEM, ITS NOTATION, AND TUNING; THE *ARCHICEMBALO*

The Tonal System

The gamut

Chapters 14-42 of Vicentino's Book I, "Concerning Musical Practice,"[14] describe all the intervals available in his system up to an octave, that is his gamut. There are thirty-one different intervals within an octave resulting from the division of the octave into thirty-one equal parts. Vicentino gives them the following names:

1. minor diesis
2a. major diesis
2b. minor semitone (the chromatic equivalent of the major enharmonic diesis)
3. major semitone
4. minor whole tone
5. whole tone
6. major whole tone
7. less than minor third
8. minor third
9. more than minor third
10. major third
11. more than major third
12. [less than fourth]
13. fourth
14. more than fourth
15. tritone
16. diminished fifth
17. more than diminished fifth
18. fifth
19. more than fifth
20. [less than minor sixth]
21. minor sixth
22. more than minor sixth
23. major sixth
24. more than major sixth
25. [less than minor seventh]
26. minor seventh
27. more than minor seventh
28. major seventh
29. more than major seventh
30. [less than octave]
31. octave[15]

Apart from those listed above, Vicentino introduces one more interval, half as large as the minor diesis, and calls it comma.[16] In order to understand the peculiar status of the comma, one has to realize that for an interval to be considered a part of a gamut it has to have a definite function in the tonal system which this gamut represents. Now a gamut does not exist in itself; it is, so to speak, the result of the constitutive structures of the tonal system which organize the gamut, in this case, of the genera and modes. Since the comma has no function whatsoever in the formation of the genera and modes, it cannot be considered a part of the gamut. It is not an interval of the tonal system but, as we shall see, it has a role to play on the level of the tuning system.

The genera

The three Vicentinian genera are introduced in Book I, Chs. 6-8,[17] where the formation of the diatonic, chromatic, and enharmonic tetrachords is discussed. The diatonic tetrachord consists of two whole tones and one major semitone. The chromatic tetrachord combines two consecutive semitones, the first major and the second minor, with a minor third. The enharmonic tetrachord consists of two consecutive enharmonic dieses, the first minor and the second major, and a major third. Vicentino adds, however, that in the enharmonic genus not only the major but also the minor semitone can be divided into two enharmonic dieses. A correct interpretation of this remark is impossible at this stage of our discussion.

There are various reasons accounting for the fact that Vicentino introduces the genera in the form of the tetrachords, the most obvious one being that he follows a well-established tradition which goes back into the classical sources. At this point, however, it is important to reconstruct his genera, and in a system respecting octave equivalence it is not possible to arrive at a clear understanding of the genera on the basis of their tetrachordal representation alone. One has to look for representation of the genera within the limits of an octave. An excellent starting point comes in Book III which deals with the modes. Vicentino enumerates there all the species of diatonic, chromatic, and enharmonic fourths, fifths, and octaves (that is, series of intervals which add up to a fourth, a fifth, and an octave, respectively) that are available in his system. The discovery of the structure common to all possible octave representations of a given genus would enable us to formulate a definition of this genus according to Vicentino. Unfortunately the theorist's examples are full of mistakes, and, for this reason, we shall first have to reconstruct painstakingly their intended forms.

Only three different species of fourths, four species of fifths, and seven octave-species are possible in each of the three genera.[18] The diatonic, chromatic, and enharmonic species of fourth are discussed in Chapters 2, 36, and 45 of Book III, respectively:[19]

DIATONIC	CHROMATIC	ENHARMONIC
1. T S T	1. S m3 s	1. d M3 D
2. S T T	2. m3 s S	2. M3 D d
3. T T S	3. S s m3	3. d D M3

(I use the following symbols: d = minor diesis;
                                D = major diesis;
                                s = minor semitone;
                                S = major semitone;
                                T = whole tone;
                               m3 = minor third;
                               M3 = major third.

Throughout this book intervallic series are always presented in ascending forms.)

In Book I, Ch. 7[20] we have been told that in the chromatic tetrachord the major semitone comes before the minor one. Now, however, we see that this is not the only possible order: in the first and second species of fourth the minor semitone precedes the major one; in the third the reverse is true.[21] The same inconsistency will be observed among the species of chromatic fifths and octaves. One has to conclude that two versions of each chromatic series are possible: in one the minor semitone always precedes the major one, in the other the opposite order is maintained. The examination of the chromatic species of fifths and octaves will show that the two orders never occur within a single series, which suggests that for Vicentino such a mixture is inadmissible. Thus I would tend to supplement the list of the possible chromatic species of fourths as follows:

1.	S	m3	s	or	s	m3	S
2.	m3	s	S	or	m3	S	s
3.	S	s	m3	or	s	S	m3

The order of the minor and the major enharmonic dieses within an enharmonic species of fourth presents a similar problem and lends itself to a similar solution. It seems that two versions of each species of fourth are possible, depending on whether the minor enharmonic diesis precedes or follows the major one:

1.	d	M3	D	or	D	M3	d
2.	M3	D	d	or	M3	d	D
3.	d	D	M3	or	D	d	M3

Furthermore, Vicentino explains that each chromatic and enharmonic species of fourth is a transformation of a diatonic one. This transformation is effected so that the lesser interval in the diatonic order (S) becomes a greater one in the chromatic and enharmonic orders (m3 and M3, respectively), whereas the greater diatonic interval (T) becomes lesser in the chromatic and enharmonic series (s or S and d or D, respectively).[22] In this way the first species of diatonic fourth is transformed into the first chromatic and the first enharmonic, the second diatonic into the second chromatic and second enharmonic, and so on. For example, we might represent the transformations of the first species of fourth in the following manner:

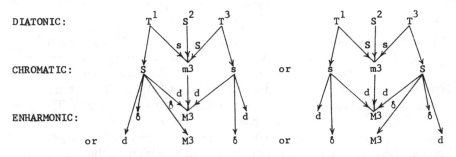

(δ = either D or dd. Superscripts are assigned arbitrarily to the diatonic intervals for reasons which will be explained later. T^1 = the whole tone which always precedes the semitone, regardless of which species of fourth is considered; T^3 = the whole tone which always follows the semitone.)

The diagram shows that each diatonic whole tone, when passing to the chromatic level, becomes subdivided into two semitones, one major and one minor. Similarly, each major chromatic semitone becomes subdivided on the enharmonic level into two enharmonic dieses, one major and one minor. The minor chromatic semitone may remain unsubdivided, changing itself into the major enharmonic diesis. We shall recall, however, the remark that Vicentino made in Ch. 8 of Book I: "Then, the enharmonic genus which I use is not divided in the same way as is that of Boethius, since he divides only the minor semitone and I divide both the major and the minor, according to what happens to be the convenient usage of various intervals and consonances in a composition."[23] Thus the minor chromatic semitone may also become subdivided into two minor enharmonic dieses. This double possibility of the minor chromatic semitone is represented on my diagram by δ which stands for: "either D or dd." It should be clear now that the two versions of each of the enharmonic species of fourth should be thus modified:

1. d   M3 δ or δ M3   d
2. M3 δ d   or   M3   d δ
3. d δ M3   or δ d   M3

Diagrams similar to the one above may also be constructed for the second and third species of fourth. In each species of fourth the diatonic semitone is changed into the chromatic minor third and enharmonic major third, the first diatonic whole tone (T^1) is changed into the chromatic semitone (major or minor) and enharmonic diesis (major or two minor ones or one minor), and the third diatonic whole tone (T^3) is changed into the chromatic semitone (minor or major) and enharmonic diesis (minor or major or two minor ones). The following is the general formula for the transformations of the species of fourths:

DIATONIC	CHROMATIC	ENHARMONIC
$T^1 \longrightarrow$ S	$\left\{\begin{array}{l} s \longrightarrow \flat \\ m3 \longrightarrow M3 \\ S \longrightarrow d \end{array}\right.$ or	$\left\{\begin{array}{l} d \\ M3 \\ \flat \end{array}\right.$
$S^2 \longrightarrow$ m3 $\Bigg\}$ or		
$T^3 \longrightarrow$ s		

Note that the vertical columns represent the only possible versions of the species of fourth. Thus if T^1 becomes s, then T^3 has to be changed into S, and vice versa.

The diatonic, chromatic, and enharmonic species of fifths are discussed in Book III, Chs. 3, 37, and 46, respectively:[24]

DIATONIC	CHROMATIC	ENHARMONIC
1. T S T T	1. S m3 s S s	1. d M3 D d d D d
2. S T T T	2. m3 S s S s	2. M3 D d d D d d
3. T T T S	3. S s S s m3	3. d d D d d D M3
4. T T S T	4. S s m3 S s	4. d D M3 d d D d

The rules of transformation from the diatonic to the chromatic and enharmonic levels remain the same: a) the small diatonic interval is changed into the large chromatic and enharmonic ones; b) the diatonic whole tone is subdivided into two chromatic semitones (major and minor), the major chromatic semitone is subdivided into enharmonic dieses (major and minor), and the minor chromatic semitone may either be changed into the major enharmonic diesis or it may be subdivided into two minor enharmonic dieses. The following diagram represents the transformations of the first species of fifth.

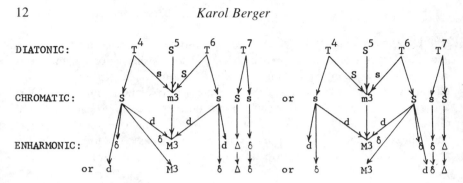

(Δ either δ d or d δ. T^4 = the whole tone which always precedes the semitone, regardless of which species of fifth is considered; T^6 = the whole tone which always follows the semitone; T^7 = the whole tone always placed between two whole tones.)

Similar diagrams may be constructed for the second, third, and fourth species of fifth. In each species of fifth the diatonic semitone is changed into the chromatic minor third and enharmonic major third, the fourth diatonic whole tone (T^4) is changed into the chromatic semitone (major or minor) and enharmonic diesis (major or two minor ones or one minor), the sixth diatonic whole tone (T^6) is changed into the chromatic semitone (minor or major) and enharmonic diesis (minor or major or two minor ones), and, finally, the seventh diatonic whole tone (T^7) is subdivided into two chromatic semitones (one major and one minor), and then the major chromatic semitone is subdivided into two enharmonic dieses (one major or two minor ones and one minor), whereas the minor one may either be changed into the major enharmonic diesis or subdivided into two minor enharmonic dieses. The following is the general formula for the transformations of the species of fifths:

ENHARMONIC		CHROMATIC	DIATONIC	CHROMATIC	ENHARMONIC	
δ		d ← s ←	T^4	s → δ		d
M3		M3 ← m3 ←	S^5	m3 → M3		M3
d	or	δ ← s ←	T^6	S → d	or	δ
$\Delta\delta$		$\Delta\delta$ ← Ss ←	T^7	sS → $\delta\Delta$		$\delta\Delta$

The reader will notice now that there is a mistake in Vicentino's fourth chromatic and enharmonic species of fifth. They should read Ss S m3 s and Δ δ δ M3 d. It goes without saying that two versions of each chromatic and four of each enharmonic species of fifth are available.

Only now does it become possible to reconstruct the intended form of seven diatonic, chromatic, and enharmonic octave-species. These are presented in Book III, Chs. 4, 38, 47, respectively:[25]

```
      DIATONIC              CHROMATIC                      ENHARMONIC

1. T S T T S T T    1. S  m3 s  S  m3 s  S  s    1. d  M3 D  d  M3 d  d  d  D  d  d
2. S T T S T T T    2. m3 S  s  m3 S  s  S  s    2. M3 D  d  M3 D  d  d  D  d  d
3. T T S T T T S    3. S  s  m3 S  s  S  s  m3   3. d  D  M3 d  D  d  d  d  D  M3
4. T S T T T S T    4. S  m3 s  S  s  S  m3 s    4. d  M3 d  d  d  M3 D  d  D  d  d
5. S T T T S T T    5. m3 S  s  S  s  m3 S  s    5. M3 D  d  d  M3 d  d  D  d  d
6. T T T S T T S    6. S  s  S  s  m3 S  s  m3   6. d  D  d  M3 d  d  M3 d  d  d  D
7. T T S T T S T    7. S  s  m3 S  s  S  m3 s    7. d  D  M3 d  D  M3 d  D  d  d
```

Vicentino explains that each octave-species results from combining one species
of fourth and one species of fifth in the following way:

```
1st species of fourth  +  1st species of fifth  =  1st octave-species
2nd   "      "    "     +  2nd   "      "    "    =  2nd    "      "
3rd   "      "    "     +  3rd   "      "    "    =  3rd    "      "
1st   "      "  fifth   +  1st   "      " fourth  =  4th    "      "
2nd   "      "    "     +  2nd   "      "    "    =  5th    "      "
3rd   "      "    "     +  3rd   "      "    "    =  6th    "      "
4th   "      "    "     +  1st   "      "    "    =  7th    "      "
```

Accordingly, the seventh chromatic octave-species has to be corrected to S s S
m3 s S m3 s, Vicentino's mistake having resulted automatically from his
previous one in the fourth chromatic species of fifth. Of the enharmonic octave-
species only the first three are free from mistakes. The correct chromatic and
enharmonic octave-species (together with the alternative variants) should read as
follows:

CHROMATIC

```
1. S  m3 s  S  m3 s  Ss      or    s  m3 S  s  m3 S  sS
2. m3 s  S  m3 s  Ss S       or    m3 S  s  m3 S  sS s
3. s  S  m3 s  Ss S  m3      or    S  s  m3 S  sS s  m3
4. S  m3 s  Ss S  m3 s       or    s  m3 S  sS s  m3 S
5. m3 s  Ss S  m3 s  S       or    m3 S  sS s  m3 S  s
6. s  Ss S  m3 s  S  m3      or    S  sS s  m3 S  s  m3
7. Ss S  m3 s  S  m3 s       or    sS s  m3 S  s  m3 S
```

ENHARMONIC

```
1. ♪ M3 d  ♪ M3 d  Δδ    or    d  M3 ♪ d  M3 ♪ Δδ    or
2. M3 d  ♪ M3 d  Δδ ♪    or    M3 ♪ d  M3 ♪ Δδ d     or
3. d  ♪ M3 d  Δδ ♪ M3    or    ♪  d  M3 ♪ Δδ d  M3    or
4. ♪ M3 d  Δδ ♪ M3 d     or    d  M3 ♪ Δδ d  M3 ♪     or
5. M3 d  Δδ ♪ M3 d  ♪    or    M3 ♪ Δδ d  M3 ♪ d      or
6. d  Δδ ♪ M3 d  ♪ M3    or    ♪  Δδ d  M3 ♪ d  M3    or
7. Δδ ♪ M3 d  ♪ M3 d     or    Δδ d  M3 ♪ d  M3 ♪     or
```

```
1. d  M3 ♪ d  M3 ♪ δΔ    or    ♪  M3 d  ♪ M3 d  δΔ    or
2. M3 ♪ d  M3 ♪ δΔ d     or    M3 d  ♪ M3 d  δΔ ♪     or
3. ♪  d  M3 ♪ δΔ d  M3    or    d  ♪ M3 d  δΔ ♪ M3     or
4. d  M3 ♪ δΔ d  M3 ♪     or    ♪  M3 d  δΔ ♪ M3 d     or
5. M3 ♪ δΔ d  M3 ♪ d      or    M3 d  δΔ ♪ M3 d  ♪     or
6. ♪  δΔ d  M3 ♪ d  M3    or    d  δΔ ♪ M3 d  ♪ M3     or
7. δΔ d  M3 ♪ d  M3 ♪     or    δΔ ♪ M3 d  ♪ M3 d
```

Having finally arrived at the correct forms of all the octave-species, we may try now to define the structure common to all seven of those in each genus. This common structure can be described in exactly those terms which I have proposed for the definition of a genus, since the consecutive intervals used and their relative positions are the same in all seven octave-species. Thus the diatonic genus according to Vicentino consists of whole tones and major semitones placed so that the semitones are separated from each other alternately by two and by three consecutive whole tones. The chromatic genus consists of minor thirds and pairs of semitones, one major and one minor, placed so that the thirds are separated from each other alternately by one and by two pairs of semitones. There are two versions of the genus, depending on which of the two possible orders within a pair of semitones is chosen, but both orders of semitones may not occur within a single series. In order to make the definition of the enharmonic genus a little less cumbersome than would be feasible otherwise, I shall use some of the symbols introduced above: The enharmonic genus consists of minor thirds and two distinct groups of dieses, *a* and *b*, placed so that the thirds are separated from each other alternately by *a* and by *b*. There are four versions of the genus:

$$
\begin{aligned}
&1. \quad \underline{a} = d \; \delta, \quad \underline{b} = d \; \Delta\delta \; \delta; \\
&2. \quad \underline{a} = d \; \delta, \quad \underline{b} = d \; \delta\Delta \; \delta; \\
&3. \quad \underline{a} = \delta \; d, \quad \underline{b} = \delta \; \Delta\delta \; d; \\
&4. \quad \underline{a} = \delta \; d, \quad \underline{b} = \delta \; \delta\Delta \; d.
\end{aligned}
$$

Note that within a single version the same interval (d or δ) always precedes the thirds and the same interval (δ or d) always follows the thirds, but the preceding and following interval always differ one from another. Thus one might correctly conclude that the enharmonic genus has only two versions (one with δ preceding, and the other with δ following the thirds), each having its two subvariants (depending on whether the subdivisions of the diatonic T^7 result in $\Delta\delta$ or in $\delta \Delta$).

It might be useful at this point to sum up the two principles which govern the generic transformations:

1. Each diatonic interval becomes subdivided or changed on the chromatic level, and each chromatic interval becomes subdivided and/or changed on the enharmonic level in the following way:
    a) The diatonic whole tone (T) is subdivided on the chromatic level either into a major semitone followed by a minor one (Ss) or vice versa (sS);
    b) The diatonic major semitone (S) is changed on the chromatic level into the chromatic major semitone (S);
    c) The chromatic major semitone (S) is subdivided on the enharmonic

level into a major enharmonic diesis followed by a minor one, or vice versa, or three minor dieses (i.e., it is subdivided into Δ = either δ d or d δ = Dd or dD or ddd);

d) The minor chromatic semitone (s) is changed or subdivided on the enharmonic level into either a major enharmonic diesis, or into two minor ones (i.e., it is changed or subdivided into δ = either D or dd).

2. Each generic series consists of seven relative positions which on the diatonic level are filled by single intervals, whereas on the chromatic and enharmonic levels each position is filled by a single interval or by an intervallic group. An interval of a given position within the diatonic series may be transformed into no more than two different chromatic intervals, or groups, and similarly an interval, or group, of a given position within the chromatic series may be transformed into no more than two different enharmonic intervals, or groups. The specific transformation made within one position at any given level may limit the possible transformations in other positions at this level according to the following formula:

ENHARMONIC 1st subvar.		CHROMATIC 1st version	DIATONIC	CHROMATIC 2nd version	ENHARMONIC 2nd subvar.	
1st ver.	2nd ver.				1st ver.	2nd ver.
δ	d ←	S ←	$T^{1,4}$ →	s →	δ	d
M3	M3 ←	m3 ←	$S^{2,5}$ →	m3 →	M3	M3
d	δ ←	s ←	$T^{3,6}$ →	S →	d	δ
$\Delta\delta$	$\Delta\delta$ ←	Ss ←	T^7 →	Ss →	$\delta\Delta$	$\delta\Delta$

(or) ... (or)

The transformational nature of the relationship between the three genera presents one of the most fascinating aspects of the whole Vicentinian system and one which is constantly emphasized by the theorist. He says, for instance:

> . . . so the nature of the division of the chromatic genus requires that the order of the diatonic be broken and that two semitones be made from one whole tone and that the incomposite interval of the minor third is made; that all those intervals do not proceed according to the natural diatonic; the nature of the enharmonic genus breaks the order of the diatonic and chromatic genera. . . .[26]

A pronouncement which is even more striking comes earlier:

> Boethius says that chromatic signifies nothing else than that you will find that the diatonic order was moved and transformed, so that first the fourth which contained this genus, which proceeded by a whole tone, a whole tone, and a semitone, now moves by two semitones and

an interval of minor third. And he does not call it chromatic only because of the differences
of the ratios, but also because of the intervals transformed from one order of intervals
into another. . .[27]

In other words, the chromatic series is not self-sufficient. It is called chromatic
not only because it contains certain intervals arranged in a prescribed order, but
also because these intervals and this order are "broken" and transformed from
the diatonic intervals and the diatonic order. The chromatic series does not exist
independently: it presupposes the more fundamental diatonic series. It is
possible to conceive of the diatonic without the chromatic. The concept
of the chromatic, on the other hand, contains the idea of the transformed
diatonic. Or still better: the diatonic *may* be "broken" and transformed into the
chromatic, whereas the chromatic *must* be a broken and transformed diatonic.
The relationship between the enharmonic and the chromatic is analogous to that
which exists between the chromatic and the diatonic. Thus the generic
transformationality establishes for Vicentino the three-level hierarchy in which:
a) the enharmonic level *necessarily* presupposes the more basic chromatic level
which in turn presupposes the fundamental diatonic; b) the diatonic contains the
possibility of the chromatic subdivision and the chromatic may in turn be
subdivided enharmonically.

Vicentino's understanding of the genera became the subject of his renowned
controversy with Vicente Lusitano. Vicentino insisted that in a composition
using the incomposite minor and major thirds along with the diatonic intervals
(the major semitone and the whole tone) all three genera were mixed, since the
thirds did not appear in the diatonic genus and represented the chromatic and
enharmonic genus, respectively. For Lusitano the presence of the thirds was not
enough reason to call the composition non-diatonic. Only with two consecutive
semitones was the boundary of the diatonicism crossed and chromaticism
introduced, whereas the presence of the enharmonic genus could be demonstrated
only with the appearance of the consecutive enharmonic dieses in the composition.

There was no basic difference of opinion between the two theorists so far as
the structure of the genera was concerned. Lusitano did not maintain that there
are no thirds in the chromatic and enharmonic genera. He only insisted (and this
was the crucial issue of the debate) that both thirds appeared first of all on the
diatonic level: the minor third was the sum of the diatonic whole tone and
semitone and the major third resulted from the addition of two diatonic whole
tones. In more general terms we could say that Lusitano, in opposition to
Vicentino, considered the sums of the constitutive intervals of a generic series as
intervals belonging to this genus.

Both theorists invoked the ultimate authority of Boethius to defend their
positions, and in fact the dispute could be resolved simply by demonstrating
whose interpretation of Boethius was correct. The primary issue of the debate,
however, was not so much the correct interpretation of Boethius as the better

interpretation of the contemporary musical practice. From this point of view one cannot but agree with the verdict favoring Lusitano passed by the judges in 1551. Lusitano's position at least enables us to determine to which genus any interval used in a contemporary composition belongs. By adhering strictly to Vicentino we would not be able even to describe the generic membership of the majority of the intervals proposed by the theorist himself, namely the minor whole tone, major whole tone, less than minor third, more than minor third, and all the intervals larger than major third.

This was precisely the argument directed against Vicentino by one of the judges in the debate, Ghiselin Danckerts. In his treatise written in defense of the judges' decision Danckerts maintained that the diatonic tetrachord consisted of a minor semitone followed by two consecutive whole tones, the chromatic tetrachord consisted of a minor semitone followed by a major semitone followed by a minor third, and the enharmonic tetrachord consisted of two consecutive enharmonic dieses (an enharmonic diesis being one half of the minor semitone) followed by a major third.[28] For Danckerts the diatonic semitone was smaller than the chromatic one, because he thought in terms of the Pythagorean tuning in which the diatonic semitone is smaller than one half of the whole tone. Intervals, argued Danckerts, could belong to several genera. The only interval which was proper exclusively to the chromatic genus was the major semitone and the only interval proper exclusively to the enharmonic genus was the diesis. The intervals which were sums of one or several minor semitones and one or several whole tones belonged to the diatonic genus.[29] Vicentino's argument, declared Danckerts, would not allow us to say to which genus a large number of commonly used intervals belonged.[30] Only the presence of a minor semitone or a diesis would betray a non-diatonic element in a composition, and, since these intervals were used neither in plainchant nor in church polyphony, it followed that this music was purely diatonic and that Vicentino's claim that modern music mixed all genera together was unjustified.[31]

However, it must be stressed that Vicentino's striking naïveté in the debate does not invalidate his whole theory of genera (in particular it leaves intact what I consider the most interesting aspect of the whole theory—his insistence on the transformational relationship between the genera) and that Lusitano's correction can be integrated with the rest of the Vicentinian system. An attempt at such an integration would have one important result: both thirds would have to abdicate completely to the semitones and the dieses their role as constitutive intervals of the chromatic and enharmonic genera. In other words, it would be possible to imagine the chromatic and enharmonic series without any thirds at all.

Vicentino was too ambitious and stubborn ever to allow consciously such a possibility. Nevertheless, at one point in the treatise he did introduce what might be treated as generic series built without any thirds. In Book I, Ch. 5 [32] he presented various "hands" with the purpose of extending the Guidonian solmization system beyond the realm of diatonicism. Each "hand" was qualified with an adjective "diatonic," "chromatic," or "enharmonic," and each could be transcribed as a series of intervals adding up to an octave. Thus, a "hand" might be treated as an example of a generic series. The "diatonic hand" (T S T T S T T or S T T T S T T)[33] conforms very well with the Vicentinian definition of the diatonic genus. Two "chromatic hands" preserve the basic diatonic framework dividing each whole tone either into a minor semitone followed by a major one or vice versa and leaving the diatonic semitones undivided:[34]

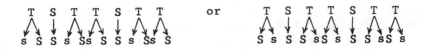

The "enharmonic hands"[35] (the number of which may be also reduced to two) preserve the basic chromatic framework and divide each major semitone either into a minor diesis followed by a major one or vice versa, whereas each minor semitone is divided into two minor dieses. Those chromatic semitones which result from the transformation of the diatonic ones are always divided into a minor diesis followed by a major one. Where a diatonic whole tone was divided into sS, there the major chromatic semitone is divided into Dd and vice versa:

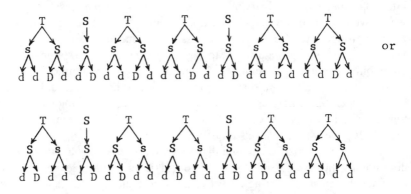

The system of "hands," although admittedly imperfect and incomplete on the enharmonic level, is a good indication of what a hypothetical compromise between Vicentino and Lusitano would look like. It demonstrates that a possibility of conceiving the chromatic and enharmonic genera entirely in terms of semitones and dieses was not completely alien to Vicentino, although I must repeat that it is hard to imagine the theorist consciously allowing such a possibility.

The modes

Book III of the treatise is devoted to the discussion of the modes. For Vicentino and for sixteenth-century theorists in general a mode is a set of characteristics that include an octave-species (that is, a generic series with a fixed starting and terminating point). In each generic series I have distinguished seven relative positions.[36] Seven different modes will be obtained in each of the three genera by assigning the beginning of a mode in turn to each position. In order to conform with the common practice Vicentino adds the eighth mode starting it at the same point as the first one:[37]

> 1st mode starts at the 4th position
> 2nd mode starts at the 1st position
> 3rd mode starts at the 5th position
> 4th mode starts at the 2nd position
> 5th mode starts at the 6th position
> 6th mode starts at the 3rd position
> 7th mode starts at the 7th position
> 8th mode starts at the 4th position

For Vicentino each mode is defined additionally by: a) a specific framework of juxtaposed fifth and fourth; b) a final. Each modal octave-species is divided into a fifth and a fourth. In the odd-numbered modes, called authentic, the fifth is placed below the fourth; in the even-numbered ones, called plagal, the opposite is true. The final of a given mode is the step which constitutes the lower limit of its fifth. The framework of juxtaposed fifth and fourth and the final is what enables us to distinguish from each other the two modes which have the same octave-species, namely, the first and the eighth.

There are twenty-four modes altogether; eight in each genus.[38] However, Vicentino mentions that musicians usually think in terms of eight modes only, since in compositional practice the genera are constantly mixed with each other.[39] In fact we shall recall that one of the results of the generic transformationality is that the genera are in constant coexistence and that one implies the real or at least potential presence of the other two. For this reason I prefer to conceive of the Vicentinian system as consisting of only eight modes, each filled with the substance of all three genera at once.

The tonal system

I have defined the tonal system as signifying the intervallic material available to the composer and the pre-compositional organization of this material.[40] Vicentino, as many other theorists of his time, organized his gamut by means of specifically conceived intervallic series—the genera and the modes. I would indicate as the most important feature of this organization the fact that it establishes a certain hierarchy among the steps of the gamut. With the genera alone the hierarchy is three-level: the steps which belong to the diatonic series are established as being more important than the rest, and the chromatic steps are elevated above the enharmonic ones. A mode introduces to the hierarchy the fourth level, even more basic than the diatonic one. It distinguishes among all the diatonic steps those two which establish the framework of the juxtaposed fifth and fourth. Finally the step which constitutes the final of the mode is additionally distinguished among the last two.

The Notation

The three basic elements of step-notation—the staff, clefs, and notes—make possible the graphic representation of the diatonic series only. Accidentals are needed in order to go beyond diatonicism. For Vicentino, the chromatic sign put on the same line or space as the note after it[41] sharpens this note (✳ or ♮ which is used only to distinguish b♮ from b♭) or flattens it (♭) by a minor semitone.[42] The enharmonic sign, the dot, put centrally above the note sharpens it by a minor diesis.[43] Finally, a comma put above the note sharpens it by a comma.

Although it is not possible to transcend diatonicism notationally without the accidentals, it does not follow that each step written without them is diatonic, nor that a step with an accidental is always nondiatonic. A step is diatonic (or chromatic, or enharmonic) only when it belongs to the diatonic (or chromatic, or enharmonic) intervallic series and regardless of the way in which it is notated. This independence of the structures of the tonal system from the manner of their notation is constantly emphasized by Vicentino. In particular he gives numerous examples of diatonic structures notated with various accidentals and repeatedly warns his readers not to confuse this manner of notation with true non-diatonicism. For instance, in Book III, Ch. 13 he gives examples of diatonic series transposed a fourth above their natural positions by means of a b♭ in the signature, and he comments:

> The fourths, fifths, and octaves discussed above you will see written below with b♭. However, for the ears there will be no transformation whatsoever different from going from b♮ to b♭ , since no changes of the intervals will occur in the process. The song will be transformed and lowered from b♮ to b♭ a minor semitone below only for the eyes. Such a composition cannot be called chromatic music, because from its beginning to end it will not have any transformation. But truly it will be possible to call it chromatic transcription, that is from b♮ to b♭ . . . .[44]

In the next chapter he appends examples of similar "chromatic transcriptions" (or transpositions, as we call them today) using three flats in the signature with the following remarks:

One ought not to speak of falsified music but rather of falsified transcription, because [although] the music is notated with four flats which [thus] to the eye seems completely transformed by the notation, to the ears there is no difference to be heard between music written with flats and that written without [flats], as I have said above; and lest anyone call this composition chromatic music, we have already explained in the first book what [sort of] thing chromatic music [really] is, which involves the change that one hears when first there is a tone and then it is transformed into a semitone, and [conversely] from a semitone into a tone, with the chromatic species and with the deprivation of progressing by natural steps. . . .''[45]

The concept of "falsified transcription" applies not only to generic, but also to modal series.[46] Chromatic modes may be transposed as well as the diatonic ones.[47] Transposition may be effected not only by means of flats, but also with sharps, enharmonic dots, and various combinations thereof.[48]

The fact that the use of accidentals does not necessarily signify the introduction of chromaticism is also stressed by Vicentino's opponent, Ghiselin Danckerts. His remarks on this topic are of particular interest to us, since they indicate the boundary between mere transposition and genuine chromaticism as seen through the eyes of a conservative Roman composer of the 1550s. At the beginning of Part III of his treatise, Danckerts relates the history of a controversy that took place during the papacy of Paul III between two Roman singers, a bass named Guido, and Giovanni, a tenor.[49] During a rehearsal of a Lamentation by Juan Escribano in which a small number of B's were flattened in the bass part Guido decided that the bass should have one flat in the signature flattening B's throughout. Giovanni protested that such a signature would flatten *ordinarily* all B's, whereas only certain B's should be flattened *accidentally*. The dispute was resolved by two singers of the Papal chapel, Constanzo Festa and Charles d'Argentilly, in favor of Giovanni. Guido appealed several times and at one point Danckerts was asked for his opinion. Danckerts, like all previous judges, thought that Giovanni's objection was correct. He argued that in the composition that was in the second mode (as the composer himself attested) there should be no flat in the signature, since such a flat, ordinarily and permanently flattening all B's, would change the species of the fourth which is proper to the second mode (A B c d = T s T) into another one (A B ♭ c d = s T T). The flats should be applied accidentally only at such points where they are necessary, for instance, in order to avoid diminished or augmented fifths or fourths, etc.

The dispute demonstrates that it was a common opinion of composers at the time that chromatic steps could be used in two manners: 1) A consistent chromatic inflection of one or several diatonic steps throughout the piece or its section did not signify the introduction of chromaticism but rather a transposition, or modulation (change of mode), or both. 2) Genuine chromaticism resulted when accidentals were not applied consistently, but sparingly and accidentally, so that they did not result in transposition, modulation, or both. Elsewhere

Danckerts gives an example which clearly shows that accidentals do not introduce chromaticism as long as the intervals are diatonic.[50] Thus both the "conservative" Danckerts and the "progressive" Vicentino distinguish between true chromaticism (the use of the chromatic intervallic series) and mere transposition.

The System of Tuning

A system of tuning is the first necessary step in the process of translating the abstract tonal system into a concrete sound-medium usable in musical practice. It gives absolute sizes to the intervals of the tonal system. The tuning system and the tonal system are to a very large extent mutually independent. A given tonal system may be tuned in many different ways. In Book I, Chs. 6-8 Vicentino describes the tetrachords of the three genera and mentions that he tunes them differently from Boethius. Nevertheless, the tetrachord retains its structural identity regardless of tuning:

> Some might say that since the genus under discussion is not composed of two sesquioctava whole tones and a minor semitone, it really should not be called diatonic. We answer that the etymology of the name derives from the fact that the diatonic genus proceeds through two consecutive whole-tone intervals and a semitone without any interruption; and not from the ratios. Boethius himself, speaking about the significance of all the three genera in Book I, Ch. 21, says that the diatonic genus is called diatonic because it proceeds through a whole tone and a whole tone and a semitone in its fourth and not because the two whole tones which this genus contains are sesquioctava. But he says diatonic, since it moves through the consecutive whole-tone intervals and the semitone. Whenever a fourth composed of two sesquioctava whole tones, or of a sesquioctava and a sesquinona whole tones and a major semitone, or of two whole tones and a semitone or whatever ratios will be seen moving through consecutive intervals of two whole tones and a semitone, this fourth will be called diatonic on account of the intervals of the whole tones and the semitone and not because of the ratios. And its species will be two natural whole tones and a natural semitone. . . .[51]

Moreover, not only can a tonal system be tuned in many different ways, but within one type of tuning an interval of the system might be represented by several different ratios, as is seen from the above quotation when two different ratios—the sesquioctava and the sesquinona—are allowed for the tuning of the whole tones of a single series, since— explains Vicentino—". . . this little difference between the two is not perceivable in singing nor in playing. . . ."[52]

The detailed description of the tuning system (or rather of two systems) advocated by Vicentino is not necessary here. For our present purposes it will suffice to indicate the most general features of the theorist's proposal.[53] He chose the most obvious way to tune his gamut, the temperament dividing the octave into thirty-one equal parts. It is interesting to note that such a temperament does not differ perceptibly from the usual meantone temperament in which the fifths are tempered by 1/4 comma.[54]. This temperament was used ordinarily for tuning keyboard instruments in the sixteenth century. Thus Vicentino's tuning of those steps which were commonly found on sixteenth-century keyboards (that is, the diatonic steps plus C♯ E♭ F♯ G♯ B♭) was practically identical with the usual one, the fact which he himself observed.[55] He was obviously satisfied with the ordinary meantone temperament of the contemporary keyboard instruments. He just wanted to extend it to those steps of his system which were not commonly found on sixteenth-century keyboards. As J. Murray Barbour put it, his "was a clever method of extending the usual meantone temperament of 1/4 comma until it formed practically a closed system."[56] Incidentally, what Vicentino called "comma," was the difference between the perfect and the tempered fifth.

The mutual independence of the tuning and the tonal systems notwithstanding, the choice of the specific tuning is not indifferent for the manner in which the system will be used in practice. The tuning makes some aspects of the tonal system practically available (or not) according to certain external criteria. Vicentino's intentions in this respect are best observed when he compares the advantages of his tuning system with those of some others. His main reference point is the Pythagorean system espoused by Boethius. Vicentino claims that in his tuning, in contrast to Boethius's, ". . . inequality of the whole tones gives birth to the convenience of being able to use the consonances of thirds and sixths, both major and minor."[57] Moreover, ". . . the fourths and fifths of Boethius are perfect and those which we use are a little blunted and scant in the tuning of the instruments."[58] The reason for this difference in tuning is

> . . . that the ancient musicians used in their practice the genera separately from each other, . . . [whereas] we use the genera and their species all together, with more consonances than they did, that is the thirds and the sixths. In order to be able to have many consonances and to use in practice many intervals, we do not think it is inconvenient to shorten the fifth and to lengthen the fourth. . . .[59]

In the Pythagorean system the fifths and the fourths are just but the thirds and the sixths are outside their simple ratios. Vicentino tempers the perfect consonances in order to make the imperfect ones more usable, more just. Moreover, the equality of his division makes those intervals equally usable regardless of transposition. Thus it is possible to use the imperfect consonances built from the steps belonging to different genera. The Pythagorean system was sufficient for a practice which did not want to employ imperfect consonances, nor mixed genera, nor transpositions, but for a practice in which all these things are used, Vicentino recommends his own system.

Besides the Pythagorean tuning, Vicentino criticizes also that type in which all semitones are equal.[60] His insistence on the importance of giving two different sizes to the major and minor semitone is significant. He wanted to underline on the level of tuning system this characteristic property of his tonal system: the existence of two different semitones.

The Archicembalo

If the tuning system was the first step in the process of translating the abstract tonal system into a concrete sound-medium usable in musical practice, the *archicembalo* is the end-product of this process. In Vicentino's superharpsichord the system materializes and musicians get the tool for its practical implementation. For the theorist the main advantage of the instrument is that it makes any transposition possible.[61] Such a situation occurs only when all the steps divide the octave into equal parts. The *archicembalo* presents all the intervals of the gamut tuned according to Vicentino's precepts, realizes the ideal of making all transpositions possible—each interval is available at each key in both directions[62] —within the limits of practicality, and makes the hierarchical organization of the genera visible in the arrangement of its keyboards. In other words, it takes into consideration the most important aspects of the theory discussed thus far.

The fifth and last book of the treatise describes the instrument. There are six rows of keys arranged in two keyboards, an octave-section of which is presented here:

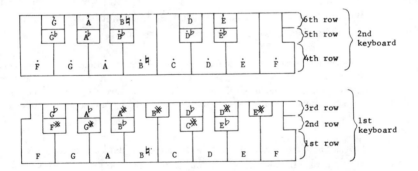

In reality both keyboards comprise three such octaves plus an E below the lowest octave in the first and fourth rows and a fifth (omitting B✻) above the highest octave in both keyboards. In the diagram I have discarded Vicentino's curious way of naming the keys since it does not correspond to his manner of notation and I have substituted one which does. Keeping in mind the principles of this notation, the reader will easily see that the first five rows of the keys do realize the thirty-one degree gamut-representation which makes any transposition possible. The keys of the sixth row are tuned a comma higher than the corresponding keys of the first row. Their function is to provide for some degrees of the gamut alternative consonances, purer than those given by the Vicentinian tuning. In particular they give perfect fifths above some steps of the first row and below those of the fourth row. The existence of such alternatives is yet another proof that in Vicentino's mind the tonal system is independent of tuning.

Another instrument, the *arciorgano,* is described by the theorist in a broadsheet which appeared in 1561.[63] Although few details of the construction are given, it was probably very similar to the *archicembalo,* judging from the author's remark that he ''has in his possession a Clavicembalo, made in the manner of the Arciorgano. . .''[64] However, they might have been different in one respect: among many advantages of the *arciorgano,* Vicentino mentions that it can play in ensemble with various kinds of instruments, such as lutes and violas, regardless of their tuning.[65] In *L'antica musica,* however, he maintained that lutes and violas which were commonly tuned so that their semitones were equal could not play in tune with instruments which had two different sizes of semitones, as did presumably the *archicembalo.*[66]

Were the *archicembalo* and the *arciorgano* tuned differently? I do not think so. Vicentino's remark should be counted among those exaggerated claims which are quite common in circulars of a promotional nature. It is also possible that the theorist decided that the chromatic and enharmonic keys would supply the steps necessary to make it approximately in tune with the lute and viola.

II. POETICS: ASPECTS OF THE COMPOSITION AND PERFORMANCE OF NON-DIATONIC MUSIC

Composition

Imitation of the words

The main objective of the first part of this chapter was to establish the nature of the tonal structures that Vicentino considered to be non-diatonic. Now I pass to the compositional and performing practice of non-diatonic music.

Vocal music rather than instrumental is usually at the center of the Renaissance musician's interest, and it is to the problems of vocal composition that Vicentino addresses himself primarily. The principle on which he insists almost obsessively throughout the treatise is that music should imitate the words. For instance, in Book IV, Ch. 36, after describing a somewhat mechanical way of inventing melodic phrases in an instrumental composition, he adds: ''This rule will not be serviceable for the composition made with words, because these themselves give the rule, as we read above in the treatise on the imitation of the nature of the words accompanied with the steps and skips and with the conso-nances.''[67] The idea that music should imitate the nature of the words is central to Vicentino's poetics, and we shall have to look closely at some of the passages in which this idea is presented in order to grasp its meaning.

What is it precisely that music should imitate? "The composer should have a refined judgment," says Vicentino, "and he should compose his compositions according to the subject and argument of the words."[68] Thus, what should be imitated are not the words themselves but rather that to which they refer, that is their "subject." Earlier he said that ". . . the composer . . . will only be obliged to give life to those words and to show by means of the harmony their passions—sometimes harsh, sometimes sweet, sometimes cheerful, sometimes sad—according to their subject."[69] The subject of the words seems to be restricted here, and also in the following most revealing passage, to their "passions":

> . . . music made upon words is made for no other purpose than to express the thought and the passions and their effects with harmony. If the words speak about modesty, one will proceed in the composition modestly and not furiously, and if they speak of cheerfulness, one does not make the music sad, and if of sadness, one does not render it cheerful, and when they are about harshness, one will not make it sweet, and when they are soft, one should not accompany them in other ways, because they will seem different than the thought. . . .[70]

Music exists to express the "passions" of the words and presumably to enhance their effects on the listener. This is not to say that the musical imitation of some other aspects of the text is totally excluded. In the passage immediately preceding the last quotation Vicentino criticizes those composers who do not take into consideration the lengths of the syllables of the text and who do not reproduce them in appropriate note values. What is even more interesting for our subject, he advocates the musical imitation of not only the temporal organization of the text but also of its pitch-organization:

> Everybody will be able to set in music his manner of singing with the intervals of the division of our instrument [that is, the *archicembalo*]. With the music used nowadays one can write no French, German, Spanish, Hungarian, Turkish, Hebrew songs, nor one in another language, because the steps and skips of all the nations of the world do not proceed according to their maternal pronunciation exclusively through the intervals of whole tones and natural and accidental semitones, but through diesis and enharmonic semitones, whole tones, and skips. So that with this division of ours we have accommodated all the nations of the world who will be able to write their accents and set them in as many voices as they will see fit.[71]

However, the idea is not pursued any further, and the theorist's emphasis throughout the treatise is certainly on the musical imitation of the passions of the text and not of its other aspects.

How is this to be accomplished? How can the passions be expressed in music? Vicentino conceives of each interval as having its own affective-expressive character, or—as he calls it—its own "nature." As we study the adjectives used to describe the natures of various intervals, we discover that they all might be arranged into two groups. The adjectives within each group are mutually interchangeable and they are opposed to those belong to the other group. Thus, an interval is described as being incited (*incitato*), cheerful (*allegro*), hard (*duro*), and harsh (*aspro*), while another is soft (*molle*), sad (*mesto*), and sweet (*dolce* or *soave*), to list only the most commonly used adjectives. The reader will recall that similar terms were used by Vicentino to describe various passions of the words. It is precisely because of the affective-expressive character of the intervals that music can refer to and express passions.

> It seems to me [says Vicentino], that the whole content of a soft and harmonious composition consists in arranging the composition according to three principal ways. Before the composer writes anything, he should pay attention to what he wants to construct the composition upon. The first way is to apply the steps and skips, incited and soft, to the subject of the words or to a musical theme [*fantasia*]. The second way is of no small importance; when the composer has arranged the steps and skips, he should accompany them with consonances and dissonances, incited and soft, in accordance with his previous arrangement of the steps and skips, so that the steps and skips are similar in nature to the incited and soft consonances. The third and last way will be that when the composer has put together the steps and skips and the consonances and dissonances, then a suitable movement will be given to that subject which communicates the argument of the words or other thoughts.[72]

The first two "ways" claim our immediate interest. The first "way" consists in choosing horizontal intervals appropriate to the subject of the words, that is to their passions, the second, in adding the appropriate vertical intervals.

The horizontal intervals

The information on the affective nature of the horizontal intervals can be extracted from Book I, Chs. 15-41.[73] It is summarized in the list below. The plus refers to the incited (and cheerful, hard, harsh, etc.) intervals, the minus to the soft (and sad, sweet, etc.), and zero to those which are indeterminate—incited and soft at the same time.

INTERVAL	ASCENDING	DESCENDING
minor diesis	−	−
major diesis and minor semitone	+	−
major semitone	−	+
minor whole tone	0	0
whole tone	+	−
major whole tone	+	−
less than minor third	−	+
minor third	−	+
more than minor third	+	−
major third	+	−
more than major third	+	−
fourth	+	−
more than fourth	+	−
tritone	+	−
diminished fifth	−	+
more than diminished fifth	0	0
fifth	+	−
more than fifth	+	−

The nature of larger intervals is not explained. All intervals with the exception of the smallest and the two indeterminate ones have one or the other of the two opposing natures, depending on whether they ascend or descend.

Vicentino does not tell us why he thinks an interval has the particular nature which he ascribes to it, nor does he explain why one and the same interval can have two opposing characters depending on its direction. He talks about the affective natures of intervals as if he were stating commonly known and accepted facts. It is my impression that the affective character of a horizontal interval depends somehow on the further direction of the melodic movement which this interval implies. If an interval is to be followed by an ascending motion it is incited; if a descending motion is implied as its continuation it is soft. Such an explanation is to a large extent substantiated by a study of the notated forms of the intervals. In Vicentino's time (and practically throughout the whole history of Western music) a flattened note implied a downward continuation of the stepwise melodic movement, whereas a sharpened note was usually followed by a motion ascending stepwise. It will be remembered that in Vicentino's notation a diatonic whole tone can be divided into five minor enharmonic dieses and that the four dividing degrees have to be noted with the following accidentals:

A note with a sharp and a dot is equivalent to the next higher note with a flat, and both forms of notation are employed. A diatonic semitone can be divided into three minor enharmonic dieses by two degrees, each of which can be notated in two equivalent forms with the following accidentals:

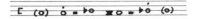

The three lower degrees dividing the natural whole tone (that is the degrees notated with a dot, or a sharp, or both) can be interpreted as sharpening the lower note which limits the whole tone. Analogically, the three higher degrees dividing the natural whole tone can be understood as flattening the higher note which limits the whole tone, although it is a peculiarity of Vicentinian notation that one of those degrees has to be provided with a sharp. The two degrees dividing a natural semitone can be interpreted as either sharpening the lower note of a semitone or flattening the higher one. If we notate all the intervals described by Vicentino as incited so that the first note of each interval is natural, we shall discover that with very few exceptions the second note of each interval is either natural or it is sharpened; that is, it implies an upward continuation of the melodic motion. Notating similarly all the soft intervals we shall see that again with very few exceptions the second note of each interval is either natural or it is flattened, implying thus that the melody should be continued downwards.

 Two additional facts support the above explanation. First, the chromatic accidentals are associated by Vicentino with affections. He says, for instance, that the two signs of b natural and b flat may be called either "square b" (*b. quadro,* that is, ♮) and "round b" (*b. rotondo,* that is, ♭), or they may be called "hard," or better "incited b" (*b. duro* or *b. incitato*) and "soft b" (*b. molle*).[74] It is characteristic that the newer of the two nomenclatures associates the two key affective descriptions, "incited" and "soft," with accidentals. Furthermore, Vicentino says expressly that ". . . each time any signs are placed accidentally in a composition, they will alter the nature of this process, and the flat will lend melancholy, the natural will make the composition cheerful, and the sharp—when it also is placed accidentally—will transform the nature of the composition. . . ."[75] Secondly, the incited intervals are associated by the theorist with upward and the soft ones with downward motion.[76] We learn about the minor third that being very weak and sad it tends to descend.[77] Of the major third it is said that because of its lively and cheerful nature it likes to ascend.[78] It is true that those observations are made about vertical intervals but it seems to me that I am justified in applying them to the horizontal ones as well, since Vicentino himself, when starting to describe the vertical intervals, says that he will not repeat which of these are incited and which are soft, since he had explained that in connection with the horizontal intervals.[79] Thus, he seems to equate the affective natures of the vertical and the horizontal intervals.

The vertical intervals

This brings us to the problem of the expressive character of the vertical intervals, the problem which—as the reader will notice immediately—is not as simple as Vicentino would lead us to believe, since a vertical interval does not have the ascending and descending forms. With few exceptions (most notable being the two thirds mentioned above) Vicentino does not say what the affective nature of any particular vertical interval is, and it is not easy to reconstruct his intentions in this respect. All we know for sure is that the major consonances (that is, major third and major sixth) are cheerful and imply upward motion, whereas the minor ones (that is, minor third and minor sixth) are sad and tend to descend.[80]

These imperfect vertical consonances seem to be decisive for the affective character of a composition.[81] In general, Vicentino considers vertical intervals to be more important as vehicles of expression than the horizontal ones:

> The whole art of music lies in knowing how to choose the movement, the steps, and the consonances according to the argument of the subject on which one has to compose, and first one should notice that the consonances are the principal among these three resources. The reason is that if the composer considers that the hearing is nourished with consonances and that if it hears the steps without consonances but with movement as when one signs alone, and that this has the steps and the movement but not the consonances, [he will realize that] this will not satisfy the ears of the listener. . . . And if the ears are better fed by consonances than by hearing a simple voice composed with the steps and with the movement, then the consonances are the principal [resource], since they will make harmony without being subordinated to steps or movement. But when the consonances are accompanied by steps and movement according to the argument of the subject, then this composition will be good.[82]

Thus, the vertical intervals are most important, the horizontal ones are subordinate, as is the temporal organization, and all three are necessary to achieve a satisfactory composition. The preeminence of the vertical intervals and the subordination of an independent melodic movement to them is worth noting, since it is reflected in the distinct interest of some composers of the second half of the sixteenth century in homophonic writing.

The genera

It is quite obvious that passions will be imitated not only by single intervals but also by larger intervallic structures such as the genera and the modes. We have noted that the expressive nature of all the intervals could be described as belonging to one of the two opposed types; some intervals were incited, others were soft. The same binary opposition pertains to the affective character of the genera. The diatonic is usually described by Vicentino as being harsh (*aspro*), whereas the non-diatonic genera are characterized together as soft or sweet (*soave*), the difference between the two being that the enharmonic is even more sweet than the chromatic. Thus, the real opposition is between the diatonic and non-diatonic genera, while the difference between the chromatic and the enharmonic is one of degree only.

The genera derive their characters from the natures of their constitutive intervals. Thus, for example, we learn that smaller steps are sweeter than larger ones when accompanied with consonances; when accompanied with dissonances the smaller will offend the ear less than the larger ones.[83] The "bad consonances" such as the diminished fifth, are more smoothly resolved in the movement of semitones than of whole tones.[84] The penultimate note in cadences gives a sweet effect when sharpened and a hard effect if left unsharpened.[85] Chromatic compositions are sweet because they avoid the step of the whole tone, which is hard and harsh.[86] In general the enharmonic diesis is sweeter than the chromatic semitone, which in turn is sweeter than the diatonic whole tone: ". . . the shorter steps will always give sweeter harmony. . . ."[87] Consequently, the chromatic series is sweeter than the diatonic, and the enharmonic is sweeter than the chromatic.[88] An example of a purely diatonic piece is characterized as full of "great harshness."[89]

The affective characteristic described above was designed to point out the nature of a genus as it relates to the natures of the other two genera. A chromatic piece is sweeter than a diatonic one, but it does not follow that all chromatic music is necessarily condemned to sweetness. Vicentino assures us that the affective range of chromatic music is quite broad and embraces sadness, cheerfulness, harshness, sweetness, and mixtures thereof.[90] The reason for this broad affective range is probably that intervals of various nature are possible within the genus.

Throughout the treatise composers are encouraged to mix various genera within one piece in order to express musically the passions of the text. Having in mind his own peculiar understanding of the genera, Vicentino maintained that contemporary composers in fact unknowingly mixed all the genera when they used the major and minor thirds together with the diatonic intervals. He urged them to take the next logical step and start using the smaller non-diatonic intervals as well. Moreover, one is allowed to mix within a single composition not only all the genera but also their diverse versions, in order to insure the maximum affective flexibility of music.[91]

The modes

Not only genera but also modes are endowed with the power to express passions. They are characterized in this respect in Book III, Chs. 5-12, and 15-22.[92] Similarly to intervals and genera, modes are classified into two opposed affective groups: the authentic modes are more cheerful than their respective plagal modes and, of course, vice versa, the plagal modes are sadder than their authentic counterparts. However, there seems to be much variation in the degree of intensity of the character within each group, and it is probable that Vicentino would consider some plagal modes to be more cheerful than even some authentic ones, although certainly not more cheerful than their authentic counterparts. Thus, the sixth mode is described as slightly sadder than the fifth but also cheerful and fierce. The reason for this cheerfulness, which—as the theorist expressly tells us—is quite uncharacteristic of the majority of plagal modes, is that the sixth mode has a major third followed by a minor one above its final. The association at this early date of what was later to become known as the major tonic triad with cheerfulness and by implication of the minor tonic triad with sadness is certainly worth pointing out.

According to Vicentino, composers should choose the mode appropriate to the passions of the text they set to music. This is deceptively a simple principle. The mode of a composition can be discovered by observing its bass part.[93] However, we learn that when in a polyphonic composition one part represents an authentic mode, another will always represent the corresponding plagal one, and vice versa.[94] Thus a polyphonic composition is never written in a pure mode but in a combination of an authentic with its corresponding plagal. How then can one match a mode with the passions of the words when one has learned from Vicentino himself that an authentic mode has a more cheerful character than its corresponding plagal? It is possible that the answer to this problem lies in the previously noticed association of the so-called major tonic triad with cheerfulness and of the minor one with sadness since such a triad is shared by an authentic mode with its corresponding plagal.

The musical architecture

Various modes may be introduced within a single composition in order to imitate diverse passions of the text. However, one mode has to be established as the basic mode of the composition, and other modes have to be treated as secondary. The form of a piece, or rather its structure (*fabrica*)—as Vicentino calls it, will be determined by its modal organization. The theorist's remarks on musical structure are so interesting that they deserve an extensive quotation:

> The broadest foundation which the composer ought to have is to consider on what he wants to construct his composition, according to the words, whether ecclesiastic, or of another subject. The foundation of this structure is to choose a tone, or mode, that will suit the argument of the words, or another musical theme, as the case may be, and on that good foundation he will measure well with his judgment and he will draw the lines of the fourths and of the fifths of this tone and of their limits, which will be the columns that will keep the structure of the composition standing. Although the fourths and fifths of other modes may be placed between these [fundamental] fourths and fifths, they [the interjected fourths and fifths] will not damage this structure when put in a few places and well accompanied in the middle of the composi-

tion. With the variety of architecture, they will [rather] embellish the structure of the composition, as good architects do who skillfully exploiting the lines of the triangle dazzle the sight of
men and by their means achieve that a façade of some beautiful palce, which in a picture is
painted very close to the sight of the onlooker, will appear to him very far without being
distant at all. This illusion results from knowing how to accompany colors with lines. Often
architects accompany diverse manners of orders of construction in one structure, as one sees
in the celebrated Vitruvius: The Doric order[95] will be accompanied by the Attic one, and the
Corinthian by the Ionic: and they are so well connected and united that even though the
manners are diverse, the practical artist using his judgment composes the structure
proportioned with various ornaments. So it happens that the composer of music can with art
make various mixtures of fourths and fifths of other modes, and he can embellish the
composition with various intervals, proportioned according to the effects of the consonances
applied to the words; and he should observe closely the tone or the mode.[96]

The musical structure is to be based on the fundamental mode, the choice of
which will be governed by the words, and the two steps which limit the
juxtaposed fifths and fourths of the mode (that is the final and the step a fifth
above the final) will serve as the columns supporting the whole structure.
Secondary modes may be introduced in the course of the composition, always
following the words. These interjected modes should not be confused with the
fundamental framework of the structure but are to be treated as ornaments
introduced for the sake of variety and expressive flexibility. It is interesting that
the art of the composer organizing the form of his work is compared with that of
a painter organizing forms in space by means of perspective, creating the illusion
of depth on a two-dimensional surface through lines converging in a single point
and marking the diminishing sizes of receding objects. There is further
comparison with an architect who is able to unite diverse orders in one structure.
The art of a composer, as that of a painter or an architect, enables him to organize
diverse elements into a structure based on a single, unifying, fundamental
principle, be it perspective or the basic mode.[97] Underlying Vicentino's thought
on musical form is the need to achieve a balance between the demand of
expressive flexibility and of a non-expressive, purely formal ideal, the work seen
as a unified whole.

Although in the last sentence of the passage quoted above the composer is
urged to observe closely the basic mode of his composition, in the passage
immediately following we learn that in certain vernacular compositions, such as
sonnets, madrigals, and canzonas, which treat numerous and diverse passions, it
is possible to start the piece in one mode and end in another, if the text so
requires. Usually, however, the piece will start and end in its basic mode, and
secondary modes will be introduced only in the middle.[98] The fifths and fourths
of the basic mode will be the ones most frequently used in the composition.[99]
Their limiting pitches—the final and its upper fifth—will be the columns
supporting the whole structure, as we have learned above. The internal and final
cadences of the piece will be built mostly on those pitches and also on the pitches
limiting the fifths and fourths of the secondary modes.[100] The skeleton of the

musical structure could be visualized as consisting of the fundamental level in which the cadences built on the pitches limiting the fifths and fourths of the basic mode would serve as points of repose—columns supporting the whole structure—and of the upper levels in which similar role would be played by the cadences built on the pitches limiting the fifths and fourths of secondary modes.

This skeleton can be fleshed out with pitch-material coming from all the genera. The mixing of genera will not introduce total chaos precisely because the piece has this firm internal skeleton.[101] Moreover, in this context it becomes possible to understand Vicentino's well-known remarks to the effect that a single composition may be performed with or without accidentals. More precisely, he indicates that a composition may be performed in three ways: 1) without accidentals; 2) with chromatic signs; 3) with chromatic and enharmonic signs; or even in five: 1) diatonic; 2) chromatic; 3) chromatic and enharmonic; 4) diatonic and chromatic; 5) diatonic, chromatic, and enharmonic.[102] Thanks to the constant internal skeleton the composition will retain its structural identity, although its affective "nature" will be somewhat changed in each performance.

One cannot overemphasize the importance of Vicentino's idea of musical form for the proper understanding of his conception of non-diatonicism. If we want to grasp not only the expressive but also the structural function of chromaticism in any musical work, we have to investigate the chromatic phenomena within the context of the whole piece. In the first part of this chapter I have tried to show the relative importance of the non-diatonic steps within the whole step-hierarchy. I hope that in the above discussion of the musical architecture I have been able to indicate the position of the genera within the overall context of the formal phenomena.

More conservative theorists of the time deplored the fact that the indiscriminate use of accidentals, the desire to mix the genera, destroyed the modal order of a composition. Ghiselin Danckerts attacked the "greenhorn composers" (*compositori novelli*) of his time for their "new manner" (*nuova maniera*), which consisted primarily in the fact that their way of using accidentals destroyed the mode of a composition:

> I shall not leave out the account of the abuse that was introduced in our time, not many years ago, by certain greenhorn composers in composition of polyphonic works. Having scorn for all good laws, orders, and ancient rules (persuading themselves that with their new laws and rules they will take away the fame from other composers), they show that they do not know the orders of the authentic and plagal modes that have to be necessarily observed in diatonic compositions so as not to enter into disorders because of which everything goes to ruin, or if they know them they show that they do not want to observe them, busying themselves only with sharpening and flattening notes beyond their ordinary intonation, in order to reduce not only the interval of minor semitone into a whole tone (e.g., b-c♯ or c′-b♭), but also the interval of the whole tone into a minor semitone (e.g., a-b♭ or d′-c♯′), or (which is worse) into a minor third (e.g., f-g♯-a). They do it without giving any reason, except that they compose in such way in a new manner. They like to do it, since they see that also others do it, and thus, one blind man leading another, they all tumble down into the ditch.[103]

Accidentals can be used occasionally when they are necessary, but not in such a way as to destroy the mode of a composition. They are used primarily to supply perfect fourths and fifths where these would be otherwise missing. But they should be introduced sparingly, so as to make it clear that they are used accidentally. Otherwise, as we already know, they will produce modulation, transposition, or both, they will destroy the mode of a composition. The innovators think they are restoring ancient genera, when in reality they just transpose semitones from their proper positions without really leaving the diatonic. Danckerts advocates the accidental use of chromatic steps, when necessary, but he abhors their modulating or transposing use.[104] Vicentino's sophisticated view of formal architecture was needed to show that the mixture of genera and modes did not have to create tonal chaos.

Norm and licence

I have suggested above that Vicentino's idea of musical architecture resulted from an attempt to accommodate two opposing impulses which for him lay behind an act of composition: on the one hand the need to express musically the diverse passions of the words, on the other the need to achieve a coherent whole, a form unified by a single, all-pervading principle. In more general terms, it is the tension between the conflicting demands of unity and variety which underlies Vicentinian poetics. On the level of form the conflict is resolved by sujecting the variety of modes and genera to a unifying skelton of the basic mode. On the contrapuntal level the analogical conflict involves what might be labeled a norm and a licence, a standard usage and a deflection from it.

Characteristically, the whole stress is put on the ideal of *varietà*. Vicentino writes against the background of contemporary Renaissance theory and practice, which emphasized such ideals as harmony, unity, and stability. He takes the existence and necessity of those ideals for granted and devotes all his energy to the propagation of their opposite, variety. His theory of counterpoint is not radically different from that *summa* of Renaissance musical grammar, Gioseffo Zarlino's *Le Istitutioni harmoniche* Part III (1558), although it is considerably less systematic. The basic difference between those two students of Adrian Willaert is that whereas Zarlino described the normal rules of counterpoint as perfected by his teacher and practiced by the composers of his own generation, Vicentino took those norms for granted, described them rather sketchily, and was much more interested in exploring the possibilities of deviating from them.[105]

In a vocal work the text justifies the licence: ". . . any wrong step with bad consonance may be used with words, according to their effects. . . ."[106] Unlimited freedom is granted in the treatment of vernacular texts; "cose ecclesiastiche" should be approached with more respect.[107] A composer's freedom is most restricted in instrumental music, since licences there cannot be justified by text. For this reason instrumental music should be as sweet and harmonious as possible, but even there variety is necessary.[108] For the same reason not all vocal compositions can be performed instrumentally.[109] But even though there are no words to guide or justify him, an instrumental composer can imitate in his works the affections of incitedness and softness.[110]

I find it impossible to show with any precision the relation between, on the one hand, the division of contrapuntal usage into normal and licentious and, on the other, the division of the genera into diatonic and non-diatonic. It is quite certain that not all use of non-diatonicism would be regarded as deviating from the norm, just as not all diatonic counterpoint is correct. One can only suppose that there would be more "norm" on the side of diatonicism and more "licence" on that of non-diatonicism. At any rate, the non-diatonic resources may be used not only with vernacular but also with ecclesiastical texts, and in instrumental works.[111]

Unfortunately Vicentino says very little about the use of chromatic and enharmonic notes in counterpoint. In a two-part composition one should avoid two consecutive vertical imperfect consonances of the same size. Accidentals are used to make one of them minor or the other major.[112] Characteristically, this is not an absolute prohibition, but rather advice for the sake of variety.[113] In general, accidentals are used to change minor consonances into major ones and vice versa and to make the consonances perfect. The composer is advised to prepare an accidental note by preceding it with a natural one a fifth or fourth above or below.[114]

The use of the non-diatonic resources is linked with the ideal of *varietà*. Mixing genera in a composition is encouraged, because it enlarges the variety of intervals.[115] Besides, it is the function of dissonances to introduce variety,[116] and the number of dissonances is obviously enlarged once the non-diatonic notes are used.

Performance

Like most theorists, Vicentino is more interested in composition than in performance. Among his scattered remarks on performance practice, some concern non-diatonic music or are otherwise relevant to our subject. I would like to mention them here.

It is worth remembering that the line separating composition and performance was much less clear in the sixteenth century than it is today. Undoubtedly the Renaissance recognized composition and performance as two distinct areas of musical activity. But the two areas overlapped and frequently it is hard to decide whether a phenomenon belongs to the field of composition or to that of performance. Indeed such a decision is quite unnecessary, if we keep in mind the fact that a Renaissance musician was likely to regard his musical activity as an uncompartmentalized whole.

The concept of movement (*il moto*) which embraces both rhythm and tempo is an example of the border phenomena I have in mind. To a certain extent the movement may be composed and notated; to a certain extent it must be left to the discretion and good sense of the performers. As already noted, movement is the third aspect of music, after vertical and horizontal intervals, which should be used to express the passions of the words.[117] In general, fast movement is used in a cheerful composition and slow movement goes well with melancholic music.[118] Its appropriateness to the words is of great importance to a successful composition, since the movement can affect the nature of intervals and change the character of the whole piece.[119] Special consideration should be given to the chromatic and enharmonic intervals that cannot be properly perceived in a movement which is too fast or too slow; they require moderate movement.[120] Performers, always observing the words, can vary the tempo within a composition.[121]

Dynamics, which—as Vicentino thinks—cannot be notated, may also vary within a single piece; in this respect, too, the text should guide the performers.[122] Vicentino's remarks concerning dynamics are not entirely clear, since the vocabulary appropriate to the problem was not yet developed in his time. In particular it is not always possible to distinguish whether the theorist has in mind the dynamic level of the performance, or the size of the performing group, or even the place of the performance. All these aspects of performance are strongly interconnected. Enharmonic music should be sung ". . . in the chambers and in a low voice. . . ."[123] The pure intonation of accidental octaves is very hard when sung in a full voice (*à piena voce*). It will be easier in chamber music which is sung softly (*piano*).[124] But in Book III, Ch. 44 Vicentino gives an example of ". . . a little cheerful motet, completely chromatic, which we sing in church on the day of the Resurrection of our Lord, so that everybody may see that the chromatic music can be sung in the churches with a loud voice."[125]

Instrumental accompaniment will help singers to solve the problems of intonation in non-diatonic music.[126] The *archicembalo* in particular is an indispensable tool for accompaniment and also for learning how to sing the unusual intervals correctly.[127] But the greatest and unprecedented advantage that the *archicembalo* and *arciorgano* have over all other instruments is that they make all transpositions possible. This means that it is possible to accompany or to answer a choir in any mode on the pitch-level convenient to the singers.[128] Vicentino discusses what he calls "chromatic transcription" (that is, transposition) always in the context of an instrumentalist who accompanies or answers singers.[129] This is the context in which the idea of transposition makes sense in a musical world which does not know an absolute pitch standard. An instrumentalist playing Vicentino's super-instruments will be able to transpose any composition to any pitch-level and thus to accommodate the singers.

The Poetics of Imitation

Imitation of the passions of the words is the basic principle of Vicentino's poetics, giving it its unity and governing both composition and performance practice. There is a chain of imitation which starts with the "subject of the words" (that is, the passions) and ends in performance. First the composer imitates various subjects of the words by devising various manners of composition. Then the singer imitates those various subjects and manners of composition by using diverse ways of singing:

> Compositions differ according to the subject on which they are made, and some singers often do not pay attention in singing to what the composition is about and sing without any consideration and always in a certain way of their own according to their own nature and habit. Compositions that are made on various subjects and various musical themes carry with them various manners of composing and thus the singer should consider the mind of the musical poet as well as the vernacular or Latin poet, and imitate the composition with the voice, and use diverse ways of singing as are diverse the manners of the compositions.[130]

The words imitate the passions; the composer imitates the words, and the singer imitates the music, and while doing so both imitate the passions. As the composer should go behind the letter of the words and imitate their spirit, so the singer should penetrate behind the letter of the musical text to its spirit. In both cases the passions constitute the ultimate reference.

The concept of imitation creates an intimate link between the art of the poet, the composer (whom Vicentino significantly calls *Poeta Musico*), and the singer. Moreover, it associates the art of singing with oratory. The singer should imitate the methods of the orator:

> The experience of the orator teaches him. For one sees by the way he delivers the oration that he speaks now loudly, now softly, now slower, and now faster; and with this he moves the listeners very much. This way of changing the measure has a great effect on the soul. For this reason one will sing music by heart in order to imitate the accents and the effects of the parts of the oration. What effect would the orator have if he recited a beautiful oration without the resources of accents, pronunciation, rapid and slow movement, and soft and loud speech? This would not move the listeners. So it should be in music, because if the orator moves the listeners with the above-stated resources, how much greater and stronger will be the effect made by music recited with the same resources accompanied by the well-united harmony?[131]

German theorists of the Baroque were to go one step further and create a musical rhetoric—the theory of composition modelled on the theory of oratory and organizing the ways in which words can be imitated into a system of musical-rhetorical figures. The basic and strong suggestion for creating a musical rhetoric are already present in Vicentino's treatise. But he was not really interested in pendantic systematization of standard figures of musical imitation and contented himself with establishing the basic principles.

III. AESTHETICS

"According to the Philosopher," says Vicentino, "all who do something, do it in order to achieve a goal. Now the goal of music is to satisfy the ears. . . ."[132] Vicentino makes it clear now and again that the final aim of all musical activity is the listener. And it is not the highest rational faculty of the listener that the musician wants to reach; he aims lower, at the sense of hearing, "the ears."

Vicentino starts his treatise by reporting the existence of the three schools of thought among ancient musical theorists. Aristoxenus based all his value judgements concerning musical matters on the evidence of the sense of hearing and did not consult reason; Pythagoras based all his judgments on pure reasoning and neglected all sensual experience. Vicentino declares himself a follower of Ptolemy, who in his judgments took into account both reason and sense.[133] Immediately after this declaration, however, he adds that he intends to show in his work many such cases in which the judgments of sense and those of reason are contradictory, which demonstrates that he is well aware that the Ptolemaic compromise is possible only when the findings of sense and reason can be reconciled. When they are contradictory no compromise is possible, and it is in such cases that Vicentino shows himself to be a pure Aristoxenian. This becomes particularly clear in his judgments concerning tuning systems, the very field that was traditionally dominated by Pythagorean rationalism. Vicentino approaches problems of tuning with "Aristoxenian" pragmatism: For example, he allows tempering of fifths, since it is useful and does not offend the hearing.[134] He also advocates the enharmonic genus, well aware that its intervals are "irrational."[135] Characteristic are his comments on the great variety of musical judgments and tastes found among various nations of the world and even among a single nation. A composer should take all those various tastes into consideration and he should try to satisfy them all.[136] For a Pythagorean rationalist the judgments of reason are universally valid and the variability of tastes can be dismissed. By taking into account the variety of human judgments Vicentino reveals himself to be an Aristoxenian empiricist and relativist.

In describing earlier the chain of imitation leading from the passions to the poet, the composer, and the singer, I left out the last link of the chain, namely, the listener. The final goal of all musical efforts is to make an effect on the listener, to move him.[137] Vicentino aims at the listener's sense of hearing, but his goal is not pure entertainment. He wants the musician to arouse the imitated passions in the listener. The chain of imitation starts and ends with passions and its goal is to affect the lower, "subrational" spheres of the listener's soul: his sense of hearing and through it his emotions.

There can be little doubt that this basic postulate of *L'antica musica* was inspired, at least in part, by the legends of miraculously powerful effects of music on emotional and moral life in ancient times. The classical reports of those miraculous effects were so widely circulated and commented upon throughout the Renaissance[138] that Vicentino, presupposing a knowledge of them on the part of his readers, referred to them casually as "those effects which, as the Authors write, were made in ancient times,"[139] without quoting any of the legends himself. It was his aim to restore the miraculous power of ancient music, the secret of which was lost, he thought, to the musicians of his time.[140]

However, Vicentino did not believe that this secret could be recaptured by an antiquarian restoration of the technical, formal, or stylistic aspects of the ancient music. For him, music was making constant progress, being more perfect in his time than ten, twenty-five, fifty, or a hundred years before, and promising a continuing progress in the future.[141] He asserted now and again the superiority of contemporary over ancient music.[142] Ancient composers, he thought, did not mix genera, whereas his contemporaries did. As a result a modern musician had a much greater variety of intervals at his disposal, and his compositions were richer. Modern tuning systems, which made such mixing of genera possible, were also superior to the ancient, Pythagorean system. Those who thought that the power of ancient music could be recaptured once the ancient music itself was restored deluded themselves, asserted Vicentino.[143] What was meant by the programmatic title of the treatise, *The Ancient Music Restored to Modern Practice,* was the restoration of the miraculous effects of the ancient music, not of its style or compositional resources.

If our music is better than that of the ancients, asks Vicentino, why cannot we make those powerful effects ourselves? The reason is that musical resources have an effect only when they are new. Their power to move diminishes as listeners get used to them.[144] Novelty is a goal as important to Vicentino as variety, and both ideals are obviously closely related. The power of ancient music will be restored not through the return to the practice of old but through the further development of the compositional resources. Vicentino's efforts to introduce the non-diatonic genera into musical practice have to be understood in this context. He thought that the musicians of his time used only the large intervals of the non-diatonic genera, that is the minor and major thirds, and neglected the small ones, the chromatic semitones and enharmonic dieses. He advocated the full employment of the non-diatonic resources not because they were used in antiquity, but because they were not used in his time; thus they were new and capable of strong effects. It was their novelty, not their antiquity, that would work wonders.

Comparing the diatonic to non-diatonic genera, Vicentino always stresses that the latter introduce the beneficial variety and novelty, which are indispensable if one wants to move listeners. Closely related to the novelty is the exclusive, unusual, "reserved" character of the occasion, place, audience, and subject suitable for non-diatonic music. The theorist informs his readers that his students and admirers ". . . realize that (as the ancient writers demonstrate) chromatic and enharmonic music was deservedly reserved for other use than diatonic, since the latter was sung during public festivals in common places for vulgar ears, whereas the former were employed among the private amusements of gentlemen and princes for refined ears in praise of great persons and heroes."[145] The novel and unusual character of non-diatonicism should be retained. The musician who masters the secrets of non-diatonicism will be famous for his unusual and rare practice.[146]

Characteristically, Vicentino's polemicist, Danckerts, was opposed to any sort of novelty in musical composition, to the introduction of non-diatonic genera, and to the belief that non-diatonic music could work wonders and restore the miraculous ancient effects. He devoted the whole Part III of his treatise to the criticism of contemporary musical innovators. One of the main novelties by means of which these composers destroyed the good old music was their indiscriminate use of accidentals introduced in the vain hope of restoring the chromaticism. Non-diatonic genera will not work greater wonders than the diatonic, and the ancient musical myths should be treated sceptically in any case, asserted Danckerts. We should follow the tradition that tells us that the diatonic is better, easier, and more practicable than the other two genera:

> The harmony of the enharmonic or chromatic order does not produce greater miracles than that of the diatonic, even though the Don Nicola [Vicentino] will willingly suggest coarse people that with his enharmonic and chromatic music he stops rivers and indomitable wild beasts better than with the diatonic (as the poets pretend that Orpheus tamed the beasts in the woods, Arion the dolphins, and that Amphion made the stones and other objects ascend and descend of themselves, building the walls of Thebes, and that others produced other effects with the harmony of their sweet concerts), if he would find a fool to believe it. Thus I conclude that one should follow the judgment of the ancient philosophers and musicians who . . . have dismissed and left unused the two genera, chromatic and enharmonic, and kept to the diatonic only as the better, easier, more practicable, more natural, and more grateful to the ears. . . .[147]

Vicentino was not a humanist.[148] He did not study the classical musical treatises which were already available at his time not only because he lacked the necessary education. He learned all he knew about ancient music from Boethius and possibly also from some humanist friends, and he was not interested in learning more. He was inspired by the legendary power of ancient music, but he did not believe that knowing ancient music would help him to regain its lost eloquence. He was really interested in the future, not in the past. His role, as he saw it, was not that of the archeologist but that of an innovator whose work would be developed and perfected by future generations.[149] He created the first musical Utopia, the first meditation on the artwork of the future, on music as it should be, not as it was.

II

Gioseffo Zarlino
and Vincenzo Galilei

In the preceding chapter I considered the treatise of Ghiselin Danckerts as an example of the mid-sixteenth-century opposition to the ideas of the leader of the chromaticists, Nicola Vincentino. When seen within a broader historical context, however, Danckerts's position as a critic of novel ideas in general and of chromaticism in particular pales beside that of Gioseffo Zarlino. The unsurpassed depth and scope of Zarlino's theoretical works and the fact that he was undoubtedly the most influential musical writer of the era make him the chief spokesman of the conservative tendencies within late Renaissance music theory. Zarlino's views deserve the careful attention of any student of late sixteenth-century chromaticism because, when contrasted with more innovative ideas, they help us to define the borderline between normal and "experimental" chromatic usages. Vicentino and Zarlino belonged to the same generation of musicians; their musical education must have been very similar since both were pupils of Willaert. Zarlino's main theoretical work appeared only three years after Vincentio's and contained many thinly veiled polemical allusions to *L'antica musica*. Zarlino, even more than Danckerts, has to be recognized as the chief defender of tradition against the innovations of Vicentino.

Gioseffo Zarlino was born in 1517 in Chioggia, a town situated in the Venetian lagoon.[1] He received his early religious and musical training from the Franciscans of his native town. He was ordained a priest by 1540 and he served as a singer at the Cathedral of Chioggia at least since 1536 and as an organist in 1539-40. In 1541 he left for Venice, where he became a pupil of Adrian Willaert. His most important theoretical treatise, *Le Istitutioni harmoniche*, appeared in 1558. In 1565 he was appointed musical director of St. Mark's, succeeding another famous pupil of Willaert, Cipriano de Rore, and he retained this prestigious post until his death in 1590. His second treatise, *Dimostrationi harmoniche*, was published in 1571 and his last theoretical work, *Sopplimenti musicali*, in 1588. A limited number of his compositions, both sacred and secular, survived.[2] He was not only a famous theorist, a composer, and a director of one of Europe's finest musical establishments, but also a teacher of many well-known musicians and theorists, among others Claudio Merulo, Giovanni Croce, Girolamo Diruta, Vincenzo Galilei, and Giovanni Maria Artusi.

I. ZARLINO: THEORY

Following ancient theorists, Zarlino defines genus as a series of three intervals which add up to a fourth and distinguishes three such series, namely, diatonic, chromatic, and enharmonic:

> . . . [Genus] is for musician a division of the tetrachord. . . . A tetrachord is an ordering of sounds comprising four steps, of which the extremes are in the sesquitertian ratio. . . . Note, however, that according to ancient musicians there were three genera of composition. The first of these they called diatonic, the second chromatic, and the third enharmonic.[3]

The diatonic tetrachord consists of a major semitone and two consecutive whole tones in ascending order.[4] The chromatic tetrachord consists of a major semitone, a minor semitone, and a minor third in ascending order.[5] The enharmonic tetrachord ascends through two consecutive dieses and a major third.[6]

In a tonal system based on octave equivalence a genus cannot be exhaustively and unambiguously defined by a series of intervals which add up to a fourth only. For an adequate definition an intervallic series dividing a whole octave is necessary. In constructing his system from several identical tetrachords Zarlino again follows the example of Greek theorists.[7] The system consists of four tetrachords (the fifth can be neglected for a moment) and a whole tone added at the very bottom. The first and second tetrachords (counting always from the lowest one), the hypaton and meson, are conjunct, that is, the highest step of the hypaton tetrachord is the same as the lowest step of the meson. Similarly, the third and fourth tetrachords, the diezeugmenon and hyperbolaion, are conjunct. The second (meson) and third (diezeugmenon) are disjunct, the interval between the highest step of the meson tetrachord and the lowest step of the diezeugmenon being a whole tone. An intervallic series comprising two identical octaves results, each octave consisting of a whole tone followed by two conjunct tetrachords. Depending on whether the tetrachords are diatonic, chromatic, or enharmonic we have the following three ascending generic octave-series:

DIATONIC:	T	S	T	T	S	T	T
CHROMATIC:	T	S	s	m3	S	s	m3
ENHARMONIC:	T	D	D	M3	D	D	M3

(M3 = major third; m3 = minor third; T = whole tone; S = major semitone; s = minor semitone; D = diesis.)

Thus the diatonic genus in Zarlino's system may be defined as an intervallic series consisting of whole tones and major semitones placed so that the semitones are separated alternately by two and by three consecutive whole tones. The chromatic series consists of minor thirds, whole tones, and major and minor semitones placed so that the thirds are separated from each other alternately by a major semitone followed by a minor one or by a whole tone followed by a major and a minor semitone. The enharmonic series consists of major thirds, whole tones, and dieses placed so that the thirds are separated from each other alternately by two consecutive dieses or by a whole tone followed by two consecutive dieses.

Zarlino's idea of how the genera are constructed was to become a standard model for many later theorists. Among those who were strongly influenced by Zarlino's work and who accepted many of his basic views was the Spanish theorist Francisco Salinas. In spite of the fact that Salinas was a Spaniard and that his *De Musica* appeared in Spain, the ideas of this writer have to be considered briefly in the present study, since he spent many years in Italy and his treatise reflects considerable familiarity with Italian musical life.

Salinas was born in 1513 and, despite early blindness, was able to become an accomplished organist and to study Greek, Latin, the arts, and philosophy at the University of Salamanca.[8] In 1538 he went to Rome in the service of a Spanish cardinal and he remained in Italy until 1561. It was in Italy that he became acquainted with a large number of Greek musical theoretical sources, becoming undoubtedly the most learned of musical humanists of his age before Girolamo Mei.[9] He returned to Spain in 1561, served as the organist of Leon in 1563-67, and taught music at the University of Salamanca in 1567-87. His monumental treatise *De Musica* appeared in Salamanca in 1577. He died in 1590.

Salinas, in spite of his great respect for Zarlino, modifies some of the Italian theorist's ideas in an interesting way and I shall mention some of these modifications in the course of the present chapter. As far as the structure of the genera is concerned, Salinas criticizes Zarlino's opinion that the chromatic series has to contain minor thirds, claiming that all diatonic whole tones may be divided in the chromatic series into two semitones:

> However, he [Zarlino] is wrong when he thinks that no more than one chromatic string has to be added to the diatonic tetrachord, and that one must proceed in this genus through the trihemitone or semiditone [that is, the minor third]. Indeed, the force of the chromatic genus lies in the fact that every tone in it is found divided into two semitones.[10]

The function of the chromatic genus is to divide each diatonic whole tone into a major and a minor semitone. Salinas considers the most commonly used accidental steps (C$\sharp$ E$\flat$ F$\sharp$ G$\sharp$ B$\flat$) to be chromatic, which demonstrates that in his chromatic series some whole tones are divided so that the major semitone is below the minor one, and some are divided by the minor semitone below the major one.[11] The function of the enharmonic genus is to allow each whole tone to be divided both ways:

> For the enharmonic serves only one function, namely, that whenever in the chromatic genus, the greater semitone is in the higher position, the lesser semitone is placed in the lower position, and vice versa.[12]

Consequently, the less common accidental steps (D♭ D♯ E♯ G♭ A♭ A♯ B♯) are enharmonic.[13]

Zarlino describes the relationship between the genera as follows:

> . . . the diatonic genus was found before any other genus; . . . the other two genera were found much later and were placed within the diatonic. Since they were put together in such a way, many ancient musicians, among them Ptolemy, Bryennius, and Boethius, were of the opinion that the last two genera were nothing but a compression of the first genus, since they called a tetrachord compressed when its highest interval was larger than the two lower ones; and this is truly a property of these last two genera. . . .[14]

This compressing of the genera was accomplished as follows:[15] The extreme steps of the diatonic tetrachord remained unchanged in the non-diatonic tetrachords. Between the second and third diatonic steps, an intermediate step was added, a minor third below the highest step. This new step, together with the first, second, and last diatonic steps, constituted a chromatic tetrachord. Then another step was added between the first and second diatonic steps, dividing the diatonic semitone into two dieses. Together with the first, second, and last diatonic steps it constituted an enharmonic tetrachord:

DIATONIC: S   T   T

CHROMATIC: S s   m3

ENHARMONIC: D D   M3

Since a minor third consists of a whole tone and a major semitone,[16] it follows from the way in which the diatonic and chromatic tetrachords are put together that a whole tone consists of a major and a minor semitone:

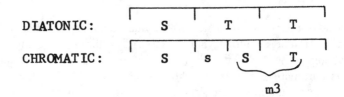

DIATONIC: S   T   T

CHROMATIC: S s S   T

m3

A major semitone consists of two dieses. Elsewhere Zarlino explains that the step added to create the enharmonic tetrachord is distant from the step added to create a lower conjunct chromatic tetrachord by a major third:[17]

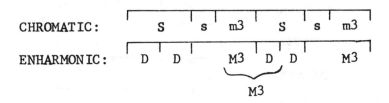

Since a major third consists of a minor third and a minor semitone,[18] it follows that a minor semitone equals a diesis. Thus a whole tone consists of three dieses. Since an octave consists of five whole tones and two major semitones, it may be argued that Zarlino's tonal system implies a division of an octave into nineteen dieses. It is possible that the same division is implied by Salinas's system as well since, as was demonstrated above, there are nineteen different steps within his octave, seven diatonic, five chromatic (C♯ E♭ F♯ G♯ B♭) and seven-enharmonic (D♭ D♯ E♯ G♭ A♭ A♯ B♭).

It will be remembered that the main issue in the debate between Vicentino and Lusitano involving the nature of the genera was whether the sums of the constitutive intervals of a generic series could be considered as intervals belonging to the genus in question or not, more specifically, whether the thirds belonged to the non-diatonic genera only, or whether they appeared already in the diatonic genus, the minor third being the sum of a whole tone and a major semitone and the major third consisting of two whole tones. Zarlino never mentions Vicentino in his writings, but his frequent polemical remarks concerning chromaticism seem often to be directed specifically against ideas presented in *L'antica musica ridotta alla moderna prattica*. The problem of thirds is discussed in *Le Istitutioni harmoniche*, Book III, Ch. 75, and predictably, Zarlino sides completely with Lusitano (without ever mentioning him or the debate explicitly), arguing very reasonably:

> Although these two intervals [that is, the major and minor thirds] are not actually found uncompounded in the diatonic genus, they are present potentially. . . . Therefore I say that the passage from one genus to another cannot be said to take place when composite intervals that are elements in another genus are used. But when the simple proper intervals peculiar to one genus and not found as simple or composite in another are introduced, this can be understood as a change of genus.[19]

Thus the use of thirds does not introduce non-diatonicism. Rather, only the presence of a minor semitone or a diesis is an unmistakable sign that the realm of diatonicism has been transcended.[20]

When the three tetrachords are put together a series of six steps dividing a fourth results:

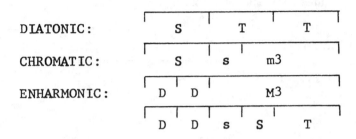

DIATONIC:	S		T		T	
CHROMATIC:	S	s		m3		
ENHARMONIC:	D	D			M3	
	D	D	s	S		T

In this new series some steps belong to several genera at the same time, others are the property of one genus only. The second lowest step appears only in the enharmonic series and the fourth only in the chromatic one. The diatonic genus is the oldest of the three and it was produced by nature. The non-diatonic genera are artificial, since they are invented by men who introduced additional steps among the diatonic ones.[21]

> Franchino Gaffurio says also that the chromatic is made artificially as an ornament of the diatonic and the enharmonic is called a perfect ornament of the natural and artificial musical diatonic and chromatic system. He says also that the diatonic tetrachord is natural.[22]

Thus the non-diatonic steps can be regarded as being incidentally arranged among the more basic diatonic ones, as serving an ornamental function in relation to the essential diatonic. The enharmonic steps seem to be even less essential than the chromatic ones. The chromatic step ornaments and ''colors'' the diatonic tetrachord:

> This (as Boethius would have it) is called chromatic, as if colored or varied, from the Greek word Χρῶμα which signifies color. It takes this name from the surface of an object which, when raised, makes it vary the color. This is well said, because when only one middle step of the diatonic tetrachord is changed and the other remain common, from such change different intervals and various ratios are born, that is, varied forms and varied sounds.[23]

It may be concluded that one of the functions of the genera is to introduce a hierarchy of relative importance among the steps of the gamut, the diatonic steps carrying more weight than the ''ornamental'' ones which belong solely to a non-diatonic series.

Similar views were expressed by Francisco Salinas, who claimed that among the genera only the diatonic was independent and self-sufficient, whereas the other two genera could not exist without the diatonic and were invented only to improve it:

Further, one also should know that these three genera stand in relation to one another as "good," "better," and "best." For just as only "good" can exist *per se*, and "better" can neither exist nor be imagined without "good," [and just as] each of these two exists in a more excellent fashion in the "best," so the diatonic alone can be found *per se*. For it forms the foundation for the others, and is annexed to them.

But although it [the diatonic] is more natural than the others, as Boethius says, it is nonetheless too hard, and the chromatic was invented to mollify its harshness. And yet this [chromatic] genus cannot be found without the diatonic, for it is nothing else than the diatonic made dense, so to speak. It receives the name [*chroma*] because it produces a more gentle and more perfect sound, as if emanating from a more perfect source. For this reason the genus is called chromatic rather than diatonic. This coincides with that which we experience on instruments struck by white and black keys.

The enharmonic also cannot subsist *per se*. But, since it is a combination of the other two genera, it produces the densest and most perfect sound. It is called not the diatonic or chromatic, but rather the enharmonic genus, because it is the best adjusted and most adaptable of all.[24]

Basing his belief on several ancient authorities, Zarlino states that the diatonic genus was the oldest of the three and that it was already long in use when ancient musicians invented first the chromatic and later the enharmonic.[25] According to Boethius the chromatic genus was invented by Timotheus of Melesia.[26] Zarlino speculates about the method in which the chromatic genus could have been invented as follows:

Although it is difficult to want to tell in what manner Timotheus may have invented or investigated this genus, since until now I could never find this matter discussed by any writer, nevertheless, it can be shown with some justification that . . . Timotheus, practicing in the diatonic genus may have attempted many times to pass with melody through the added tetrachord [that is, the synemmenon tetrachord which was conjunct with the meson], touching after the mese [that is, the highest step of the meson and the lowest of the synemmenon, a] the trite synemmenon [that is, the second lowest step of the synemmenon, b ♭], then passing from it to the paramese [that is, the lowest step of the diezeugmenon, b ♮], arriving also at the paranete synemmenon [that is, the second highest step of the synemmenon, c'] or the trite diezeugmenon [that is, the second lowest step of the diezeugmenon, c'] which are both the same step, even though it changes the name depending on which tetrachord it belongs to. Then, considering that the passage made through these steps yielded a certain variety, . . . he sought to make melody through every tetrachord in such a manner. . . .[27]

The synemmenon tetrachord of the system is conjunct with the meson.[28] When the steps of the diezeugmenon and synemmenon diatonic tetrachords are added to each other a chromatic tetrachord results.[29]

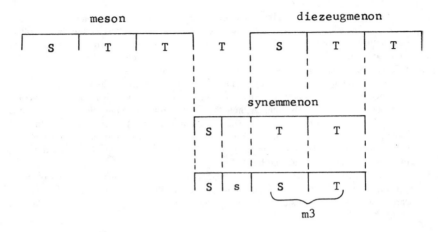

In other words, Zarlino thinks that a chromatic tetrachord was generated by Timotheus when he combined the steps of diezeugmenon and synemmenon tetrachords. Since these are both identical diatonic tetrachords and one may be regarded as a transposition of the other, the process which gave birth to the chromatic tetrachord can be understood as the process of transposition of the diatonic series and of adding up the steps from the transposed and untransposed series. As the result, the diatonic genus is considered by Zarlino to be more basic and important than the non-diatonic ones:

> It is honest and just to put this genus before the other two as more noble and excellent, since the others derive their being from it. The diatonic virtually contains the chromatic and enharmonic and at the end actually produces them, but not the reverse. It was truly just that Ptolemy gave all preeminence to this genus, since as the generator it is doubtless much more noble than what it generates.[30]

The method of transposition of the diatonic series can help us to understand not only how the non-diatonic genera might have been produced, but also the rationale behind the form of the keyboard proposed by Zarlino in *Le Istitutioni*. I have established that in Zarlino's tonal system a minor semitone consists of one diesis, a major semitone of two, and a whole tone of three. Thus a diesis is the largest common denominator of all the intervals of the three genera. If we represent an interval by a number which shows how many dieses it contains, we could represent the set of all intervals and their sums (that is, the gamut) produced by the diatonic series as follows: 2 (S), 3 (T), 5(m3), 6(m3), 8 (4th), 9 (tritone), 10 (dim.5th), 11 (5th), 13 (m6), 14 (M6), 16 (m7), 17 (M7), 19 (8). If we now want to construct such a series of steps that every interval of the gamut is available in both directions on every step, we must make these steps equidistant with the distance between two consecutive ones being the largest common denominator of all the intervals of the gamut, that is, diesis. In other words, if we want to construct such a series of steps that any species of the diatonic genus can be built by means of these steps in both directions starting at any step, we have to divide an octave into nineteen dieses by means of nineteen equidistant steps. The same series of steps will also enable us to build in both directions any species of the non-diatonic genera starting at any step. Thus, transposing an octave-species of the diatonic genus so that it starts at every step of the original series and also at every new step added by the transpositions, we shall finally arrive at a series of nineteen steps dividing the octave into dieses. The method of transposing a diatonic octave-species and adding up the untransposed and transposed steps produces not only the non-diatonic genera but also such a division of an octave which makes possible transpositions of all the octave-species of all three genera to any step dividing this octave.

"One should always note," says Zarlino, ". . . that these steps are put with some utility and order in an instrument when they are placed in such a way that they have in one or the other direction a corresponding consonant step at a fifth or a fourth or a major or minor third. . . ."[31] The utility of non-diatonic genera is that when their steps are combined with diatonic ones consonances may be obtained at these diatonic steps where they are not ordinarily available and, moreover, these non-diatonic steps make transpositions of modes possible which are of great help to organists who have to play a mode in the register which is convenient for the singers whom they accompany.[32] It seems to me that for Zarlino a perfect instrument should allow a transposition of any mode into any step of its keyboard. Toward the end of *Le Istitutioni*, Part II, the theorist describes such perfect "Clavocembalo" which was made for him by Dominico Pesarese in 1548 in Venice.[33] The picture of the instrument shows that it has two identical octaves each containing nineteen keys:[34]

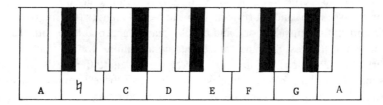

In the notation employed by Zarlino chromatic signs placed before a note move it up (✖) or down (♭) by a minor semitone and the enharmonic sign (✗), which Zarlino thought he invented, placed before a note moves it up a diesis.[35] It can be assumed that the dark keys of the upper row are the ones which were commonly found in sixteenth-century keyboards, that is, B♭, C♯, E♭, F♯, and G♯, and that the white keys of the upper row provide the remaining steps that are needed in order to have each diatonic whole tone divided not only by a major semitone followed by a minor one *or* the reverse, but by a major followed by minor *and* the reverse, and also in order to have each diatonic semitone divided into two dieses:

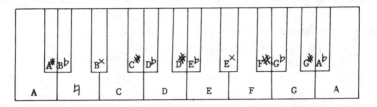

Such keyboard makes possible any transposition of any octave-species of any genus. Thus it is truly a perfect embodiment of Zarlino's tonal system.

The question remains how this instrument is to be tuned. Zarlino assumes that, at least to a certain extent, the intervallic structures of a tonal system are independent of a tuning system. This can be inferred from the fact that he presents several different possible tuning systems for diatonic, chromatic, and enharmonic tetrachords, suggesting thereby that a diatonic series, for instance, remains diatonic regardless by what specific ratios its intervals are represented.[36] This is the sense in which the revealing remark that Zarlino makes about the chromatic tetrachord should be understood:

> Although its ratios are very different from those which Boethius gives them, this is of little importance. Diversity of genus is born only from mutation or variation of the intervals which can be best made by going upwards through a semitone as the first interval, another semitone as the second, putting finally a minor third as the third interval.[37]

Although various tuning systems are possible, some of them are better than others. Zarlino's criterion of a perfect tuning system is that both its perfect (that is, the octave, fifth, and fourth) and imperfect consonances (the major and minor thirds and sixths) must be good and usable, that is, acceptable to both reason and sense. He criticizes the ancient Pythagorean tuning for its lack of usable imperfect consonances. Contemporary composers regard the thirds and sixths as consonances and a tuning system which will make these intervals consonant is required.[38] A simple consonance, for Zarlino, must be represented by a multiple or superparticular ratio expressed by means of numbers from 1 to 6 only, the privileged position of 6, the *numero senario*, deriving from the fact that it is the first perfect number.[39] The sixths do not conform to these criteria, since they are not simple consonances, but rather sums of the fourth and thirds.[40] The true ratios of the simple consonances are born from the harmonic division.[41] The harmonic division of the octave (2:1) yields the fifth (3:2) and fourth (4:3), and the harmonic division of the fifth gives the major and minor thirds (5:4 and 6:5). The fourth and major third give major sixth (5:3), the fourth and minor third give minor sixth (8:5).

Zarlino believes that the perfect tuning system in which the consonances have these ratios is the syntonic tuning of Ptolemy[42] in which the diatonic tetrachord consists of a major semitone (16:15), followed by a major whole tone (9:8), followed by a minor whole tone (10:9).[43] Since the major semitone is 16:15 and the minor third is 6:5, the minor semitone of the chromatic tetrachord has to be 25:24. And finally, since the major third is 5:4 and the first of the enharmonic dieses in the enharmonic tetrachord has to be of the same size as the minor semitone,[44] that is 25:24, the second diesis must be 128:125. Thus in the enharmonic tetrachord the first diesis is major and the second minor.

A diatonic octave in the syntonic tuning will have the following ratios:

9:8	16:15	9:8	10:9	16:15	9:8	10:9
A	B♮ c	d	e	f	g	a

It is easy to notice that it lacks a pure fourth between A and d (and, of course, a pure fifth between d and a) and a pure minor third between d and f (and a major sixth between f and d'). The problem is solved when the synemmenon tetrachord is added to the system and another d is created a comma (81:80) lower than the first one:

9:8	16:15	9:8	10:9	16:15	9:8	10:9
A	B♮ c	d	e	f	g	a

16:15	9:8	10:9
A	B♭ c	d↑

⌊⌋ = comma 81:80

This time, however, an impure major sixth appears between B♭ and g, which can be improved only when another B♭ is added a comma higher than the first one. According to Zarlino, in unaccompanied vocal performance the voices always sing pure consonances and the troublesome comma can be disregarded.[45] In such instruments, however, which cannot vary pitch continuously, that is, primarily in keyed and fretted instruments, the problem of comma must be approached in one of the two ways. Either many steps will have two versions distant by a comma, or, in order to avoid the multiplication of steps, the comma will be divided and distributed among many intervals, that is, a temperament will be introduced.

The first solution is presented in a curious keyboard instrument which Zarlino described in his last work, *Sopplimenti musicali* of 1588 and claimed to have it made for himself many years ago.[46] The keyboard has two identical octaves with diatonic and chromatic keys regularly found in sixteenth-century instruments (C $\sharp$, E $\flat$, F $\sharp$, G $\sharp$, B $\flat$), with the addition of alternative keys for D, B $\flat$, E $\flat$, and F $\sharp$:

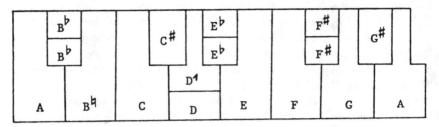

Since the lower d^1 is placed on the keyboard above d, it can be assumed that an analogous solution was chosen for the double chromatic keys. I have already explained why two different d's and two different B $\flat$'s were necessary. Of the two f $\sharp$'s one supplies a minor third below a (and a major sixth above A), the other, which is a comma higher, supplies all other pure consonances which are possible between f $\sharp$ and other keys. I see no necessity for two e $\flat$'s and I do not understand why Zarlino added the lower one. The consecutive intervals of the octave are tuned as follows:

16:15	81:80	25:24	16:15	25:24	16:15	81:80	256:243	81:80
A	B$\flat$	B$\flat$	B$\natural$	c	c$\sharp$	d^1	d	e$\flat$	e$\flat$

25:24	16:15	25:24	81:80	16:15	25:24	16:15
e$\flat$	e	f	f$\sharp$	f$\sharp$	g	g$\sharp$	a

The same solution was chosen by Francisco Salinas for his perfect keyboard instrument containing all three genera, which he claimed to have ordered to be constructed in Rome and which was still in his possession in 1577.[47] Like Zarlino, Salinas considers the just intonation to be the most perfect system of tuning.[48] As a result he has to introduce within his diatonic series two D's a comma apart.[49] Two of his chromatic steps, B $\flat$ and F $\sharp$, must have two versions distant by a comma[50] and, similarly, two of his enharmonic steps, G $\flat$ and A $\sharp$, must have two versions.[51] Since, as I have already indicated, the combined steps of Salinas's three genera produce a series of nineteen different steps within an octave, the double versions of the five steps listed above produce a keyboard with twenty-four steps within an octave and such was undoubtedly the keyboard of Salinas's perfect instrument. In view of Salinas's admiration for just intonation it is understandable that he criticizes the *archicembalo* of Nicola Vicentino (without mentioning his name expressly) for employing the 31-division of the octave, that is a division bearing no relationship to just intonation.[52]

Zarlino admits that his instrument is very difficult to use and that a temperament is a much more practicable solution, since it allows reduction of the number of keys without reducing the number of usable consonances.[53] A temperament changes the true ratios of intervals so slightly that hearing is not offended.[54] In *Le Istitutioni* Zarlino describes a temperament in which fifths are diminished by 2/7 comma, thirds by 1/7 comma each, major whole tones by 4/7 comma, whereas minor whole tones are enlarged by 3/7 comma (thus the major and minor whole tones have the same size), and major semitones are enlarged by 3/7 comma. Only the minor semitone and, naturally, the octave are left untempered.[55] Another temperament, which according to Zarlino is very good and easier to accomplish,[56] is described in *Dimostrationi harmoniche*.[57] It diminishes fifths by 1/4 comma, minor thirds by 1/4 comma, major whole tones by 1/2 comma, it enlarges minor whole tones by 1/2 comma (thus the major and minor whole tones have the same size), and it enlarges major (and presumably also minor) semitones by 1/4 comma each. Major thirds and octaves are left pure. Both temperaments seem to be intended for an ordinary keyboard of twelve keys within an octave and at least the first one is also prescribed for Zarlino's *Clavocembalo* of nineteen keys per octave. Neither the ordinary meantone temperament of 1/4 comma nor the 2/7 comma variety of meantone temperament correspond perfectly to the 19-division of an octave, but, in J. Murray Barbour's words, "most of these varieties of the meantone temperament will have a smaller deviation [from the equal temperament] when applied to a keyboard with 19 or more notes to the octave than upon the usual keyboard."[58] While the 2/7-comma temperament seems to be more suitable for the multiple division, it is inferior to the ordinary 1/4-comma system when applied to a keyboard of twelve notes to an octave.[59] Both temperaments are also advocated for keyboard instruments by Francisco Salinas who, in addition, invented the 1/3-comma temperament which produced an almost precisely equal division of the octave into nineteen intervals.[60]

I have argued above that Zarlino's thought implies a certain degree of independence of the tonal system from the tuning system. It must be admitted, however, that this independence is only implied and never explicitly stated in the theorist's works. For this reason any reconstruction of the tonal system implied by these works involves some interpretation on the part of a historian. It seems to me that I owe the reader an explanation of why I have decided to treat the differentiation of the whole tone into major and minor sizes and the differentiation of the diesis into major and minor sizes as phenomena which belong to the level of the tuning system and not of the tonal system. Two intervals can be treated as truly different only when they are meant to be used differently by musicians. There is no trace of such a functional differentiation of the major and minor whole tones in Zarlino's work; on the contrary, the following remarks seem to prove that in composition they are treated as one and the same interval:

When we find in counterpoint two parts separated by one of these intervals, we may say that they are separated by a large whole tone or a small one; or we may say that the distance between them is a major second. For this is the term used by practical musicians to distinguish it from the minor second, which is the large semitone.[61]

Thus, it seems to me that on the level of the tonal system there is one whole tone which gets two different sizes in the vocal syntonic tuning, the difference being again obliterated in both of Zarlino's instrumental temperaments.

The problem of the diesis is somewhat different, since it is not supposed to be used in composition at all. As we shall see below, only an enharmonic step (but not an interval) can be used in instrumental practice when a diatonic piece is played in transposition. Since diesis is musically useful only as the smallest interval in a series of steps (keyboard) which allows transposition, and since such a series is best when it divides an octave into equal parts, it seems logical to assume that on the level of tonal system there is only one diesis which gets two different sizes in the syntonic tuning when it is theoretically expanded to accommodate all three genera.

On the other hand, the difference between the major and minor semitones is very real already on the level of the tonal system, since the major semitone, being diatonic, is allowed in composition, whereas the chromatic minor semitone is not. At this point, however, we have crossed the boundary between theory and practice.

II. ZARLINO: POETICS

Even when he discusses genera from a purely theoretical point of view, it is evident that Zarlino highly favors the diatonic above the non-diatonic. Diatonic genus is more noble and excellent, it is oldest, natural, it is the generator of non-diatonic series, and, consequently, it is essential, whereas they are merely ornamental. Thus it is not surprising to learn that in Zarlino's theory of composition the non-diatonic genera play a very limited role. The theorist's ideal is a diatonic work. Non-diatonic elements are allowed only exceptionally. The circumstances in which they are allowed, however, deserve careful consideration of any student of sixteenth-century chromaticism. Thanks to the unprecedented thoroughness of its contrapuntal theory and to the prestige it enjoyed in the latter part of the sixteenth century, *Le Istitutioni harmoniche* is deservedly considered the most important work on the art of musical composition of its time. For us its conservative point of view, its lack of sympathy toward innovations of chromaticists, is only an advantage, because it affords us an insight into what a well-informed but conservative Italian musician of the third quarter of the sixteenth-century would have considered a normal and justifiable use of non-diatonic elements and which ways of going beyond strict diatonicism would be for him extravagant, experimental, or simply inadmissible. Thus Zarlino's views on the proper use of chromaticism in composition give us an indispensable standard of normalcy against which the degree of novelty, both theoretical and practical, of his more daring contemporaries can be measured.

Zarlino's ideal is a basically diatonic and modal composition. Non-diatonic steps are allowed only when they do not destroy diatonicism and, above all, when they do not change one mode into another or disrupt the modal framework of a composition altogether. In other words, they are allowed only when introduced accidentally and temporarily. Attempts of "some musicians today" to write a purely chromatic of enharmonic composition were severely censured by Zarlino. He devoted the last nine chapters of the Part III of *Le Istitutioni*, as well as many asides throughout his writings, to the rebuttal of the opinions of "chromaticists," naming no one, but aiming clearly at Nicola Vicentino, whose *L'antica musica* appeared three years earlier. For Zarlino only diatonic genus can be used without going beyond its natural steps.[62] Non-diatonic genera cannot be used in their pure forms, that is without steps belonging to another genus, without the loss of many consonances which are necessary to produce perfect vertical harmonies appropriate in a polyphonic composition. "We may therefore conclude that it is impossible to use the last two genera simply and independently and to obtain the perfect harmony without the steps peculiar to the other genera."[63] It is not possible to compose a perfect piece in a pure chromatic or enharmonic genus, "as some have dreamed."[64] The use of pure non-diatonic genera was possible in the monodic style of the ancient Greeks, but not in modern polyphonic music.[65] This last idea was criticized by Francisco Salinas: "Also he [that is, Zarlino] seems to be mistaken when he says that the chromatic genus can be separated from the diatonic, and was sometimes used apart from the diatonic."[66]

Zarlino contrasts the ancient monodic ideal which aims at melodic variety (hence the variety of ancient tuning systems and genera) and the modern polyphonic ideal which needs all consonances, perfect and imperfect (and hence utilizes the only tuning system that renders imperfect consonances pure, namely, the syntonic tuning), in order to produce smooth "harmony," that is movement of several parts together.[67] It is true that if one accepts Zarlino's understanding of the structures of the generic series, steps within a purely diatonic series have more consonances above and below them than steps within a purely chromatic or enharmonic series, and that, consequently, it is easier to write good counterpoint using only diatonic steps than employing the steps belonging only to the chromatic or enharmonic series. In polyphony Zarlino's diatonic is self-sufficient, whereas his chromatic or enharmonic are not. A defender of consistent non-diatonicism could refute Zarlino's argument only if he rejected the theorist's understanding of how generic series are constructed, or if he attacked Zarlino's counterpoint and polyphony in the name of the idealized monodic style of the ancient Greeks, or in the name of new rules of counterpoint. Meanwhile the

theorist could maintain that the chromaticists did not understand the real nature
of the genera and deluded themselves that their compositions were purely
chromatic or enharmonic when in fact

> they use not only the steps of the genus in which they say they are composing but also
> steps proper and peculiar to other genera and still others that are altogether foreign. . . .
> Since these works fail to meet the given requirements, they cannot be said to be composed
> in these two genera as used by the ancients; rather they are in a genus invented by them
> [modern chromaticists] and subject only to their own whims.[68]

Since Zarlino's diatonic genus, in opposition to his chromatic and
enharmonic, is self-sufficient, and since in theoretically established hierarchy of
the genera the diatonic plays a fundamental part, it follows that non-diatonic
steps can be used within a basically diatonic composition only in accidental and
temporary manner so that they do not introduce a permanent mutation into a
non-diatonic genus. Thus it is particularly annoying when a non-diatonic step is
too frequently substituted for a diatonic one.[69] Zarlino's general precept is that
one may use non-diatonic steps but not non-diatonic genera:

> Let no one be surprised by my saying we use the steps from these [non-diatonic] genera while
> proceeding in the manner described. We actually do use their steps but not the genera
> themselves. We use the parts but not the whole.[70]

Zarlino has in mind two situations in which such use of non-diatonic steps
but not of the whole genera is possible. First, a purely diatonic composition
may be transposed by an organist to a register convenient for the singers
whom he accompanies, so that he will use black keys. Second, in an untransposed diatonic composition non-diatonic steps may occasionally be used
when a required consonance cannot be supplied otherwise. In this case one
should avoid, however, non-diatonic melodic intervals:

> The use of the steps or even an interval, provided it is harmonious, may be conceded, since
> their effect is good; this constitutes the use of parts. It is not legitimate, however, to use the
> whole, that is, all the steps of a genus and all its intervals. To do so leads to a poor effect. I
> refer to the use of all the steps and intervals that a musician considers to be part of one genus
> and of no other in the melodic lines of the parts of a composition. To use steps from a genus,
> on the other hand, means to accommodate parts of it to the melodic lines of diatonic
> compositions, proceeding with intervals found or possible in the diatonic genus. This has
> been successfully accomplished by many. Excluded from this usage, though, are the steps
> proper to the chromatic and enharmonic, the small semitone and the diesis.[71]

We may infer from these words that consistent employment of non-diatonic
intervals in melodic lines would be considered unusual at the time when *Le
Istitutioni* was being written.

    There are, hypothetically speaking, three general situations in which non-diatonic steps can be used within a basically diatonic composition. First, a diatonic piece may be transposed by an instrumentalist for the convenience of accompanied singers. Second, a non-diatonic step may be used accidentally within a diatonic framework. Third, an introduction of non-diatonic steps within the course of a work may indicate that a transposition or a modulation, that is, a mutation of one mode into another, and a simultaneous transposition was made. Zarlino's attitude concerning the first two cases was briefly discussed above. As far as modulation is concerned, Zarlino considers it "a vice some composers practice."[72] Even more deplorable for him is such indiscriminate use of non-diatonic steps that modal identity of a composition (created primarily by means of cadences which should normally be made on the final and a fifth and third above the final of a mode)[73] is altogether destroyed. This is one of the main charges directed by Zarlino against modern chromaticists.[74]

If modulatory use of non-diatonic steps is not advised, an accidental and temporary use which does not change genus or mode permanently is possible. A good indication of what is such an accidental, non-modulatory usage is provided in the following passage:

> It is quite true that taking a tetrachord out of a composition and putting in it another may be made in two ways: first, when the step b ♭ , which is the trite synemmenon is put accidentally once or twice between the mese [a] and paramese [b ♮] in only one part of the composition, that is, in a small section of the tenor or of another part (but not in every part). In this case we can say that taking out the diezeugemenon tetrachord which starts on the step b ♮ , that is, on paramese and putting in the synemmenon which starts on the step a, which means putting in the step b ♭ mentioned above, does not have the power of transforming one mode into another and that such tetrachord put within the composition is not natural but accidental. . . . But the second way takes place when in the whole composition, that is, in every part, we use the synemmenon instead of the diezeugmenon and we sing this composition using b flat instead of singing it using b natural. When this tetrachord is placed in such a way . . . it is not placed accidentally within the composition but is natural and the mode is called transposed. . . . Such tetrachord has the power to transform one mode into another.[75]

Thus a non-diatonic step used once or twice in a single part can be understood as being used accidentally. On the other hand, persistent use of a non-diatonic step in every part introduces a transposition, or a mutation of genus, or a change of mode.

Since Zarlino allows the use of non-diatonic steps only in so far as they do not destroy the diatonic genus or the mode of a composition, it might be asked why does he find them useful at all. The advantage he sees in their use in composition is that

> by combining their steps with diatonic steps we can use the perfect harmonies and at the same time obtain with the steps of these genera many imperfect consonances, major and minor, at many points in the diatonic scale where they are not ordinarily available, as is apparent to anyone who has experience in composition. These steps are at times wanted to create a harmony that corresponds to gay or sad words.[76]

Within the limits of strict diatonicism certain consonances are not available at certain steps. This deficiency can be overcome by means of non-diatonic steps. The increase in the number of consonances available at every step is desirable for reasons of text expression as well as for strictly technical, contrapuntal ones.

One of Zarlino's requirements for every good composition is that it "shall complement the text, that is the words. With gay texts it should not be plaintive, and vice versa; with sad subjects it should not be gay."[77] The most important role in complementing the text with music is played by imperfect consonances. The major imperfect consonances are lively and cheerful by nature, the minor ones are sweet, smooth, sad, and languid.[78] Thanks to non-diatonic steps it is possible to change, for instance, a natural major imperfect consonance into a minor one when the text calls for a sad effect, and vice versa.

Besides these demands of text expression, there are also purely contrapuntal reasons which make the increase in the number of consonances at every step desirable:

> Through the aid of chromatic steps we may achieve good, sonorous harmonies and escape poor relationships in the diatonic, such as the tritone, semidiapente, and similar intervals that result from simultaneous singing, as I have shown already. Without the chromatic, many harsh harmonies and awkward lines would be heard. Although the poor relationships could be avoided with only the diatonic steps, it would be rather more difficult to do so, particularly while seeking, as one should, to vary the harmony. It follows that the use of the steps mentioned will render the modes sweeter and smoother.[79]

More specifically, chromatic steps provide perfect consonances where these cannot be obtained with diatonic steps alone, and thus the prohibited augmented and diminished octaves, fifths, and fourths can be avoided.[80] When two parts move in parallel thirds or sixths, it is advisable to vary the size of these consonances so that the major alternate with minor ones,[81] and chromatic steps may be needed to do this. Zarlino notes that the minor semitone "is used mostly when two parts ascend or descend together in thirds."[82] Finally, chromatic steps are useful when one wants to change the size of an imperfect consonance so as to make it conform to Zarlino's rule to the effect that, with minor exceptions, "the composer moving from an imperfect to a perfect consonance must be certain the imperfect one is actually the nearest."[83] It is necessary, however, to violate this rule occasionally, so as to avoid a violation of an even more important rule. "Let us remember, then, that our obligations to the rules do not extend to impossibilities," warns Zarlino.[84] The function of chromatic steps was understood similarly by Salinas who saw their usefulness in the fact that they supplied consonances on such steps where these were missing within the purely diatonic system and thus mollified the harshness of the diatonic.[85]

Non-diatonic steps are useful not only in composition but also in performance:

With the steps of these genera we can moreover transpose modes into higher or lower registers. Such transpositions are very necessary to chapel organists, who must at times move a mode from one register to another according to the voices available. This could not be done without the aid of these steps. Although the steps are often used on such occasions, it does not follow that they are other than diatonically treated.[86]

Zarlino distinguishes clearly between a mere transposition of a diatonic piece and a true mutation into a non-diatonic genus. The concept of transposition explains the use of accidentals and non-diatonic steps in notation and performance of a diatonic piece. The concept does not apply to purely vocal music as long as there is no recognizable pitch standard. It does apply, however, to instrumental music, and it is particularly useful when instruments have to play in the register which is convenient for accompanied singers.

It should be recalled that Zarlino regarded non-diatonic genera as the result of the process of transposition of the diatonic series and that he constructed his perfect keyboard with nineteen keys to an octave in such a way that it made possible a transposition of any mode to any key. Within the context of the whole *Le Istitutioni* it may be assumed that the theorist invented his unusual and complicated keyboard to provide harpsichordists and organists with a perfect accompanying tool. This might explain why Zarlino, although opposed to any consistent non-diatonicism, bothered to create an instrument so eminently suited for experiments in chromatic and enharmonic music. However, certain remarks that the theorist makes about his instrument seem to indicate that this is not the complete explanation. Zarlino states that he has constructed the instrument "in order to see in what manner the chromatic and enharmonic harmonies could succeed."[87] Moreover, he adds that "this is an instrument in which every excellent player will be able to practice not only diatonic but also chromatic and enharmonic harmonies, when he will be able to restore them to ancient modes, or when in our times they [the non-diatonic harmonies] will turn out better and sweeter than that which is heard [in compositions of some modern composers]."[88] It is clear from these remarks that Zarlino aimed not only at an instrument which makes all transpositions possible but also at one on which practical experiments in truly chromatic and enharmonic music could be made. The remarks seem also to indicate that although Zarlino was not opposed to such experiments in principle and even possibly made some himself, he did not think that attempts of his contemporaries to write non-diatonically were successful. It is probable that in 1548, when he constructed his instrument, Zarlino entertained hopes similar to those of Vicentino, hopes of restoring non-diatonic modes to modern practice, and that only subsequently he decided that it was not possible to create good non-diatonic music within the framework of the polyphonic ideal.

Regardless of whether this conjecture is correct or not, one can hardly escape the impression that Zarlino, although he ultimately rejected chromaticism, or, rather, allowed its use on a very limited scale, was profoundly interested in exploring and defining the possibilities of non-diatonic tonal resources. His somewhat ambiguous attitude toward chromaticism reflects, I think, an inner tension which seems to be one of the most characteristic traits of the musical thought of his time, the tension between ''formal'' and ''expressive'' ideals of music, between the ideals of a work of music which is a pleasing, regularly organized, harmonious whole and one which strives to imitate and cause passions. I have described the same tension as it appeared in the theory of Nicola Vicentino.[89] Neither theorist was able to resolve the tension completely. Vicentino, the defender of chromaticism, emphasized the ''expressive'' aspect of musical art, Zarlino, who rejected radical chromaticism, unmistakably preferred the ''formal'' aspect. However, in both cases it was the matter of preference rather than exclusive choice and in both cases certain attempts were made at reconciling the opposed principles. It is as if the theorists felt that both principles were indispensable and that they mutually defined one another through their opposition.

Characteristically, Zarlino defines most clearly the musical ideal he wants to defend within the context of his lifelong polemic with the chromaticists. One such definition can be found in *Dimostrationi harmoniche*, Ragionamento IV, Proposta XI. The treatise purports to record a series of conversations which supposedly took place in Venice in the spring of 1562 in which three Venetian musicians, Zarlino, Claudio Merulo, and Adrian Willaert, a visitor from Ferrara, Francesco Viola, and a certain Desiderio, an amateur from Pavia, participated. During the conversations various problems of music theory were considered under the expert guidance of Zarlino. However, in the aside directed against chromaticists which I have mentioned the theorist conspicuously remains silent. One gets a definite impression that Zarlino wants to put the great authority of three famous contemporary musicians, Willaert, Merulo, and Viola, behind his critique of chromaticism. Willaert starts with Zarlino's customary charges to the effect that, first, modern composers who claim to write chromatic pieces do not understand the true structure of the genus and, instead of inserting just one step between the second and third steps of the diatonic tetrachord in order to make it chromatic, add chromatic steps haphazardly wherever they want; second, they do not observe any mode; and third, they break the rules of counterpoint by using the prohibited diminished and augmented intervals.

Salinas refers to this passage when he says that Zarlino

> introduces Adrian Willaert as a speaker in the fourth dialogue of his *Dimostrazioni*, who bitterly inveighs against those who wish chromatics to be found in his musical compositions in such a way that movement may be made through lesser semitones, the steps of the chromatic genus. He is right in scolding these people; for, indeed, the force of the chromatic genus is not such that it requires us to move through steps as short as these.[90]

Then Merulo says to Willaert:

> Sir, you have laboured greatly together with many other good musicians more ancient than you to bring music to a certain manner or form which would combine some gravity and majesty. But with these [modern chromaticists] your endeavour became almost vain, because not only do they not observe good precepts of the art, but they also teach and exhort others to break what is good and well-organized and to do worse things than they do themselves. And when they do something which transgresses the good and beautiful of music, they cover themselves with the shield of ignorance and say that these things are done in the chromatic genus, although they neither do it, nor know what it is.[91]

Zarlino's ideal, as embodied in music of his teacher, Adrian Willaert, is characterized by a certain manner of "gravity and majesty." It is the ideal of a harmoniously balanced work, organized according to the traditional precepts of composition, preserving the unity of mode, and obeying rules of counterpoint. It is opposed to expressive excesses of modern chromaticists and to their disregard of traditional rules.

However, this is not to say that the idea of expressing affections by musical means is totally repugnant to Zarlino. On the contrary, he considers the musical imitation of textual subjects an important goal of a composer. The process of composition should start with careful consideration of the words.[92] In a polyphonic vocal composition, which Zarlino, following Plato's terminology,[93] calls *Melodia*, the text (*Oratione*) is the principal component, whereas harmony (*Harmonia*), or simultaneous movement of several parts, and rhythm (*Numero*) are secondary.[94] If the text imitates matters that are gay or sad, the composer should choose his musical resources, such as mode, harmony, and rhythm, according to the nature of these matters and thus imitate musically the passions of the text.[95] Non-diatonicism has an important role in musical imitation of passions, since, as has been pointed out, it greatly enlarges the range of affective devices and in general its use introduces certain softness, whereas purely diatonic composition produces harsh and manly effects.[96] It is principally for the purpose of text expression that Zarlino allows certain limited use of non-diatonicism.

Thus Zarlino's ambivalent attitude toward non-diatonicism, his severe censure of chromatic experiments on the one hand, and his reluctant acceptance of carefully controlled chromaticism on the other, can be explained as the result of his attempt to achieve a compromise between the conflicting demands of the "formal" and "expressive" ideals of music. There can be no doubt, however, that he was willing to compromise only so long as the demand for text expression did not result in compositional licence, in transgressing the traditional rules. Music should imitate and excite passions, but not to such an extent that the harmonious balance and restraint, *gravità*, as well as modal unity or precepts of counterpoint are disturbed.

This emphasis on traditional rules rather than on innovation for the sake of text expression is well illustrated by Zarlino's attitude toward the opinion of the "chromaticists" who contend that any interval whatsoever, and not only the traditionally accepted consonances and dissonances, may be used in music, since

> the voice is capable of forming any interval, and it is necessary to imitate ordinary speech in representing the words as orators do and ought. Therefore it is not inappropriate to use all these intervals to express the ideas contained in the words, with the same accents and other effects we employ in conversation, so that the music might move the affections.[97]

Predictably, Zarlino rejects such suggestions:

> It would be possible to include such things comfortably in one voice of a composition, where these accents, properly used, would have a good effect. Were this voice combined with others, however, the result would compel one to seal one's ears.[98]

In polyphony only a limited number of intervals may be used, even though human voice and some instruments can intone many more.

III. ZARLINO: AESTHETICS

There is a motif which constantly reappears in Zarlino's writing, namely, the suggestion that various recent innovations, such as the imitation of the methods of orators, or chromaticism, might be viable if musicians returned to the monodic style of the ancients but not in modern polyphony. Near the end of Part III of *Le Istitutioni* and of his long "rebuttal to the opinions of the chromaticists"[99] Zarlino concludes

> that nothing good can be accomplished outside of our [that is, diatonic] genus, used, as we are accustomed to, with chromatic and enharmonic steps where appropriate. Only if we return to the practice of the ancients and coordinate meter, melody, and words can we use these genera otherwise.[100]

Zarlino might refer here to his belief that in antiquity a particular genus was coordinated with particular metric feet, since "the nature of the genera did not consist simply in melody, but [also] in the feet of the text."[101] But, more significantly, it is the imitation of the text and of its affections by means of melody and meter that he has in mind. Ancient monody makes such imitation possible to a much larger extent than modern polyphony, since the latter has to obey certain autonomously musical rules. We have already seen that for Zarlino the requirements of polyphony exclude both consistent non-diatonicism and imitation of oratory.

Thus Zarlino indirectly suggests that the future of chromaticism is linked with the restoration of monody and with increased emphasis on imitation of the words, with a return, therefore, to ancient musical ideals. Zarlino himself, however, was very far from advocating a return to the ancient monody, since for him modern polyphony was obviously superior. In comparison with music of the ancients, modern music was in a state of almost unsurpassable perfection.[102] It is characteristic of the historical awareness of the age that those who, like Nicola Vicentino, looked back to restore certain aspects of ancient music, were at the same time looking forward to change modern practice, whereas those like Zarlino whose attitude toward the ancient past might be described as reverent but indifferent defended the present against innovations. Thus Zarlino compared modern chromaticists to Herostrates, since they wanted to become famous while destroying traditional precepts.[103] Zarlino, although full of admiration for ancient musicians and theorists, in particular Ptolemy, who for him was the highest authority in musical matters, thought that his own times far surpassed antiquity thanks to the achievements of Willaert and others in composition and to his own in theory. And the superiority of modern music lay in his opinion in the perfection of its "harmony," simultaneous movement of parts.

A doubt concerning the alleged superiority of modern music could be aroused by stories of miraculous effects which music had in ancient times:

> But if ancient music was so imperfect (as I have demonstrated above), it does not appear believable that musicians could have produced such various effects in human souls as are reported in the histories. . . . It appears even less believable, since today, when it has been brought to such perfection that one almost cannot hope for anything better, one does not see it have any of the effects mentioned above.[104]

To such objections Zarlino answers that, although ancient musicians did truly achieve miraculous effects, "also at the present time music is not deprived of the power to achieve such effects."[105] Later Zarlino adds that "music never ceases in various modes and times to work and produce various effects. . . . Thus we see also in our days that it excites in us various passions as it did in ancient times."[106] Such remarks are designed to counter any attempt to return to ancient practices, an attempt which in Zarlino's time was usually justified by the desire to recover the miraculous power of ancient music.

Zarlino's particular scorn is directed against those who claim that the effects of ancient music were due to the use of non-diatonic genera. He argues that the effects are possible also in the diatonic genus, and further that all aspects of musical composition, and not only genera, contribute to the imitation of the passions.[107] Zarlino affirms the greater nobility and importance of the diatonic and criticizes the chromaticists who falsely attribute to the ancients the belief in a special, exclusive, noble character of non-diatonic music:

> Whence some people make me laugh when they say, giving no reason nor any authority, that this [diatonic] genus was used by the ancients at public festivals for common ears, and that the other two were put in use among private gentlemen. I think, however, that they had never seen Ptolemy, and even if they had, they did not understand him.[108]

Zarlino's aim in this clear reference to Vicentino[109] is to discredit the reformer's authority to speak about the music of the ancients so that his ideas concerning ancient practice might not be used to justify innovations.

It is important to realize that when Zarlino claims that modern diatonic music is capable of equally powerful effects as those for which ancient music was famous, he does so in order to take away from the reformers their crucial argument rather than to indicate what he himself considers the most important aim of music. For the "effects," important as they are, do not seem to constitute the real goal of music in Zarlino's thought. The superiority of modern polyphony over ancient monody lies not in its power to move listeners but in its "harmony." And "harmony" is the pivotal concept of the theorist's aesthetic thought.

> Speaking universally, music is nothing but harmony, and we may say that it is that agreement from which Empedocles proposed all things were generated; it is a concord of discords, meaning a concord of diverse things that can be joined together.[110]

This universal harmony or *musica mondana* finds its microcosmic parallel in *musica humana*, which harmonizes diverse parts of the human soul and body.[111] Both these kinds of music find in turn their analogy in the harmony of actually sounding vocal and instrumental music, "harmony which arises from sounds."[112] These various kinds of harmony and analogies between them are possible thanks to the fact that the harmonious concord in which diverse elements are joined together can be conceived as a proportion and that such a proportion can be expressed by means of a numerical ratio. In audible music harmony arises in the form of consonant relations between two or more different sounds (this is called improper harmony and is perfect when there are more than two sounds, or imperfect when there are only two) and between two or more simultaneous melodies (this is called proper harmony and again may be perfect when there are more than two melodies, or imperfect when there are only two).[113]

For Zarlino harmony is the essence of music, and whether music can excite passions or not is of secondary importance. He has nothing against the musical imitation of passions so long as it does not interfere with what is essential—the harmony. It is only natural for him to prefer polyphony to monody, since only in polyphony is what he calls "proper harmony" possible. Similarly, since harmony arises from consonant relations between sounds, and since consonances must be expressable by multiple or superparticular ratios within the *senario* (except for the "compound" sixths), it is only natural for Zarlino to beware of non-diatonicism, not only because the pure non-diatonic genera are less rich in consonances than the diatonic one, but also because non-diatonic steps introduce "consonances" which do not have true ratios.

In the previous section of this chapter I have suggested that it is possible to see the whole musical thought of the second half of the sixteenth century as a struggle to resolve the fundamental tension between the "formal" and "expressive'' ideals of music. It is possible now to formulate this tension, as it appears in Zarlino's writings, more precisely as the opposition between music which is ''harmony'' and music which is a method of achieving ''effects.'' The theorist resolves the tension not by banning the imitation of passions altogether, but by subjugating it completely to the essential ideal of harmony. ''Harmony'' and ''effects'' constitute the most basic aesthetic alternative facing any theorist of that time.

Vincenzo Galilei was born around 1520 in Santa Maria a Monte near Florence, son of an impoverished nobleman.[114] An accomplished lutenist, he became a protégé of a wealthy and influential Florentine patron, Giovanni de' Bardi (1534-1612).[115] Thanks to Bardi's encouragement and help, Galilei was able to start serious theoretical studies with Gioseffo Zarlino in Venice in the early 1560s and to travel extensively. When he returned to Florence in 1572, Galilei had enough experience in musical practice and theory to serve as an authority on theoretical matters to Bardi and a group of musicians, poets, and amateurs whose informal gatherings in Bardi's house came to be known as the *Camerata*. The group, which started to meet at least in 1573, suffered a gradual decline in the late 1580s and ceased to exist in 1592 when Bardi moved to Rome, counted among its members, besides Bardi and Galilei, Giulio Caccini and Piero Strozzi. Other musicians who might have been associated with the group were Jacopo Peri, Alessandro Striggio, Cristoforo Malvezzi, Emilio de' Cavalieri, and Francesco Cini. The attention of the Camerata was focused on the ancient Greek music and the possibility of its revival. This interest of the group led Galilei to explore the nature of ancient music in a more detailed and systematic fashion than was ever done before. He deplored the lack of familiarity with ancient theorists among modern practical musicians and blamed on it the fact that music did not undergo the rebirth which characterized other branches of science and art.[116] Galilei himself, however, lacked the necessary philological training for such an exploration of ancient authors and had to seek help of more qualified scholars. In 1572 he initiated a correspondence which was to last for the next ten years with a Florentine humanist Girolamo Mei (1519-94) who since 1559 resided in Rome.[117] Mei, a pupil of famous philologist Piero Vettori (1499-1585) and himself an immensely learned and respected student of ancient letters, directed his attention to the study of ancient Greek music in 1561 and, by the time Galilei wrote him asking a number of questions concerning Greek music, he had already studied practically every Greek theoretical treatise that is known today. Mei's interpretation of the nature of Greek music and his explanation of the reasons why it was superior to modern practice had a decisive influence on the Camerata. Mei's views are reflected in Bardi's *Discorso mandato a Caccini sopra la musica antica e 'l cantar bene* of 1578.[118] Galilei, whose initial theoretical views were strongly influenced by Gioseffo Zarlino, became completely converted to Mei's way of thinking as the result of the correspondence and two personal encounters with the humanist. Galilei's *Dialogo della musica antica, et della moderna* which appeared in Florence in 1581 or 1582,[119] the theorist's most influential work and consequently the fullest statement of the Camerata position, developed Mei's suggestions into a full-length attack on the theories of Gioseffo Zarlino, initiating a polemic which was to last until Zarlino's death in 1590. Zarlino answered the *Dialogo* with his *Sopplimenti musicali* in 1588 which in turn provoked Galilei's response, the *Discorso intorno all'opere di messer Gioseffo Zarlino da Chioggia, et altri importanti particolari attenenti alla musica* (Florence: Giorgio Marescotti, 1589). Zarlino's cause was further defended by his pupil, Giovanni Maria Artusi, in two unpublished treatises of 1588 and 1590.[120] Toward the very end of his life, in 1591, Galilei wrote another critique of Zarlino's *Sopplimenti*, which, however, remained unpublished.[121] The last four years preceding his death in 1591 Galilei spent writing not only his polemical treatises but, more importantly, his monumental *Trattato dell'Arte del Contrapunto* (1588-91).[122] The treatise which represented Galilei's most mature thoughts on musical matters unfortunately remained unpublished.[123]

IV. GALILEI: THEORY

In spite of the increasingly acrimonious tone of their polemic, one should not overlook the fact that on some issues which he considered to be of minor importance Galilei tacitly accepted the opinions of his great teacher. Thus, so far as the tonal system is concerned, Galilei did not agree with Zarlino's modal theory, while accepting implicitly his views on the structure of the genera. Describing various ancient ways of tuning a diatonic, chromatic, and enharmonic tetrachords,[124] or the differences between these tetrachords,[125] Galilei reveals no difference between his and Zarlino's understanding of the intervallic structure of each tetrachord.[126] There is also no disagreement on the way in which tetrachords are combined to form the two-octave disjunct and conjunct systems.[127] As a result, there can be no difference between the theorists' understanding of the intervallic structure of each genus.[128]

Their views on the relationship between the genera are also very similar. The extreme steps of tetrachords are common to all three genera.[129] The difference between the diatonic and chromatic tetrachords consists in the third lowest step which in the chromatic tetrachord should form a minor third with the highest step, while in the enharmonic tetrachord the lowest interval of the diatonic is divided into two parts and the third lowest diatonic step is omitted.[130] It may be concluded that Galilei tacitly accepts both the gamut implied by Zarlino's theory and the way in which this gamut is organized on the generic level.[131]

Like Zarlino, Galilei believes that both thirds belong to the diatonic genus and that they were used in diatonic compositions both before and after the non-diatonic genera were discovered. And, like his teacher, he considers as exclusively non-diatonic intervals the enharmonic diesis and chromatic semitone (that is, the second lowest interval of the chromatic tetrachord).[132] The *Dialogo* reveals so little interest in the problems of non-diatonicism that, not surprisingly, Galilei seems to be unaware that the generic membership of the thirds was once hotly debated by Vicentino and Lusitano.

As regards the relative importance of the genera, Galilei seems to accept the common notion of the diatonic steps being most basic and the non-diatonic ones being less essential. This can be inferred from the fact that he considers a non-diatonic genus to be a "compression" *(una spessatione)* of the diatonic, since chromatic steps divide the diatonic whole tones, and enharmonic steps divide the diatonic and chromatic semitones. Consequently, it is clear (says Galilei) that the diatonic was used first, later the chromatic, and last the enharmonic.[133] The non-diatonic steps add color to the basic diatonic structure:

> . . . The musician uses the diatonic not otherwise than the painter uses drawing. . . . The perfect drawing of the diatonic is later colored by the musician with the chromatic. Finally, he gives it the ultimate perfection (as far as sound and harmonies are concerned) by means of the enharmonic.[134]

The diatonic is the most important, stable, excellent, and oldest genus. Second in importance is the chromatic, and, third, the enharmonic.[135]

Throughout his writings Galilei uses accidentals in the same sense in which they were used by Zarlino.[136] But if there was no basic disagreement between the theorists so far as the structure of the genera and the notation were concerned, there was certainly a profound difference of opinion on the nature of the tuning system used in modern practice. In fact the problem of the tuning system constitutes the core of the whole Galilei-Zarlino controversy. It will be remembered that according to Zarlino the perfect tuning system, that is, the system in which consonances have their true ratios, is the syntonic tuning of Ptolemy.[137] The disadvantage of this system, however, consists in the fact that it produces many intervals in two sizes, differing by a comma, depending on which step an interval is constructed. In tuning instruments which cannot vary pitch continuously this difficulty has to be resolved either by supplying many steps with two versions distant by a comma, or by means of a temperament which divides the comma and distributes its parts among many intervals. While admitting the necessity of resolving the problems created by the troublesome comma in tuning instruments, Zarlino claimed that in an unaccompanied vocal performance voices always sang pure consonances and the problem of the comma could be disregarded. Galilei most emphatically disagreed with this claim and, quite justifiably, refused to see any essential difference between instrumental and vocal performance. It was Girolamo Mei who had shaken Galilei's original agreement with Zarlino's claim. Mei insisted that since the syntonic tuning was consistently rejected in favor of the Pythagorean one by all theorists before Zarlino, it was the Pythagorean tuning that was still the basis of contemporary practice. More importantly, in a letter written in 1578, Mei suggested to Galilei that he check the tuning used in modern practice experimentally. Such an experiment must have convinced Galilei that neither the Ptolemaic nor the Pythagorean tuning systems were in use.[138] In the *Dialogo* Galilei painstakingly lists and discusses the ''comma-problems'' (he calls them "Paradoxes" —*Paradossi*) which appear in the syntonic tuning.[139] Since the difference of the comma is perceptible, and since the ear does not perceive that in modern practice intervals are sung in two sizes different by a comma, it follows that the tuning system used by composers, singers, and instrumentalists is not the syntonic of Ptolemy.[140]

What is it, then? The fretted string instruments use the intense diatonic and chromatic tonikon tuning of Aristoxenus, that is, an equal temperament in which the octave consists of six equal whole tones, each consisting of two equal semitones, the approximate ratio of each semitone being 18:17.[141] According to J. Murray Barbour, Galilei's is ''the first really practical approximation for equal temperament'' and most probably it represented the contemporary practice.[142] Zarlino criticized Galilei sharply for giving only an approximate method of arriving at equal temperament and himself presented three geometrical methods for finding the proper placement of frets.[143] In this Zarlino followed Francisco Salinas, the first to propose a geometrical method for achieving equal temperament.[144] According to Barbour, Salinas was also the first to give precise mathematical definition of equal temperament.[145] Zarlino and Salinas, like Galilei, discuss equal temperament as appropriate for fretted string instruments. In keyboard temperament the whole tones are divided into two unequal semitones,[146] but, as in all practical temperaments, inequality of whole tones is avoided.[147] Keyboard instruments use the 2/7 comma variety of meantone temperament, in which (taking the syntonic tuning as the point of departure) fifths are diminished by 2/7 comma, thirds by 1/7 comma each, and the major whole tones by 4/7 comma, and minor whole tones and major semitones are augmented by 3/7 comma each, leaving the minor semitones and octaves unchanged.[148] Galilei considers this to be the most perfect temperament possible for keyboard instruments and claims to be its inventor.[149] However, as Zarlino indignantly pointed out in his *Sopplimenti*, this temperament was already described in *Le Istitutioni*.[150] Galilei describes also, but does not favor, the ordinary meantone temperament of 1/4 comma recommended by Zarlino in his *Dimostrationi*.[151]

The most noticeable difference between the two temperaments (equal and meantone) consists in the fact that only in the meantone temperament does one hear the difference between the major and minor semitones.[152] As a result of this difference lutes and violas cannot play together with keyboard instruments.[153] Equal temperament is closer to perfection than meantone temperament. Not only are its perfect consonances closer to their true ratios,[154] but also, thanks to equal temperament, each diatonic and chromatic step has any diatonic and chromatic interval below and above it which makes any transposition possible. Galilei maintains:

> On the contrary, in the string distribution used by keyboard instruments, which is different [from the one used by the lute], many [of these intervals] are commonly lacking. Because of this the player of this [keyboard instrument], however practiced and skilled, cannot transpose a composition either below or above by a whole tone or semitone—transpositions that are done most often, I would say—while such a composition is very easily and usefully transposed in the lute.[155]

In the *Discorso* he makes an even more eloquent plea for equal temperament, praising it for its equal semitones. Thanks to this equality all inconvenient and musically useless discrepancies between steps which we today call enharmonically equivalent disappear.[156] If equal temperament has purer perfect consonances and makes all transpositions possible, why do we not use it for keyboard instruments as well, asks Galilei? Because equal temperament, when applied for keyboard instruments, reveals certain defects. Some of its imperfect consonances are too sharp, for example. This happens probably because we are accustomed to hear keyboard instruments in meantone temperament and also because the strings of a keyboard instrument produce a more violent sound than those of a lute.[157]

Galilei was not the only theorist of the time to admire the perfection and usefulness of equal temperament. Zarlino reports that a friend of his, Don Girolamo Roselli of Perugia, a monk at Monte Cassino, and then (that is, around 1588 when *Sopplimenti musicali* appeared) the abbot of S. Martino in Sicily, in his *Trattato della musica spherica* (probably never published and, so far as I know, no longer extant) extolled the division of an octave into twelve equal semitones over all other divisions

> as the one which has taken away all difficulties from singers, instrumentalists, and composers, since [thanks to equal temperament] they can commonly start to sing or to play on whichever of the twelve steps they wish, according to the usage of practicing musicians, ut-re-mi-fa-sol-la, circling through all the notes, making (as he says) spherical music. They will be able to finish any composition comfortably where they started, as if in perpetual motion. All instruments will be able to keep their temperament and play together, and organs (as he says) will not be made either too high or too low in pitch.[158]

Roselli here praises equal temperament primarily for making any transposition of a diatonic composition possible and for allowing keyboard instruments to play together with fretted instruments, that is, for reasons similar to those of Galilei. In fact, Galilei might have had Roselli's *musica sferica* in mind when, praising equal temperament in his counterpoint treatise, he said that "thanks to its chromatic steps, any step in it has, both above and below, any interval used in counterpoint." For this reason he esteemed equal temperament "no less than the mathematician esteems the sphere above other solid figures."[159]

Wind instruments and voices adapt to either temperament, depending on whether they are accompanied by fretted or by keyboard instruments.[160] The Galilei-Zarlino controversy, however, is concerned not with instrumental temperaments, but with the tuning system used in an unaccompanied vocal performance. According to Galilei, this is neither the pure ditoniaion of Pythagoras (since its thirds and sixths are dissonant), nor the pure syntonon of Ptolemy (for reasons stated above), but a temperament similar to the syntonon. It has only the octave in its true ratio, all other intervals (including the whole tones) having always the same size, and the natural semitone larger than 16:15.[161] Owing to the inequality of semitones the temperament used in unaccompanied singing is closer to that used for the keyboard instruments than to the one used for the lute.[162]

It might be mentioned that long before Galilei the difficulties involved in the use of just intonation in modern practice were observed and described by the scientist Giovanni Battista Benedetti. In two letters addressed to Cipriano de Rore and written probably around 1563, but published only in 1585, Benedetti demonstrated that the problems which arise in just intonation are caused by its unequal semitones and whole tones and consequently advocated equal temperament as the best solution.[163]

V. GALILEI: POETICS

Galilei's relative indifference toward non-diatonicism is equally evident in his treatment of purely theoretical problems and in his ideas concerning musical practice. I must stress that it is indifference, not hostility, as if for him and possibly the group of musicians to which he belonged, chromaticism had ceased to be a controversial issue requiring a critique or defense and became an accepted feature of musical composition. Galilei is neither for nor against chromaticism. In the *Dialogo* he scarcely mentions it at all. He tells us only that chromatic steps were introduced in order to provide perfect and imperfect consonances on those steps where they were lacking in a purely diatonic system.[164] "At least they were introduced for such a reason, although badly used."[165] Chromatic steps (added to diatonic ones) are sufficient to create every consonance below and above every step in the diatonic and chromatic genera. In the counterpoint treatise, which represents Galilei's most mature thoughts on problems of composition, his opinion concerning the usefulness of chromatic steps is basically unchanged:

> The minor semitone considered in itself is of little importance in counterpoint. . . . Neverthe-
> less, when it is applied to other intervals, its use is not only convenient to the contrapuntist,

but is is very necessary for the perfection of harmonies, . . . thanks to the power given to it by practicing musicians, which is to make imperfect consonances that ordinarily are minor among the common diatonic steps, to make them—I say—major whenever the contrapuntist pleases, and to make the major ones minor.[166]

The enharmonic step dividing the diatonic semitone into two enharmonic dieses was uselessly added because nobody has been able to put it into practice.[167] The uselessness of enharmonic steps is also confirmed in the counterpoint treatise,[168] and in the "Discorso intorno all'uso dell'Enharmonio et di chi fusse autore del Cromatico" which was conceived as an appendix to it. In the latter Galilei expresses his disbelief in the supposed excellence of the enharmonic and argues that it cannot satisfy the ear because the number of intervals which are satisfying to it is limited and because the enharmonic diesis is contrary to the nature of singing and disproportionate with our sense of hearing.[169] No one in modern times was able to reintroduce the enharmonic genus in such a way as to convince his listeners of the genus' excellence, says Galilei,[170] and he cites the unsuccessful attempts of Nicola Vicentino:

Don Nicola Vicentino, a man of no little reputation in musical practice, played a keyboard instrument which besides the two ordinary rows of keys, that is, the diatonic and the chromatic, had one more which enabled him to play the enharmonic (normally understood) whenever he wanted. The same Don Nicola had also some students who, while he played especially the enharmonic, sang this sort of music composed by him. He let this music be heard in all principal cities of Italy and I have heard it in various times and places many times. Let it be the sign of whether this music pleased or not that after his death it was practiced neither by his students nor by anybody else. One of these [students] named Jacomo Finetti I saw again in Venice in [15]60. Besides playing keyboard instruments better than ordinarily, he sang very well as a contralto. Among other things he told me that, wanting to find employment, he had to leave the enharmonic of his teacher and pay attention to other things. As I have said, such music was never sung without the instrument named above and if by misfortune one of the singers lost his way while singing, it was impossible to put him back on the right track. I have seen this to happen in Ravenna. . . . Thus, this kind of music necessarily required such an instrument that guided the voices of the singers through unknown tracts (not to say through precipitate cliffs) and did not let them proceed according to the nature of singing and through a straight path. These particular sounds of the enharmonic . . . could not but be unpleasant to the sense. Don Nicola left many of these compositions, both in print and in manuscript. He also left more than one of those keyboard instruments. Also his pupils remained who through a long study understood this practice no less than their teacher. After his death the music was not sung any more and the instruments were no longer played in that manner, and his students . . . abandoned completely this enharmonic, not finding anybody who wished to listen to it. Don Nicola stayed in the service of the Cardinal of Ferrara and let many important gentlemen listen to his music. Let no one believe that he was introduced to them to let them listen only to the enharmonic, but also to the diatonic and chromatic. In these two genera he composed many beautiful works. . . . But when it came to the enharmonic, some have praised it . . . not to be accused of ignorance, and others because of respect inspired by the greatness of his patron. But time, the true judge of things, demonstrated by experience that this music so divided did not please, as it was abandoned in favor of that which was not so divided in minor parts.[171]

Thus Galilei dismisses the enharmonic genus as completely impracticable, but accepts the chromatic one as both practicable and useful. Its usefulness consists in the fact that it enriches the diatonic with missing consonances and makes transpositions possible. Although Galilei criticizes the practice of transposing a composition "to strange, unsingable pitches which are completely out of the ordinary and full of artifice," as some impertinent contrapuntists do "in order to have a larger field in which to boast about themselves and their abilities to those who are more ignorant than they are, as if [their deeds] are miracles," he does not mean to censure the practice of transposition when it is done for a good purpose: "skilled organists customarily do this [that is, transpose] to accommodate the choir, by a tone, a third, or another interval by means of accidental signs."[172] It will be recalled in this context that one of the main reasons why Galilei considered equal temperament to be superior to meantone temperament was that only the forme made many transpositions possible.

Is the usefulness of the chromatic steps limited only to the fact that they enrich the diatonic and allow transpositions, or is it possible to use them also in a purely chromatic composition? In answering this question Galilei follows Zarlino, arguing that in modern polyphony only the diatonic genus may be used in its pure form, because the other two genera, when used without the diatonic, contain a lesser number of consonances, which are so necessary in a polyphonic composition, between their steps.[173] Having accepted Zarlino's views concerning the structure of the genera, Galilei had to accept this conclusion also. Galilei follows Zarlino further in asserting that the ancients have used each of the three genera in their pure form and that they could do it because they did not employ polyphony but sang monophonically.[174] The mixture of the genera was neither practiced nor even considered by the ancients before Ptolemy "who, compared to these ancients, is modern in a certain way."[175] This was also Girolamo Mei's opinion, since in one of his letters to Galilei he wrote:

> Concerning what you desire to know, whether the chromatic and enharmonic genera of the ancients so praised by them could have been played each one by itself, I believe that one can certainly give a positive answer, in the same way as in singing, understanding, however, singing and playing as was customary in ancient times, of a single air, and not of many airs together, that is, in plainchant and not in counterpoint; otherwise the answer has to be negative.[176]

VI. GALILEI: AESTHETICS

As I have pointed out, anybody attempting to defend consistent non-diatonicism (that is, not just the use of non-diatonic steps within a diatonic framework, but such an employment of non-diatonic steps which produces a purely non-diatonic composition) against Zarlino's arguments had either to reject the theorist's understanding of how generic series were constructed, or to substitute ancient monody for modern polyphony.[177] Galilei chose the second alternative. But by the time he did so, chromaticism ceased to be a burning controversial issue and, although Galilei did accept the link between monody and pure (not just temporary and accidental) non-diatonicism established by Zarlino, his postulate of the return to monody was certainly not motivated by the consideration that such a return made purely chromatic or enharmonic composition again possible. His polemic against polyphony was motivated by much more fundamental aesthetic considerations, not by the desire to reinstate consistent non-diatonicism which could at best be just one of many methods designed to bring the new aesthetic postulates into practice.

> . . . the practice of music, I say, was introduced by men for the reason and ends which all learned men agree upon. It arose simply to express the conceits of the mind with greater efficacy in celebrating the praises of gods, geniuses, and heroes, just as the origin of our [music] for several voices may be partially understood through the ecclesiastical *cantus firmi* and plainsongs, and to impress them, then, with equal force upon the minds of mortals for their benefit and comfort.[178]

Throughout his writings Galilei reiterates his most fundamental aesthetic postulate: The function of music is "to express the conceits of the mind" and "to impress them with equal force upon the minds" of listeners. The "conceits" that are being expressed and impressed are first and foremost passions or affections. This "expression" and "impression" is done for the sake of listeners' benefit, conceived not in terms of pleasure, but in terms of moral uplifting.

According to Galilei, these aesthetic postulates governed the music of the ancients, and they should be restored to guide modern practice as well. The *Dialogo* starts with a brief summary of Galilei's views concerning music history. With the breakdown of ancient culture the perfect musical doctrine of the Greeks in which music was taught "not only as delightful to life, but also as useful to virtue" was lost for a very long time.[179]

> [Men] persisted in such blindness until first Gaffurio, then Glarean, and after him Zarlino— truly the princes of this modern practice—began to investigate what music might really be, and to seek to extricate it from the darkness where it had been entombed. That part which they understood and valued, they brought little by little to the end result in which it is found; but it does not seem to any men of intelligence that they have restored it to its ancient state.[180]

This modern practice, later identified with polyphony, started, according to Galilei, some hundred fifty years before his own time, that is, around 1430, and in the short time was brought to perfection:

> All the better practical musicians of our times agree in believing and saying that from that time until the present, [music] has attained the highest [state of] perfection that man could possibly imagine. Even since the death of Cipriano Rore, a truly unrivalled musician in this practice of counterpoint, it has gone into decline rather than into advancement.[181]

The rules of modern counterpoint were established in practice by Adrian Willaert, in theory by Zarlino, and they were finally perfected by Cipriano de Rore, "the prince . . . of contrapuntists."[182] Giovanni de' Bardi expressed similarly high regard for Cipriano de Rore as the one who perfected polyphony and even indicated the way in which music should be developed in the future to conform more closely to the ancient ideal:

> In composing, then, you will make it your chief aim to arrange the verse well and to declaim the words as intelligibly as you can, not letting yourself be led astray by the counterpoint like a bad swimmer who lets himself be carried out of his course by the current and comes to shore beyond the mark that he had set, for you will consider it self-evident that, just as the soul is nobler than the body, so the words are nobler than the counterpoint. . . . The divine Cipriano, toward the end of his life, was well aware how very grave an error this was in the counterpoint of his day. For this reason, straining every fibre of his genius, he devoted himself to making the verse and the sound of the words thoroughly intelligible in his madrigals. . . . For this great man told me himself, in Venice, that this was the true manner of composing and a different one, and if he had not been taken from us by death, he would in my opinion have restored the music combining several melodies to a degree of perfection from which others might easily have returned it little by little to that true and perfect music so highly praised by the ancients.[183]

According to Galilei modern polyphonic music achieved a perfection of sorts, but it certainly did not restore music to its ancient state. So far as theory is concerned, this "has been attained in our time by Girolamo Mei, a worthy man, to whom all musicians and all scholarly men should render thanks and honor."[184] Galilei's own aim is to restore ancient music not only in theory but also in practice.

Galilei's critique of modern music was inspired by Girolamo Mei, who claimed that music of his contemporaries was inferior to that of the ancients since it did not arouse passions but sought merely to delight the ear with harmony. Mei blamed the emotional insipidity of contemporary compositions on the fact that they were polyphonic, and he advocated the return to the ancient methods of pure monody. Before coming under the influence of Mei, Galilei accepted Zarlino's view that the aim of music was to delight the ear with harmony. In his letter of 1572 Mei wrote to Galilei:

> . . . you are of the opinion that music should have as its object to delight the ear with harmony and that for this reason the same must have been the object of ancient music. Now if you mean the delight that is born from the sung air which when well accommodated, expressing the concept it ornaments, and producing by its means . . . the affection, cannot but be pleasant to listen to, I easily agree with you. But since your words seem to be strongly determined in favor of the pure sense of hearing, since you use and repeat many times the terms "sweetness" and "sweet" as [indicating] the aim of music, especially concerning the consonances, it occurred to me that you might see perhaps only this delight that today one sees as being openly proposed to our musicians as the goal which is only this delicacy, to call it with this name, which does not have any other more profound goal than to satisfy purely the ear

upon hearing . . . and that since you presuppose this goal of theirs to be true, you consequently interpret the term and word "harmony" not as the thread and order and mode of the
air of the composition . . . but, being preoccupied—as I estimate—with the modern usage, as
above all the quality of the consonances that one hears between many diverse airs. Now this I
judge to be not only completely opposed to the aim of ancient [music] (as I have said above),
but also it is a thing by its nature contrary to the intention of the ancient music and
consequently of its artists. This obvious, and not at all natural concern, diverting the minds
and occupying it with another consideration. does not permit the instrument of the voice,
given to man with all its diverse qualities especially for the perfect expression of his thoughts
and affections, to fulfill its function neither agreeably nor without hindrance. Therefore I
believe that the proposed goal, imitating the very nature of the instrument which they used,
was not the sweetness of the consonances to satisfy the ear (since there is no testimony nor
any evidence by the authors about the use of these in their singing) but the complete and
efficacious expression of everything he wanted to make understood . . . by means and through
the aid of high and low sounds . . . accompanied with the regulated temperament of the fast
and slow, articulating the sections of his works according to the one and the other quality so
that each one by itself through its proper nature was accommodated to some determinate
affection. . . . And that this must have been the true goal and proper aim of the ancient
musicians is certainly demonstrated and confirmed beyond doubt by the fact that their art was
at the beginning joined very closely with poetry, since the first and best were both musicians
and poets. Now it is certain that poetry has imitation as its proper goal and aim. . . .[185]

The extent to which the above-quoted words influenced Galilei is apparent
to any reader of the *Dialogo*. Galilei contrasts the aesthetic ideals and practice of
the ancients with those of the modern polyphony. Polyphony was first developed
by ancient cithara players whose aim was to delight the sense of hearing and
whose methods consisted in the use of diverse harmonies, that is, perfect and
imperfect consonances and dissonances, between the parts of their compositions.[186] Polyphony is acceptable so long as it remains a property of instrumental
music only. But the transgression of modern music consists in the fact that it
accepted the aims and methods of polyphony as obligatory for all music, vocal and
instrumental alike, thus neglecting the most important duty of music, which is the
expression of the thoughts contained in the text and not the harmony of the parts.[187]
There can be no doubt that the goal of instrumental counterpoint, the delight
of the sense of hearing, is much lower than the educational, moral aim of ancient
vocal music:

If the goal of our practicing contemporaries is (as they say) to delight the sense of hearing with
the diversity of the consonances, . . . then let this goal of delighting with the variety of their
harmonies be abandoned to these instruments, for they are capable of no more, since they are
devoid of sense, motion, intelligence, speech, discourse, and soul. But [let] men who have
been furnished by nature with all these wonderfully noble, excellent abilities seek by means of
them not only to delight but, as imitators of the good ancients, to improve as well, for they
have the ability to do this.[188]

The aim of music is not to delight the ear, but to improve men by reaching their
emotional and rational faculties through the expression of affections and conceits

of the mind. Ethical, emotional, and intellectual content of music is more important than any sensual pleasure it brings. Galilei asserts the primacy of reason over sense in more than one way. Not only is it more important for music to express the text which carries intellectual content than to delight the ear, but also the judgment of reason is more trustworthy in musical matters than the pronouncement based on sensual experience only. Reason allows us to know intervals more exactly than sense alone and reason is a better guide concerning what is desirable and what is to be avoided in music: "Although the senses know black and white, and bitter and sweet, they are unable to discern that one thing is desirable and another is to be avoided."[189] Reason is more important than sense and expression of the text is more important than the sensual pleasure afforded by polyphony. Modern composers who imitate the instrumental contrapuntists "deprived of the most noble, most important, most principal parts of music, which are the conceptions of the mind expressed by means of the words . . . . have captivated reason as the slave of their appetites."[190]

The method of polyphony, the rules of counterpoint, not only do not help to express the text; they make such expression impossible.[191] The mind beguiled by pleasure provided by counterpoint cannot consider the words and cannot be moved to any affection.[192] This is not to say that the impediment of polyphony consists simply in the fact that it obscures the words. According to Galilei, ancient instrumental music did arouse the affections even though no text was involved:

> Strozzi: Did the mere sound of an artificial instrument have the power to evoke any effect in the listener? Bardi: Do not doubt it at all . . . that the sound of an instrument made by art without the use of words had—according to what I pointed out to you above and as Aristotle says—the nature to imitate good character and to possess it itself, and very great power to produce in the minds of the listeners most of the affections which were pleasing to the skillful player.[193]

The problem with polyphony is that it not only obscures the words but also treats the same words in contradictory fashion. Music can express affections mainly through an appropriate range of the voice and rhythm and tempo. Since in polyphony the same words are sung by voices of different range and in various rhythms no affection can be produced.[194] Zarlino is wrong when he regards "harmony" as involving relationship between several parts. "The ancient Greeks . . . understood harmony to be the beautiful, graceful progression of the melody of the composition."[195] Harmony is necessary in musical expression, but it is the harmony of a single melody, not of several parts. To summarize: polyphony impedes an unambiguous expression of affections, because "the diversity of sound, with regard to highness and lowness, together with the difference of movement and of interval produces variety of harmony and affection."[196] Similarly, Giovanni de' Bardi suggested that modern counterpoint, though appropriate in instrumental music, was inimical to what should be a musician's real goal, namely, to dispose the mind of the listener to a moral quality.[197] Needless to say, both Bardi and Galilei were inspired in their critique of polyphony by Girolamo Mei.[198]

In his most mature work Galilei somewhat modified his position and tried to reach a compromise between strict monophony and polyphony. In the little discourses which he appended to his counterpoint treatise he still disapproved of many voices singing various lines at the same time, but he no longer wished to banish the vertical harmonies altogether. The ancients sang soloistically, but always accompanied by an instrument which together with the voice created harmony. The texture advocated by Galilei consists now of a single vocal line accompanied by consonant vertical harmonies of an instrument the highest line of which doubles the vocal melody.[199] Instrumental consonances are necessary since they not only give pleasure, but also help to communicate the passions of the soul:

> To deprive music of consonances, especially these produced by artificial instruments, is the same as to deprive painting of the pleasure of colors. As the painter with various colors paints from nature various things produced by nature and art, as if deceiving the eye so that to reassure himself of the truth he often resorts to the sense of touch, so similarly the musician, with variety of intervals and in particular of consonances communicates to the intellect all the passions of the soul, especially shaped appropriately by the text. Those, however, that are deprived of the use of the consonances, are deprived also of any delight that the sense of hearing might desire from the musical intervals. . . .[200]

Since the sole aim of modern music "is nothing but the pleasure of the ear, and that of ancient music is to produce in someone else the same affection one feels oneself,"[201] it is no wonder that modern musicians, even when they endeavor to imitate words in their inadequate and ridiculous ways, cannot produce the marvellous and virtuous effects for which ancient musicians were famous.[202] Modern musicians at best imitate single words, whereas the ancients tried to convey the sense of the entire text: "What is meant today by the imitation of the words is not the whole concept and sense of the entire text, as was the case among the ancients, but the significance of the sound of a single word," wrote Galilei.[203]

> Notwithstanding all the consummate excellence of the modern music practice, one does not hear or see today the least sign of those things which ancient [music] achieved. One does not even read that it achieved such things fifty or a hundred years ago when it was not so common and familiar to men. Neither its novelty, therefore nor its excellence has ever had the power with our practicing contemporaries to produce any of those virtuous, useful, convenient effects which ancient [music] produced. Whereupon one necessarily concludes that either music or human nature has been changed from its original state. . . .[204]

When Galilei argues that novelty does not produce effects, he must have in mind the kind of enthusiasm for the efficacy of new devices which we have encountered in the work of Nicola Vicentino. He also disagrees with those "who claim that the music of the ancients, in comparison with theirs, was a joke to be ridiculed. The amazement which they caused with this [music] in the souls and minds of men resulted or evolved only because they were insensitive or boorish."[205] This cannot be true, says Galilei, since the miraculous effects "have been told to us by the worthiest, most famous writers, outside of the music profession, which the world has ever seen."[206] Another proof of the excellence of ancient music in comparison with modern is the much higher social and intellectual status of musicians and music among the Greeks.[207] Modern music is practiced "by people who are ordinarily of little or no value; who will not tell where and of whom they were born, so to speak; who have no possessions, or very few; and who cannot even read without difficulty,"[208] and it is enjoyed by the common man who is always ignorant of what is good and true.[209] The ancients had known several kinds of music (the instrumental polyphony was their invention, after all) but their philosophers approved only such music that inclined the soul to virtue as worthy of free men, whereas the kind that was practiced only to give pleasure to the sense of hearing they contemptuously left for common plebs.[210]

Since I have already noticed Galilei's lack of interest in non-diatonic genera, it should not be surprising that he says little about their text-expressing possibilities and that most of what he says is fairly conventional. Thus we learn that the ancients achieved the virile and energetic effects most efficiently in the diatonic genus, whereas the chromatic was suitable for soft and effeminate effects. Even less virile was the enharmonic.[211] Certain harshness of the diatonic resulted from the fact that some of its steps lacked perfect consonances above or below.[212] According to universal opinion the virile diatonic and delicate chromatic were still in use in Galilei's time.[213]

In spite of Galilei's lack of interest in chromaticism I thought it was necessary to devote some space to his musical ideas for the following reasons. Galilei was probably the most important and influential theorist of his generation. In his treatise on counterpoint he codified some of the basic precepts of new practice and in all his writings expressed certain aesthetic principles which were to become the orthodoxy of the future. By directing these principles against those of Zarlino, Galilei indirectly helped to remove the most powerful arguments against chromaticism. Galilei's ideas were indirectly favorable for the further development of chromaticism not only in this negative way. The most fundamental feature of Galilei's aesthetics, the insistence on music as the art of emotional expression, makes him the true successor of Nicola Vicentino. Galilei's position on many issues was anticipated by Vincentino. For example, similarly to Vicentino, Galilei urged musicians, both composers and performers, to learn the proper methods of text expression from orators and actors.[214] It is quite understandable that this idea, in particular the suggestion that performers should imitate gestures of theatrical actors, was severely criticized and scorned by Zarlino.[215] The profound differences between Vincentino and Galilei cannot be ignored, but their agreement on the ultimate sense of music makes them allies. And while for Galilei chromaticism ceased to be the controversial issue, the earlier theorist firmly established the association between chromaticism and the aesthetics of musical expression. Both theorists had the same aim—to arouse passions by means of music—but while Vincentino expected chromaticism to be the proper method of achieving this aim, Galilei, following Mei and his understanding of the musical practice of ancient Greeks, put his hopes in monody.

III

Ercole Bottrigari and
Giovanni Maria Artusi

The two Bolognese authors discussed in this chapter belong to the last generation of sixteenth-century theorists. They both witnessed and commented upon the last phase of the process of profound technical, stylistic, and aesthetic change which led to the creation of the musical Baroque. They had the opportunity to see more clearly than their predecessors the direction this change was taking, and for this reason their writings, even though containing few truly original ideas, illuminated the practice of their contemporaries in an interesting way.

Ercole Bottrigari was born in Bologna in 1531.[1] He received a well-rounded humanistic education in disciplines which ranged from the ancient letters to architecture, perspective, mathematics, and astronomy. He also studied composition with Bartolomeo Spontone, the *maestro di cappella* of the Bolognese church of San Petronio. In 1576 he left Bologna for Ferrara where he spent eleven years and had the opportunity to gain a first-hand acquaintance with the most advanced trends in musical composition and performance practice. He returned to Bologna in 1587 and spent the rest of his life in the city and in his suburban villa in San Alberto where he died in 1612.

During this last period of his life he wrote several treatises on music and translated into Italian numerous works of ancient theorists. His first book on music appeared in Bologna in 1593 under the title of *Il Patricio*.[2] In this book he criticized his Ferrarese friend, famous Platonic philosopher and humanist Francesco Patrizi, for the way in which Patrizi interpreted the Aristoxenian divisions (tuning systems) of diatonic, chromatic, and enharmonic tetrachords.[3] Bottrigari's criticism was further amplified in an anonymous treatise entitled *Del libro chiamato il Patricio overo de' Tetracordi d'Hercole Butrigario*.[4] Patrizi's interpretation of Aristoxenus was in turn defended against Bottrigari's criticism by Giovanni Maria Artusi in the "Considerationi musicali," the second part of a treatise which Artusi dedicated to Bottrigari, *Seconda parte dell'Artusi overo delle imperfettioni della moderna musica*, published by Giacomo Vincenti in

Venice in 1603. Bottrigari responded the following year in an unpublished letter of some hundred fifty pages, *Aletelogia di Leonardo Gallucio à' benigni, e sinceri lettori. Lettera apologetica.*[5]

Bottrigari's second book on music, *Il Desiderio overo de' concerti di varii strumenti musicali*, was also attacked by Artusi. The book was first published by Ricciardo Amadino in Venice in 1594 under the name of Alemanno Benelli, an anagram of the name of one of the interlocutors in the dialogue, Bottrigari's friend and prominent Bolognese musician, Annibale Melone. In 1599 Gioambattista Bellagamba published the second edition in Bologna, this time under Bottrigari's name and with a preface explaining the anagram. Artusi criticized certain ideas of the treatise in his *L'Artusi, overo delle imperfettioni della moderna musica* published by Giacomo Vincenti in Venice in 1600 and one year later he brought forth the third edition of *Il Desiderio* with a dedicatory letter for the Bolognese Senate and with a foreword claiming that the true author of the treatise was Annibale Melone.[6] Bottrigari answered this claim indignantly next year with an unpublished *Lettera di Fiderico Verdicelli a' benigni, e sinceri lettori in difesa del Sig.^e Caval:^e Hercole Bottrigaro contra quanto in pregiudicio della rifutazione di lui ha scritto un certo Artusi in due sue lettere una per dedicatoria all'Illmo Senato di Bologna l'altra à i cortesi lettori sotto la data di Milano à 12 di luglio 1601 & stampate in Milano appresso gli stampatori archiepis.*[7] and he responded to Artusi's criticism of *Il Desiderio* with a dialogue *Antartusi* which is no longer extant.[8]

Bottrigari's third important work on music was his massive unpublished treatise of 1599, *Il Trimerone*, discussing ancient and modern modes and the history of musical notation.[9] In his dialogue *Antartusi* Bottrigari claimed that Artusi plagiarized his discussion of modes in *L'Artusi, overo delle imperfettioni della moderna musica*, Ragionamento II, pp. 49-69.[10]

Bottrigari's final important treatise on music was published in 1602 under the title *Il Melone*.[11] The first part of the treatise was devoted to a discussion of the dispute between Vicentino and Lusitano, the second part (*Il Melone secondo*) was a refutation of the criticism directed by Gandolfo Sigonio, a musician from Modena and a friend of Annibale Melone,[12] against some compositions of Nicola Vicentino and against his treatise. Sigonio's "Discorso" was also published in Bottrigari's book.

Giovanni Maria Artusi, Bottrigari's persistent polemical opponent, was a canon of S. Salvatore in Bologna from 1562 until his death in 1613. He was a student and follower of Gioseffo Zarlino. His penchant for polemics found its expression not only in his criticism of Bottrigari and in two unpreserved treatises directed against Vincenzo Galilei, but most importantly in his famous attack on Claudio Monteverdi.[13] In his *L'Artusi, overo delle imperfettioni della moderna musica* of 1600 Artusi printed and critically analyzed several examples from then still unpublished madrigals of Monteverdi without quoting the text or mentioning the composer's name. Monteverdi was defended by a certain l'Ottuso Accademico in two letters, one from 1599 no longer extant and another from before 1603 printed by Artusi together with his answers in *Seconda parte dell' Artusi overo delle imperfettioni della moderna musica* of 1603.[14] Monteverdi answered Artusi in 1605 in a letter prefacing the Fifth Book of his Madrigals.[15] Artusi retorted with an unpreserved *Discorso musicale* published under the pseudonym of Antonio Braccino da Todi probably in 1606, and Monteverdi was in turn defended by his brother Giulio Cesare in a "Dichiarattione della lettera stampata nel Quinto Libro de' suoi Madrigali" published in Claudio's *Scherzi musicali* of 1607.[16] Artusi had the last word in his *Discorso secondo musicale di Antonio Braccino da Todi per la dichiaratione della lettera posta ne' Scherzi musicali del Sig. Claudio Monteverde* published by Giacomo Vincenti in Venice in 1608.

I. BOTTRIGARI

Bottrigari's views on the structure of the genera emerge most clearly in his *Il Melone*. The treatise is a response to a letter of Annibale Melone, written on May 21, 1591 and printed at the beginning of the text, in which Bottrigari's friend defends the position assumed by Nicola Vicentino in his dispute with Vicente Lusitano, that is, the opinion that the use of the thirds introduced elements foreign to pure diatonicism. Bottrigari assumes a construction of the genera essentially identical with that described earlier by Zarlino: the diatonic, chromatic, and enharmonic tetrachords consist of ascending major semitone and two whole tones (diatonic), major and minor semitones and a minor third (chromatic), and two dieses and a major third (enharmonic), and the tetrachords can be combined into disjunct and conjunct systems in all three genera. In other words, the generic octaves of the disjunct system use the following steps:[17]

DIATONIC:	B		c		d	e		f			g	a	b
CHROMATIC:	B		c	c$\sharp$		e		f		f$\sharp$		a	b
ENHARMONIC:	B	B^X	c			e	e^X	f				a	b

In the conjunct system b$\flat$ is added to the diatonic (since the diatonic synemmenon tetrachord is a b$\flat$ c' d') and both b$\flat$ and d' are added to the chromatic (the chromatic synemmenon tetrachord being a b$\flat$ b$\natural$ d'). Bottrigari argues that a composition which uses only the steps of the diatonic octave is purely diatonic, a composition using only the steps of the chromatic system is purely chromatic, etc. Consequently, he claims that neither Vicentino nor Lusitano were right. Vicentino was wrong to assume that incomposite thirds could not be used in a purely diatonic composition, but he was right to assert that contemporary compositions did not use the pure diatonic genus, since they mixed diatonic and chromatic genera, using in a single composition such steps as c♯ and f♯ (which are particular to the chromatic genus only) and d and g (which belong exclusively to the diatonic).[18]

A pure diatonic composition, according to Bottrigari, can use neither minor semitone nor diesis, a pure chromatic composition can use neither diesis nor d and g.[19] At the end of *Il Melone* (pp. 39-46) Bottrigari presents as an example of purely chromatic composition a madrigal *a 4* of his own based on Petrarch's sonnet "Il cantar novo e 'l pianger delli augelli." In the first part of the madrigal he uses the purely chromatic disjunct system, that is, the steps B, c, c♯, e, f, f♯, and a only, and in the second part he introduces also the synemmenon tetrachord of the conjunct system, using additionally b♭ and d'.

In *Il Desiderio* Bottrigari explained that both diatonic and chromatic structures may be transposed, which accounted for the use of such steps as, for example, e♭ or g♯, and which in effect meant that the only firm criterion of non-diatonicism was the use of a minor semitone or a diesis, since such steps which in the untransposed system were chromatic could become diatonic in a transposition and vice versa.[20]

Bottrigari is best known for his description in *Il Desiderio* of various tuning systems used by various types of instruments and of problems created by this variety of temperaments in performances involving large and varied instrumental forces. His observations, though very interesting for their detailed description of performance practices he witnessed in Ferrara, are not really new. Like several writers before him, Bottrigari observes that keyboard instruments are tuned according to the syntonic tuning of Ptolemy and tempered, probably meaning one of the varieties of meantone temperament described by Zarlino, whereas the fretted string instruments are tuned according to the intense tuning of Aristoxenus, that is, equal temperament.[21] The main difference between these two types of instruments is that the former have two different semitones, whereas the latter have all their semitones equal. This difference accounts for the fact that it is difficult to have a perfectly united ensemble when these two types of instruments are used together.[22] Ensemble is not impossible, since the intonation of the fretted instruments can be altered a little depending on where one touches the fret, but the perfect concord between these two types of instruments is very difficult to achieve.[23] Bottrigari adds also that fretted instruments, thanks to the equality of their division, can transpose freely, whereas the number of possible transpositions is limited on keyboard instruments, because of their unequal semitones.[24]

One of the most interesting sections of *Il Desiderio* is the description of instruments in possession of the Duke of Ferrara, among them the *archicembalo* of Nicola Vicentino "called the 'Arch-musician' because he renewed the study of the three genera, two of which were almost forgotten, I don't know if I should say by men or only by practical musicians, whereas by theoretical or speculative musicians, of whom there are so few today, they are and always will be remembered."[25] Bottrigari adds that, when played, the instrument makes "a strange sound," (*un nuovo udire*) but "it is used only rarely because of the great difficulty in the tuning and maintenance of it and also in the playing of it."[26] Nevertheless, it renders new harmony, "when Luzzasco, principal organist of his Highness, touches it delicately in several compositions of music composed by him for this instrument only."[27] The tuning system prescribed by Vicentino for his instrument is then criticized because it has been made "by Aristoxenian practice rather than by true and good Ptolomaic theory." [28] Bottrigari probably refers to the fact that Vicentino's instrument extends the approximate "practical" meantone temperament to create an equal division of the octave, instead of using the "true" intervals of just intonation. Finally, he mentions that "in addition to this one there exist only two other similar Archiorgans, as he called them. One is in Rome, made to the order of the Cardinal of Ferrara of blessed memory, Uncle to His Highness, benefactor and patron of Don Nicola, and under his care; and another similarly made, but under the supervision of Don Nicola, is in Milan, where its maker died the year following the atrocious plague [1575-76]. . . ."[29]

Bottrigari's views on compositional practice are interesting, since they represent an attempt to come to terms with the critique levelled against polyphony by Vincenzo Galilei. Bottrigari certainly knew Galilei's *Dialogo della musica antica, et della moderna*, since he mentioned it in his earliest musical treatise, *Il Patricio*.[30] In *Il Melone Secondo* he repeated some of the arguments against counterpoint when he answered Gandolfo Sigonio's charge against Vicentino's madrigals to the effect that they lacked contrapuntal inventiveness and relied too much on homophony. Contrapuntal inventiveness, said Bottrigari, gives pleasure to professional musicians, but not to all listeners. Besides, it makes the text incomprehensible, creating an impression of "the chatter of plebeians and base persons" (*cicalamento delle persone plebee, & vili*), an impression aimed at by Alessandro Striggio in *Il cicalamento delle donne al bucato*, in imitation of Clément Janequin's *Le Caquet des femmes*.[31] However, unlike Galilei of the *Dialogo*, Bottrigari is not ready to ban polyphony altogether. He wants to avoid the excesses of counterpoint, but to preserve at the same time the Zarlinian ideal of "harmony," that is, of simultaneous movement of parts, and he finds the suitable compromise in homophonic texture since it does not destroy harmony and it helps to express the words. The parts may occasionally abandon strict homophony, but they should not do it too often. As the best example of what he has in mind Bottrigari cites the madrigals of Cipriano de Rore, "universally esteemed to be not only the most artful, but also the most lovely and polished composer of music in our time."[32]

Despite his attempts to achieve a compromise between the ideals of harmony and of the expression of the words, Bottrigari was definitely on the side of these musicians who felt that the ultimate goal of music was to express the passions of the text. He was against purely instrumental music since, being textless, it failed to express the affections:

> To this very important warning I think it best to add that no concert of instruments should ever be given without the addition of a human voice—always a voice well suited to the subject of the song. This is to avoid the music and the concert being called "mute" by connoisseurs and intelligent listeners, or as Aristotle calls it, and Plato calls it more clearly and better in the *Laws*, the "bare" sound of the Cithara or the Aulos, which they say resembles the sounds made by animals. This is because of the failure to express the *affetti* and because of the poor pronunciation of the words. From the words, especially when they are well mimed by a good musician, truly comes the great part of the emotions aroused in the minds of the listeners.[33]

It is to be expected from the theorist who sides with the trend of musical thought that conceives of music primarily in terms of its expressive possibilities that he will advocate the use of non-diatonic resources in composition. Bottrigari will not disappoint us in this respect. In *Il Melone* he takes issue with Zarlino's contention to the effect that in the polyphonic style of modern music pure chromaticism is impossible.[34] He agrees with Zarlino that no modern composer thus far was able to use pure chromatic and enharmonic genera successfully, but he does not think that this is impossible and, as a proof, he presents his "purely chromatic" madrigal "Il cantar novo."

Moreover, Bottrigari argues that the use of non-diatonic genera is not only possible but highly desirable. It was not for nothing that the ancients, in particular Plutarch, described the miraculous effects that these genera produced. The true use of these genera was forgotten after the ancient times not because they were useless, but because of their perfection. Non-diatonic genera were not as commonplace and natural as the diatonic, they were all produced by art, whose works are more difficult than the products of nature. Fortunately, the knowledge of these genera was preserved in ancient theoretical writings and as soon as these are studied and understood properly, the genera will be revived in the same way in which ancient letters, paintings, sculpture, and other arts have been revived. This has not been accomplished until today not because the non-diatonic genera are useless, but because they are not used properly. In short, Bottrigari values the artificial and difficult non-diatonic genera high above the diatonic and he connects the revival of these genera with the humanistic revival of ancient music and its miraculous powers.

II. ARTUSI

More clearly than most of his predecessors, Giovanni Maria Artusi makes a distinction between ancient and modern ideas of the structure of the genera. The genera described by Zarlino are the genera of the ancients. The tetrachord the limiting steps of which are common to all three genera is filled in the diatonic genus by a major semitone followed by two whole tones in ascending order (for example, B C D E). In the chromatic tetrachord the third diatonic step is moved a major semitone down producing an ascending series of a major and minor semitones followed by a minor third (B C C $\sharp$ E) and a presumably similar process of lowering diatonic and chromatic steps produces the enharmonic tetrachord consisting of two dieses followed by a major third (B B $^{\times}$ C E).[35] As a result the ancient tonal system consists only of the following steps within an octave: B, B $^{\times}$, C, C $\sharp$, D, E, E $^{\times}$, F, F $\sharp$, G, A.[36] Modern compositions, however, use other steps as well, for instance, D $\flat$, D $\sharp$, E $\flat$, G $\sharp$, A $\flat$, which do not belong to the system.[37] Contemporary composers consider each diatonic step as being capable of sharpening and flattening by means of an appropriate accidental.[38] Clearly, the moderns understand the genera differently from the ancients. Only the diatonic is common to the ancient and modern systems. The essence of the modern chromatic is the division of the whole tone into two semitones and the essence of the modern enharmonic is the division of the semitone into two dieses:

> Note that one should not consider the constitution of the three genera to lie in the division of the fourth, as was formerly done, but only in the division of the diatonic genus. The constitution of the chromatic genus lies in the division of the whole tone and that of the enharmonic, in the division of the semitone. One should be divided into two semitones and the other into a minor semitone and a diesis, although both are called by the name of diesis.[39]

Modern chromatic and enharmonic tetrachords do not contain incomposite thirds and in this respect they are superior to the ancient.[40] Artusi recalls the debate of Vicentino and Lusitano, correctly describes the problem as consisting in whether the thirds were diatonic or not, and, like every theorist discussed in this book, takes Lusitano's side.[41] Artusi's verdict does not bespeak his "innate conservatism," which "rebelled against the novel and visionary concepts evoked by Don Nicola's imagination," as one historian reflecting modern musicology's somewhat oversimplified portrait of Artusi the Conservatist would have it,[42] but, on the contrary, it shows that in the debate between the concept of the genera based on ancient authorities and the concept based upon observation of modern practice the theorist was ready to side with the modern idea of the genera and to consider it superior to the ancient one.

On the other hand, Artusi is much less enthusiastic about another feature which differentiates modern practice from the ancient one. The moderns, taking no heed of the "good rules" (*buone Regole*) of the ancients, divide each diatonic whole tone both by means of a sharp (for example, C C $\sharp$ D) and of a flat (for example, C D $\flat$ D). As a result, modern compositions are not purely diatonic, or chromatic, or enharmonic, but employ a mixture of all three genera.[43] Consequently, Vicentino was right to affirm that modern music mixes all genera, even though he did so for the wrong reasons:

> I want to tell you in conclusion that Don Nicola was right to assert that the music which was sung and played was a mixture of various genera. But since he did not know the true causes, it was good that he lost the wager made with Lusitano.[44]

Probably the most interesting aspect of Artusi's theory was his clear realization that contemporary composers failed to differentiate either between the major and minor whole tones or between the major and minor semitones. As regards the whole tones, all instruments have them equal, and, according to Francisco Salinas to whom Artusi approvingly refers, the whole tones used in singing are also equal.[45] Close observation of contemporary practice rather than reading of other theorists convinced Artusi that also semitones used by the modern composers were equal. This conclusion followed from the fact that the moderns divided indiscriminately every whole tone by means of both the sharp and the flat:

> While I consider that the most modern practitioners do not recognize any difference between whole tones nor between semitones but divide all with sharps and flats, . . . I also think that they themselves do not know what is the tuning system that is sung and played, although one can judge that they think they follow Aristoxenus, who had divided the whole tone exactly into two equal parts. The most certain proof of this will be provided by the composition for two parts by Mr. Adrian [Willaert]. . . . Not far from it will be many madrigals by [Costanzo] Porta, Cipriano [de Rore], Gabrieli, and so many others. . . .[46]

The fact that modern composers divide every whole tone indiscriminately by means of both the sharp and the flat indicates that they think in terms of equal temperament in which equal whole tones are divided into equal semitones. The most important proof is provided by Willaert's famous "chromatic duo" (it might in fact be called "enharmonic quartet"), *Quid non ebrietas*.[47] The duo, relates Artusi, is notated in such a way that it seems to end on a seventh (e-d') between the parts, but in fact it ends on an octave since the e has to be read as e♭♭. The same conclusion was reached by the theorist Giovanni Spataro in his letter of September 9, 1524 addressed to another theorist, Pietro Aaron (and, like the duo itself, printed by Artusi), except that Spataro assumed (incorrectly, according to Artusi) that the piece should be interpreted in the Pythagorean tuning and consequently proved that the final octave was too large by a comma. In the Pythagorean tuning the whole tone (for example, D-E) is divided into two unequal semitones, the diatonic minor semitone (for example, D-E♭ or D♯-E) and the chromatic major semitone (for example, D-D♯ or E♭-E♮). When this tuning is assumed, the double flat lowers a step by two major semitones, that is, by an interval a comma larger than the whole tone. Consequently, Spataro concluded that the final octave of the duo was too large by a comma. Spataro's reasoning, argued Artusi, was correct, but his assumption of the Pythagorean tuning for the duo was not. To assume that the duo presupposed the syntonic tuning of Ptolemy (that is, the just intonation) was also incorrect, since in this tuning the double flat lowered a step by an interval a comma smaller than the whole tone. Since it is clear that Willaert wanted to finish the piece on a perfect ocatve, concludes Artusi, he must have presupposed a tuning system in which a double flat lowers a step precisely by a whole tone, that is, a system in which there is no difference between a diatonic and chromatic (or major and minor) semitones, that is, the Aristoxenian equal temperament used by fretted string instruments. One cannot but agree with this conclusion.[48]

The example of the duo shows clearly that what Artusi has in mind when he claims that the indiscriminate dividing of every whole tone by both the sharp and the flat in modern compositions shows that their composers think in terms of equal temperament is the phenomenon called today the enharmonic equivalence of two notes. Only when equal temperament is presupposed will E$\flat\flat$ be equivalent to D, or C$\sharp$ to D$\flat$. The examination of the duo and other modern compositions convinced Artusi that their composers treated such differently notated steps as equivalent and that consequently they must have presupposed equal temperament.

The practice of transposition is for Artusi another proof of the fact that modern music presupposes equal temperament. Many transpositions are possible only in the equal temperament and not in the just intonation.[49] The range of transpositions is limited on keyboard instruments because of their unequal semitones.[50] In sum, the music which uses many accidentals would be full of imperfections, if just intonation were used. In order to avoid these imperfections, particularly in transpositions, a tuning system is required which divides the octave into equal parts and in fact such an equal temperament is used today, "even though they [modern practitioners] neither know it [the equal temperament], nor are able to explain it."[51]

Artusi's claim that modern music presupposes equal temperament implies that in his view the modern chromatic divides all diatonic whole tones into equal semitones and that the modern enharmonic could be understood in exactly the same way in which it is understood in our own time, as the enharmonic equivalence of differently notated steps. This is why Artusi can state that modern music mixes together all three genera, since it divides indiscriminately every whole tone by means of both the sharp and the flat.

Artusi was undoubtedly the first to arrive at such a clear understanding of the tonal system presupposed by the music his contemporaries. It has to be stressed, moreover, that Artusi not only states the fact that modern music presupposes equal temperament, but also in many places referred to above advocates this temperament as best suited for contemporary practice. However, his views on this subject are not entirely consistent. He starts his *L'Artusi, overo delle imperfettioni della moderna musica* with a consideration, modelled on Bottrigari's *Il Desiderio*, of the reasons why it is difficult for different types of instruments to create a good concert and comes to conclusions similar to Bottrigari's: Different types of instruments use different tuning systems. While the human voice and some wind instruments can sing and play in any system of tuning and temperament, the keyboard instruments have major and minor semitones and the fretted instruments have equal semitones, this being the reason why the keyboard and fretted instruments should not perform together.[52] Normal keyboard instruments lack certain steps, for instance, D ♯ available only on Vicentino's *archicembalo* which according to Artusi, was in the possession of Antonio Goretti of Ferrara at the time when the fictitious conversation recorded in his treatise supposedly took place, that is, in late 1598.[53] Artusi does not make clear whether he approves of such multiple divisions as Vicentino's and he expressly disapproves of equal temperament for keyboard instruments, stating, as Vincenzo Galilei before him, that equal temperament, when applied to a harpsichord, offends the unaccustomed ear:

> If one could bring the harpsichord to the temperament of equal whole tones and similarly equal semitones, one would hear a strange harmony. I recall having tempered a whole octave of a harpsichord with a lute as exactly as it was possible, but the sound, being outside of its natural temperament, offended the sense of hearing exceedingly. [54]

Thus in his treatise of 1600 Artusi was not ready to endorse equal temperament completely. Moreover, in the second part of the treatise, published in 1603, Artusi came to criticize certain contemporary composers for using intervals such as the diminished seventh or the diminished fourth in vocal compositions.[55] Such intervals, being enharmonically equivalent to the consonances of the major sixth and the major third, were acceptable in music intended for equally tempered instruments, such as the lute, but they were false and inappropriate in vocal music. Clearly, in 1603 the theorist was no longer ready to accept the fact that also vocal music could be conceived in terms of presupposed equal temperament and fell back upon the old Zarlinian doctrine of natural (presumably just) intonation of vocal music.

> . . . although [the voice] may be bent in whatever way, it cannot justly divide the whole tone into two equal parts and sing these in such a way that they make the effect heard on instruments. It seems to me an error that the inventors of such confusions fill paper with those things that cannot be employed by nature without its offence, only to appear of clever genius, not taking into account that natural things are different from accidental ones.[56]

Farther on, Artusi shows that certain intervals, different in vocal intonation, are identical (or, as we say, "enharmonically equivalent") in an instrumental equal temperament in which there are only twelve different intervals.[57]

Artusi's attitude toward equal temperament was undeniably ambivalent. It is to his great credit that he recognized the fact that this temperament was presupposed by the musical practice of his contemporaries, even though he was finally able to accept its use only in instrumental music and, probably under the influence of his revered teacher Gioseffo Zarlino, asserted that the voice should use a "natural," presumably just, intonation with its major and minor semitones.

Other aspects of Artusi's theory which are of interest to a student of chromaticism are fairly conventional. Like almost all previously discussed theorists, Artusi is aware that the use of accidentals does not necessarily mean that a composition is chromatic. It can be a transposed diatonic work. Chromaticism is, in effect, introduced only when the chromatic intervallic series is used.[58] Consequently, Artusi criticizes the author of *Il Desiderio*, whom he calls Benelli according to the anagram used in the first edition of 1594, for believing that the term "chromaticism" was derived from the colored black keys. Not only was it possible to use the black keys and remain within the diatonic, argued Artusi, but chromaticism was invented earlier than keyboard.[59] Any composition can be transposed upwards and downwards by any interval. Transpositions do not change intervallic structures used within a composition and consequently can be only seen, not heard.[60]

Artusi's description of the relationship between the genera uses the same terms that Francisco Salinas used earlier:[61]

> Besides, I should like you to know that these genera have among themselves this agreement and relation that the best has to the better and this to the good. The good can stand by itself and can exist without there being a better and a best. But the better can be better only in relation to the good, and the best cannot exist by itself without the better and the good. Thus the good is the origin and foundation of the better and the best, and both the good and the better find perfection in the best. Thus we say that for our purpose the diatonic can stand and exist by itself, because it was created by nature and was used for a long time in its natural being. . . . One sees that this [chromatic genus] can in no way stand by itself alone without the diatonic, since it is nothing but a compressed diatonic. Because it mollifies the harshness of the latter, it acquired the name of the better and more perfect. Similarly, the enharmonic cannot exist by itself, because it, like the chromatic, is built upon the diatonic, but it is more compressed than the chromatic.[62]

Artusi's attitude toward chromatic experiments is certainly negative: "Who leaves an old road for a new one is often deceived," he says, quoting a popular proverb. "This happened to Don Nicola Vicentino, who wanted to introduce into singing all three genera but, because of the difficulty of such a thing and the little pleasure it gave the sense of hearing, he did not have the happy success he expected. . . ."[63] This, however, does not mean that Artusi would ban the use of non-diatonic steps altogether. His attitude toward chromaticism is in fact very similar to Zarlino's. Non-diatonic steps may be used temporarily and accidentally, since such use does not make a composition non-diatonic. But when one particular non-diatonic step is used too persistently or when a whole chromatic intervallic series is employed, this indicates that the chromatic genus has been introduced and that the composition mixes genera.[64] Artusi reproaches composers for making such mixtures, since he considers them to serve no purpose but to satisfy a composer's whim.[65] The chromaticism was introduced to mollify the harshness of the diatonic or, more specifically, to supply consonances on such diatonic steps where these are ordinarily missing.[66] Thanks to these additional consonances chromatic steps can enrich the harmony of a composition; they should thus ornament the diatonic genus, not destroy it.[67]

Like Zarlino, who used to call compositions of the chromaticists derisively "your whims" (*vostri Capricci*),[68] Artusi accuses those who use chromatic steps more boldly than he preferred, of using them for no purpose but "to satisfy their whims" (*per scapriciarsi*).[69] It was an accusation of this kind that Claudio Monteverdi had in mind when he claimed "that I do not compose my works at haphazard."[70] A modern composer, like those of old, declared Monteverdi, "builds upon the foundation of truth."[71] His practice, like the practice of older masters, is based upon certain principles, but these principles differ from those that guided the older practice. Monteverdi contrasted the newer, second practice which, as his brother explained, "was first renewed in our notation by Cipriano de Rore . . ., was followed and amplified, not only by the gentlemen already mentioned [that is, "the Signor Prencipe di Venosa, Emilio del Cavaliere, Count Alfonso Fontanella, the Count of the Camerata, the Cavalier Turchi, Pecci, and other gentlemen of that heroic school"], but by Ingegneri, Marenzio, Giaches de Wert, Luzzasco, likewise by Jacopo Peri, Giulio Caccini, and finally by loftier spirits with a better understanding of true art . . .," with the older, first practice "finally perfected by Messer Adriano with actual composition and by the most excellent Zarlino with most judicious rules."[72] In technical terms, the difference between the two practices lies in the different manner of employing consonances and dissonances in counterpoint. These different manners of composing, however, are influenced by fundamental aesthetic considerations. Giulio Cesare Monteverdi explained that

> By First Practice he [Claudio Monteverdi] understands the one that turns on the perfection of the harmony, that is, the one that considers the harmony not commanded, but commanding, not the servant, but the mistress of the words. . . . By Second Practice . . . he understands the one that turns on the perfection of the melody, that is, the one that considers harmony not commanding, but commanded, and makes the words the mistress of the harmony. . . .[73]

The "melody" in the above passage is the union of the words, the harmony, and the rhythm. Referring to Plato's *Republic*, 398D, Monteverdi's brother explains the term:

> Of this [melody] Plato speaks as follows: "The song is composed of three things: the words, the

harmony, and the rhythm''; and, a little further on: ''And so of the apt and the unapt, if the rhythm and the harmony follow the words, and not the words these.''[74]

Thus in the Monteverdian opposition of the first and second practice one has to see not only two different contrapuntal styles, but more fundamentally, the same opposition which, as I have indicated before, underlies the whole late sixteenth-century Italian theory, the opposition between the idea of music as harmony and as a medium expressing the words.

Artusi, like Zarlino, whom Monteverdi pointed out as the codifier of the first practice, defends the idea of music as ''harmony,'' as an independent, abstract tonal order governed by consonant relations between sounds and between melodies. This harmony brings pleasure, which is the aim of music:

> The goal of the musician and that of the poet are all one. . . . The goal of the poet is to be useful and entertaining. Hence the goal of the singer or player is to be useful and entertaining.[75]

The Horatian precept to unite the delightful with the profitable was also pointed out as the goal of music by Zarlino,[76] and we have seen his opponent Galilei criticizing modern music for seeking no other aim than pleasure of the sense. Answering a letter of Monteverdi's defender, L'Ottuso Accademico, Artusi explained that while the ancient music had the power to move affections, modern music could not achieve this but could bring pleasure.[77] Artusi must have said this in answer to L'Ottuso's claim that the new manner of composition was designed to excite passions. In fact, in his second letter L'Ottuso explained:

> However, it is not necessary for this music to effect the miracle of raising the dead. It will certainly cause an affection, that is, a desire by the novelty of its part movement. . . .[78]

When Monteverdi says that in the second practice the words are the mistress of the harmony and rhythm he advocates the idea of music subordinated to the expression of the text or, more precisely, to the expression of the passions conveyed by the text. While the music of the first practice was to unite the delightful with the profitable and had the concept of ''harmony'' at its center, that of the second practice was to move the affections and to subordinate the ''harmony'' to this goal.

Behind the second practice was the desire to give music the affective power it was supposed to have had in ancient times. But unlike Galilei of the *Dialogo*, neither Monteverdi nor his defenders were interested in reconstructing ancient compositional techniques. L'Ottuso expressly said in his letter that new music ''will cause an affection . . . by the novelty of its melody'' and that it was important to invent new devices rather than to imitate the ancient ones.[79] Like Vicentino before him, Monteverdi hoped that novelty rather than antiquarian reconstruction will renew music's emotional effectiveness.

IV

Conclusion

The second half of the sixteenth-century was a period of incessant musical polemics, starting with the debates among Vicentino, Lusitano, and Danckerts, continuing with Zarlino's attacks on Vicentino and later with his polemic with Galilei, and culminating in Artusi's many-sided controversies with Galilei, Bottrigari, and Monteverdi. The theorists of that time were able to define their positions most clearly when they were defending them against those of other theorists. The incessant debates were not mere explosions of quarrelsome characters. What seems today an indecently acrimonious wrangle may have been a perfectly acceptable manner of debating at the time; the issues were felt strongly, because they were truly important.

If theorists were divided over some issues, there were also numerous points of agreement. These points of agreement, often unstated but accepted silently as presuppositions of an argument, are of particular interest to us, since they make possible, at least to a certain extent, a reconstruction of the way in which music was commonly heard and experienced at the time. Such a hypothetical reconstruction (to be undertaken presently) is necessary, if the technical function of late sixteenth-century chromaticism is to be explained. I believe that it should take into consideration the late-Renaissance modes of musical experience as they are revealed by contemporary theory, but should not be afraid to go beyond the conceptual framework proposed by this theory when it does not make the experience fully conscious, when it does not explain it adequately.

It is my first assumption that a sixteenth-century musical work is a unified, coherent whole and that to understand it is to grasp the principle of this unity and coherence, to demonstrate what makes this particular collection of various pitches a unified, coherent, and meaningful organization.

My second assumption is that in the sixteenth century this coherence is primarily the result of tonal organization, that is, the organization of various pitches, and that the organization of other values (temporal, dynamic, and timbral), although it may contribute to the overall coherence, is less essential. The coherence of a sixteenth-century work must be grasped primarily in terms of its tonal organization. It is necessary to recognize that chromaticism is one aspect of tonal organization. To understand the function of chromaticism within tonal organization, one has first to understand the basic principles of the sixteenth-century tonal organization itself.

My third assumption is that these basic principles of tonal organization are pre-compositional, that they are common to all, or most, sixteenth-century compositions and are taken for granted by composers even before they start to write. These basic principles will be called the tonal system, that is, the set of all pitches and intervals available to a composer and the way in which it is pre-compositionally organized.

Since sixteenth-century music does not know an absolute pitch-standard, a pitch is not defined in absolute terms (as an absolutely determined point in the pitch-continuum), but only relatively, by its intervallic relations with other pitches. To avoid confusion with modern terminology, I have used the term step for such a relatively defined pitch. Italian theorists of the era used the term "string" (*corda*) in this sense.

Since steps are defined by means of intervals, and not the reverse, it follows that intervals are logically prior to steps and that it is possible to discuss the tonal system entirely in terms of intervals, that is, as a set of all intervals available to a composer (that is, the gamut) and its pre-compositional organization. Octave equivalence is basic to the sixteenth-century intervallic system; two intervals distant by an octave are equivalent and, consequently, two steps distant by an octave are equivalent.[1] It follows that the gamut consists of all intervals possible within the octave.

What is the gamut of sixteenth-century music? The notation used at the time employs seven diatonic (that is, unsharpened and unflattened) notes with the possibility (at least theoretical) of chromatic lowering and raising of each, or most, of these notes by means of a flat or a sharp. Certainly more than twelve, and possibly even all twenty-one, different notes are used in practical sources. Although it can be reasonably assumed that the musicians of the Renaissance were able to notate all the steps and intervals they were using, it does not follow that all differently notated steps and intervals were indeed different. It is not inconceivable that it was possible to notate the same steps and intervals in several different ways.

I believe that this was indeed the case. This can be demonstrated by the existence of pieces which use what is called today enharmonically equivalent form of notation, that is, which show that the same step can be notated in several different ways. An example which comes immediately to mind is Adrian Willaert's chromatic duo *Quid non ebrietas* discussed in the preceding chapter. It will be recalled that the piece is notated in such a way that it seems to end on a seventh e-d' between the tenor and soprano. It is significant that although contemporary theorists disagreed on how to interpret the piece, there was no disagreement on one point: a double flat had to be applied to the tenor's final e according to *musica ficta* rules so that the piece might end on the octave d-d', as Willaert had intended. This was the opinion of both Spataro who interpreted the piece according to Pythagorean tuning system and Artusi who argued that an interpretation according to Aristoxenian temperament was appropriate. It follows that e♭♭ and d were commonly considered to be equivalent in principle, even though not necessarily in every tuning system. More generally, double flats (or sharps) lowered (or raised) a note so that it was equivalent to a diatonic note a whole tone lower (or higher). This common assumption had, as Artusi demonstrated, one serious presupposition: it presupposed that an accidental lowered or raised a note by exactly one half of a whole tone. Thus it can be further deduced from Willaert's example that if among two diatonic notes distant by a whole tone the lower one was sharpened and the higher flattened, the result would be an enharmonically equivalent notation of one step. That this was indeed so can be demonstrated by an unambiguous example of such enharmonically equivalent notation in Luca Marenzio's famous madrigal *O voi che sospirate:*[2]

There can be little doubt that the vertical intervals notated as A♭- g♯ ', d♭- c♯ ', and G♭- f♯ ' (all on strong beats) are intended to represent consonant octaves and their equivalents.

Such examples of enharmonically equivalent notation demonstrate that even if musicians used notation which allowed flattening and sharpening of all seven diatonic notes, in fact only twelve different equidistant steps and twelve different intervals (the semitone and its multiples) were employed.[3] Different ways of notating a step reflected different ways in which a step was used. In particular, after a sharpened note one could expect a continuation of the melodic movement upward and after a flattened note the reverse, if the melodic movement was stepwise. Similarly, if a composer had to choose between a normally notated melodic consonance versus a normally notated vertical consonance, he usually made the choice in favor of the former. These, however, were just notational tendencies and one should not expect them to be applied very consistently.

The question of the relationship between the tonal and tuning system should be discussed here. The tonal system is to a large extent independent of a specific tuning system that is applied. Sixteenth-century theorists show that identical intervallic structures of the tonal system (for instance, the genera) may be tuned in many different ways. Moreover, it is a well-known fact that several tuning systems were used throughout the sixteenth century. Besides, even today practical intonation of intervals in performance can vary to quite a considerable degree without making such performance unsatisfactory, since we perceive such slightly differently intoned intervals as identical from the point of view of the tonal system.

Thus various tuning systems may be used in practical application of a given tonal system. It does not follow, however, that these various tuning systems are all equally good. The perfect tuning system that is implied by the sixteenth-century tonal system is equal temperament. Much of the sixteenth-century repertory may be satisfactorily performed with intervals tempered differently. It is only in certain chromatic pieces that equal temperament becomes absolutely necessary. Such pieces make explicit the perfect tuning method only implied by the sixteenth-century tonal system in general. The fact that late Renaissance composers thought in terms of equal temperament was first demonstrated by Artusi, even though the virtues of this temperament were praised and discussed by several theorists before him. For various reasons, such as attachment to tradition, and lack of truly compelling necessity, it took musicians and theorists another hundred years or so to accept equal temperament universally. Much of the repertory did not absolutely require equal temperament. Moreover, fretted string instruments were gradually replaced in the seventeenth century by unfretted ones, making possible the simultaneous use of bowed string and keyboard instruments in one ensemble without forcing keyboard instruments to adopt equal temperament.[4]

Sixteenth-century theory organizes the intervals of the gamut on several levels. First, the intervals are organized into the diatonic series, which is "circular," that is, has no beginning nor end, and consists of consecutive whole tones and semitones placed so that the semitones are separated from each other alternately by two and by three consecutive whole tones. This way of understanding diatonic structures can be deduced from all theorists discussed in this book. It makes possible a negative definition of what is non-diatonic, even though the theorists differ considerably in their specific definitions of the chromatic and enharmonic genera.

Although the theorists did argue about the structure of the chromatic "genus," they all gave definitions which involved the division of a whole tone into two consecutive semitones. By the end of the sixteenth century some theorists recognized the obvious fact that in modern practice the chromatic "genus" was nothing more than the division of diatonic whole tones into two semitones.

The enharmonic "genus," the structure of which was also debated, is of lesser interest, since it found almost no application outside of theoretical sources. So far as the Renaissance practice is concerned, the term "enharmonic" may be used in the same way in which it is used today, to signify the enharmonically equivalent forms of notation.

It should be observed that the diatonic genus contains all the intervals of the gamut: individual intervals of the diatonic series and the sums of the consecutive intervals give the semitone and all its twelve multiples up to the octave. The so-called chromatic "genus" or "scale" yields no new intervals. Thus the chromatic does nothing more than make explicit the interval- and step-content present implicitly in the diatonic series.

The method thanks to which the chromatic potential implicit in the diatonic is made explicit is transposition. Chromatic series can be generated from the diatonic one when the latter is fixed on a specific pitch-level and then transposed as many times as is necessary in order to have any one step of the series correspond to each of the specific pitches produced by the original fixing and by all previous transpositions. Putting together all original and transposed pitches will produce the twelve-step chromatic series.

It would require a seperate investigation to see whether this was indeed the way in which chromaticism historically emerged. For the present purpose it suffices to note the intimate connection between chromaticism and transposition. Many sixteenth-century theorists point out that the transposed diatonic using many accidentals in notation should not be confused with the true chromatic. A step that belongs to a diatonic intervallic series is diatonic regardless of how it is notated; other steps are purely chromatic. All theorists who describe the relationship between the genera assert that it creates a definite hierarchy of importance between steps: the truly chromatic steps are somehow less important, less fundamental, less stable than the diatonic ones.

The genera represent the first level on which the intervals of the gamut are organized. The intervals of the diatonic series are further organized into what sixteenth-century theorists (following their Greek and medieval predecessors) called "octave-species." Any interval within the diatonic series may be chosen as a fixed point of departure, transforming the "circular" series into a "linear" one with a fixed starting point and a fixed end at the octave's distance and giving the consecutive intervals of the series absolute positions instead of the relative ones it had before. Seven different octave-species result.

These octave-species are further organized into modes. Sixteenth-century theorists seem to agree that a mode is an octave-species divided into two parts, a species of fifth and a species of fourth. If the species of fifth is below the species of fourth, a mode is called authentic, if their order is reversed it is called plagal.

Even before Vicentino and Zarlino theorists asserted that in polyphonic music neighboring parts use, one the authentic and the other the corresponding plagal mode. In other words, in a polyphonic composition the distinction between the authentic and plagal is irrelevant; it is the distinction of ambitus only. What is important are the species of fifth and fourth that are being used, not their order. Since one of the octave-species cannot be divided into species of perfect fifth and fourth, there are only six different polyphonic modes.[5]

The modal division of an octave-species produces hierarchical differentiation among the diatonic steps: The lower limit of the species of fifth, called the final of the mode, is the most important diatonic step, the upper limit of the species of fifth is second in importance. It is on these steps that most important structural cadences of the piece will be constructed. Some theorists, most notably Zarlino, distinguish also the step which divides the species of fifth into two thirds as a suitable point on which to construct cadences.[6] If Zarlino's observation is correct—and I think it is—one might say that a mode is primarily a division of an octave-species into species of fifth and fourth and secondarily a division of the species of fifth into two thirds. These two divisions distinguish three steps as being most suitable cadential points and consequently more important than other diatonic steps, namely, the final as the most important step, the fifth above the final as second in importance, and the third above the final as third in importance.

Note that the divisions of octave-species correspond to the hierarchy of intervals commonly accepted in the sixteenth century. Thanks to the principle of octave equivalence, the octave is the most important interval, the point of reference of the whole system. The primary division of the octave-species corresponds to two perfect consonances, the fifth and the fourth. The secondary division of the species of fifth corresponds to two imperfect consonances, the third and the sixth, both of which can be either major or minor depending on which species of fifth is divided. Other intervals are dissonances.

The pre-compositional organization of the tonal system results in hierarchical differentiation among intervals and among steps. Certain intervals and certain steps are more fundamental, more perfect, more stable than others. Among intervals these are (in the decreasing order of perfection) the octave, other perfect consonances, imperfect consonances, and finally dissonances. Among steps these are the final, the fifth above it, the third above it, other diatonic steps, chromatic steps. The coherence of any particular work is grounded in these pre-compositionally established hierarchies. A piece of music is based on a mode and a hierarchy of steps within this mode creates the multi-level hierarchy of steps within the piece. More important steps are stable "centers" to which less important steps are subordinated with the final as the ultimate point of reference. However, a composition does not have to use the tonal material of just one mode. Most theorists of the era affirm this fact, even though some find it deplorable. An analyst can expect to find in a sixteenth-century composition a modulation, that is, a change of mode, a transposition of a mode, and a simultaneous modulation and transposition. It is his duty to show on which mode and transposition a given area within the piece is based, and to explain how these various areas are combined with one another. To accomplish the first part of his task, he will observe primarily which species of fifth and fourth and secondarily also which species of thirds are used, both horizontally and vertically, at any given point within the piece. The second part of his task, the explanation of how areas based on different modes and transpositions are combined to create a coherent whole, is more difficult.

Among the theorists whose work is discussed in this book Nicola Vicentino was the only one to address himself seriously to this problem. He not only recognized it as a problem, as did many others, but also had the theoretical imagination and artistic experience that enabled him to solve it. Discussing the structure of a piece which uses many modes, Vicentino made clear that such a piece has to be based on a single fundamental mode to which other modes have to be subordinated.[7] The most important structural cadences of the composition will be constructed on the final and other basic steps of the fundamental mode. In the course of the piece cadences may also be constructed on steps belonging to other modes, for the sake of variety and embellishment of the fundamental structure of the composition provided by the cadences built on the basic steps of the fundamental mode. Areas based on secondary modes will be subordinated to this fundamental structure. The skeleton of the musical structure could be visualized as consisting of the fundamental level in which the cadences built on the most important steps of the basic mode would serve as points of repose—pillars supporting the whole structure—and of upper levels, in which a similar role would be played by the cadences built on the most important steps of secondary modes.

Vicentino suggests that we should regard the relationship between areas based on various modes (or transpositions) as being hierarchical: one mode is fundamental, others are subordinated to it, still others may presumably be subordinated to these, etc. I find his suggestion truly brilliant. Coherence within a piece of music based on a mode is generated by the pre-compositionally established multi-level tonal hierarchy which makes certain steps into stable "centers" to which other steps are subordinated. Similarly, a composition which uses many modes and transpositions can be made into a unified, coherent whole only if hierarchical relationships are established between these various modes and transpositions, when certain of these are subordinated to others. As a matter of fact, the coherence of a total composition based on several modes is the result of the same principles which establish coherence within an area based on a single mode; it is generated by the same principles of the tonal system.

In other words, the pre-compositional principles of the tonal system estab-

lish a specific hierarchy of steps within each area based on a single mode within a
composition. In order for a total composition to be coherent, these separate
hierarchies will have to create a more fundamental hierarchy of two or more levels.
Since all steps of a mode are ultimately subordinated to the final, the relatonships
between several modes and transpositions are basically the relationships between
their finals, that is, their finals will enter into the same type of hierarchical
organization as steps of a single mode do. Any step within a composition is either
the central point of a mode, or is subordinated to such a central point, or both. An
analyst will want to elucidate the function of each step within the total hierarchy.

The above outline is offered as a hypothesis which would have to be tested
analytically to prove its usefulness. At present nothing more than just a brief
example of such an analytical test can be given. The example is the much-
discussed prologue to Orlando di Lasso's *Prophetiae Sibyllarum*:[8]

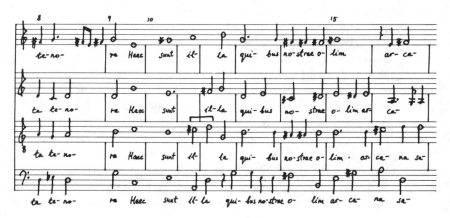

Edward E. Lowinsky described this piece as an example of "triadic atonality":

> Here is a music in which extreme chromaticism and constant modulation within a triadic texture erode any sense of a stable tonal center. . . . In the first nine bars of the prologue to the prophecies Lasso uses all twelve tones; he builds triads on ten different degrees, six of which result in harmonies foreign to the mode—if we take the mode as Mixolydian since the piece ends on G. Lasso strays as far as B-flat major and C minor in one direction, and B major in the other. This phrase, although beginning on a C major and ending on a G major chord, has no stable frame of tonal reference. Through the excessive modulation within so small a space we lose all orientation.[9]

One cannot disagree with the characterization of the texture of the piece as "triadic," as least as long as the term remains purely descriptive. Four-part consonant "triads," almost all of them full, in root position, and with the prime doubled, completely dominate the strictly syllabic setting and are enlivened by very brief ornamental dissonances only before the three main cadences (mm. 8, 16-17, and 24). The result of this singlemindedly austere texture is that modal species are articulated locally primarily in vertical rather than horizontal terms. Since a consonant triad is a harmony consisting of the three most important steps of a mode, each triad emerges locally as the main event defining the mode in its immediate area. Incidentally, this is why it justified to use the anachronistic concept of "triad" which made its appearance only in the early seventeenth century[10] in a discussion of a mid-sixteenth-century composition, in spite of the fact that the theory contemporaneous with it conceives of "triadic" harmonies as mere sums of intervals rather than harmonies unified by a central root.[11] A triadic harmony, whether theoretically recognized or not, has the power of defining a mode by emphasising its most important steps and, consequently, of projecting its own prime as the central point of reference for all intervals, analogous to the final of the mode. It is certainly not an accident that Johannes Lippius, who coined the term "harmonic triad" (*trias harmonica*) and who was among the earliest theorists to understand the full implications of the concept, related it very closely to the concept of the mode.[12]

The principal analytical problem of the prologue is to establish whether individual triads-modes merely succeed one another without being truly connected and without creating a coherent unified whole (as would be the case in "triadic atonality"), or whether it can be demonstrated that the composer took pains to impose on the manifold of triads an intelligible and audible multi-level hierarchical order whereby the roots (finals) of individual triads (modes) articulate a mode of a more fundamental level, the whole process repeating itself as many times as is necessary to subordinate all triads ultimately to a single modal center. I believe that, while it is hard to deny that the piece through its extreme chromaticism and exploration of distant tonal areas makes heavy demands on a listener, it is possible to demonstrate the existence of a sophisticated hierarchical design which not only imposes a sense of coherence and unity on the piece as a whole and on its constituent parts but also, thanks to its careful correlation with the text, subtly parallels and illuminates various nuances of the poem's structure and meaning.

A success of an analysis based on a theory positing the existence of a hierarchy of structural levels depends to a large extent on whether the events belonging to a single level have been correctly chosen and distinguished from those belonging to other levels as well as on a correct evaluation of relationships between levels. This can be accomplished only if the style of the analyzed composition is taken into consideration. In the case of a syllabic and homorhythmic setting, such as Lasso's prologue, initial clues will most likely be provided by the structure of the poem. Indeed, one notices immediately that the endings of the three lines of the prologue's text correspond with the three strongest cadences in the piece, the only ones preceded by brief ornamental dissonant disturbances in the otherwise strictly syllabic, consonant, and homorhythmic texture (mm. 9, 18, 25). These three main cadential points, on G, C, and G respectively, constitute the most fundamental structural level and provide an unmistakable framework of modal reference (I-IV-I in G-Mixolydian or -Ionian) for the entire composition. (Roman numerals in the diagrams below signify the diatonic degrees of a mode [and diatonic consonant triads built upon these degrees] starting with, and ascending from, the final. Arabic superscript followed by an accidental indicates a chromatic inflection. Capital letters signify major triads, small letters—minor triads.)

Let us examine in detail the first section, mm. 1-9. It not only ends, but also starts in G-mode, the initial triad on the fourth degree of the mode, C, being subordinated to the following triad on the first degree, G.[13] Beginning the piece rather unusually with the progression IV-I, Lasso subtly anticipates the importance of the fourth degree within the basic tonal plan of the piece (I-IV-I).

The most important textual caesura corresponds with the implied comma in

m. 5 after the word *chromatico*. This point of articulation in the text, combined with metrically strong placement of the accompanying chord and with the following rest in the tenor (the only internal rest in the whole analyzed section), gives special prominence to the E-triad at the beginning of m. 5. E-triad is additionally emphasised by the deliberate analogy with the central G in m. 2. Namely, it is repeated in the same rhythm in which G-triad was repeated previously. As a result, the first triad after the textual caesura, f ♯ in m. 5, which is the only potential rival of E in architectonic importance since it opens the second half of the verse, is clearly heard as subordinated to E which emerges as the main event between the G-triads in mm. 2 and 9. Thus, the basic structure of the section seems to be:

Measure:	2	5	9
Triad:	G	E	G
Structure:	I	VI^{3}♯	I

The progression is chromatic because the E-triad does not belong to the same diatonic series as the G-mode (regardless of whether this mode is Mixolydian or transposed Ionian). Thus, the progressions from the end of m. 2 to the beginning of m. 5 and from there to the beginning of m. 9 must involve transpositions and perhaps also modulations. The very first triad after G in m. 2, B in m. 3, introduces a chromatic progression in the soprano and, consequently, it cannot belong to the diatonic G-mode. However, together with the following two triads (c ♯ and E, mm. 4-5), it can well belong to a single diatonic series, different from the one represented by the first two chords of the piece. Since the final triad of this progression, E, is the local goal of the tonal motion, the previous two triads are subordinated to it. Thus, while the first two measures express the untransposed G-mode (or C-mode transposed a fifth up), mm. 3-beginning of 5 express the C-mode transposed a major third up. While both units viewed separately are diatonic, the second is chromatic in relation to the first. This chromatic relationship between the two units is expressed most immediately by the chromatic semitone progression in the soprano between the last triad of the first and the first triad of the second unit (d′-d ♯ ′). The latter triad (B) may be interpreted as the chromatic pivot-chord between the two units, being simultaneously V in the second unit and III$^{5}_{3}$♯ or III^{3} ♯ in the first.

We have seen that the two units differ not only in their respective levels of transposition of the diatonic series, but also in their respective modal centers (G and E) and that the second of these centers is subordinated to the first one (as VI^{3}♯ to I). Consequently, the triads subordinated to the second center (which, in relation to them, becomes a local I) must represent a different, and less fundamental, structural level from all the other triads of both units:

Measure:	1	2	3	4	5
Triad:		C	G	B	c♯	E

Structure: 2nd level: (V)   [VI]   I

1st level: (IV)   I   [III$^{3}{}_{\#}^{5\#}{}_{?}$]   VI$^{3\#}$

(On any single level parentheses and brackets enclose events of decreasing structural weight. Thus, on the first level IV has been interpreted as being structurally less prominent than either I or VI$^{3\#}$, and the chromatic III as carrying even less weight than the diatonic IV.)

The most important architectonic points in the return from E back to G are the first f♯-triad in mm. 5-6, since it initiates the new motion and since it is repeated, and D-triad in m. 8, since it is embellished and prolonged to last a whole measure. These two triads receive so much emphasis that the intervening chords are experienced as being subordinated to them. Consequently, the analyst should avoid the trap of interpreting the G-triad in m. 6 as representing the return of the original modal center. The D-triad is a diatonic or chromatic member (V$^{3\#}{}_{?}$) of G-mode, and the f♯-triad—a diatonic member (II) of E-mode. It is also the pivot in the return, since it may be interpreted as the chromatic VII$\hat{1}^{5\#}{}_{\#?}$ of G or the diatonic III of D:

Measure:	5		8	9
Triad:	E	f♯	D	G

Structure: 3rd level: (III)   I

2nd level: I   (II)

1st level: VI$^{3\#}$ [VII$^{1}{}_{\#?}^{5\#}$] (V$^{3}{}_{?}^{\#}$) I

(On the third level I interpret f♯ as being subordinated to D and not the reverse, since D is metrically stronger.)

The progression from f♯ to D involves the melodic descent in the soprano from a' through g' and f' to f♯'. The melodic motion from g' to f' is supported by the triadic motion down the circle of fifths from G to C (under g') and from F to B♭ (under f'). The result is a strict sequence of two units. In each unit the appearance of a new melodic note over the first chord gives this chord a slightly greater weight and subordinates the second chord to it (as IV to I):

Measure:	5	6		7		8
Triad	f♯	{D}	G C	F	B♭	D
Structure: 4th level:		{V}	I (IV)	I	(IV)	
3rd level:	(III)		[IV	III¹ ♮]		I

(D has been enclosed in braces because, taking as it does the weakest metric position and being the first inverted triad heard thus far, it leads a much less independent existence than other triads. It exists only because the note d′ is introduced in the alto one beat "too early" in order to avoid parallel fifths with the bass.)

Nothing in the first half of the analyzed section (mm. 1-5) allows us to recognize whether the central tonality represented the untransposed G-mode or the C-mode transposed a fifth up. The "key signature" was of no help not only for the obvious reason that it cannot be heard, but also because we know far too little about the function of accidental signatures in sixteenth-century music to assume their consistent and systematic use to indicate modal transpositions. In the second half of the section (mm. 5-9) both the Mixolydian and the Ionian versions of the seventh scale-step are used prominently. My analysis demonstrates, however, that f♯- and D-triads are structurally more important than F. As a result, we hear the melodic f♯′ in the soprano in m. 8 as a diatonic step and we hear the preceding f′ as its chromatic alteration. It is, incidentally, quite likely that a sixteenth-century theorist would consider the piece to represent the Hypomixolydian mode. In doing so he would follow the obvious traditional clues provided by the final, the signature, and the emphasis on the fourth scale-step, that is, the plagal reciting pitch. Even he, however, would probably *hear* the f′ in m. 7 as a chromatically lowered step.

Only now are we in a position to appreciate the subtlety with which Lasso set his text ("The songs which you hear sung in a chromatic manner"). (See chart on p. 110. The braces around c in m. 8 indicate that this triad, like D in m. 6, leads a much less independent existence than other tirads, due to its context, weak metric position, and inversion. It is in fact no more than a chromatic neighbor-note embellishment of the prolonged D.) The most striking feature of the section, and the one which contributes most to our difficulty in hearing it in "tonal" rather than "atonal" terms, is the sudden chromatic modulation in mm. 3-5. The unexpected shift is fully justified by the text, since it corresponds precisely with the word *Chromatico*. While the modulation from G to E is chromatic, the return from E through D to G is diatonic since it is effected by means of pivot-chords which are diatonic members of modes between which they mediate. Consequently, the return offers less opportunity for "atonal" hearing. The only difficulty is

	1	2	3	4	5	6	7	8	9
Measure:	1	2	3	4	5	6	7	8	9
Triad:	C	G	B	c♯	E	f♯	{D} G C F B♭	D {c} D	G
Structure: 4th level:							{V}		{VII¹ ♮}I ³♭)I
3rd level:					I		I	(V	
2nd level:			(V) [VI]			(III)	(IV)		)I
1st level:	(IV)	I	[III³ #]		VI³ # [II)	(II) [VII⁵ #]	[IV III¹ ♮] ⁵♮	I	)I
Text: Soprano:	Car-	mina	Chro- ma-		tico	quae au-	du- dis la- ta	te-	no- re
Other parts:	Car-	mina	Chro- ma-		tico	quae au-	mo- dis du- la-	ta	no- re

introduced by the progression down the circle of fifths in mm. 6-7 and it may be the text again (*modulata*) which offers a possible justification for the corresponding musical procedure.

Observe further, that in the text the usual syntactic order has been disturbed by the displacement of the adjective *Chromatico* from the position before the noun it modifies, *tenore*, to the middle of the verse. This displacement has two important results. It gives the displaced word, *Chromatico*, an extraordinary prominence, and it creates a "syntactic gap" between *Chromatico* and *tenore*. Both these textual features have their musical counterparts. Chromaticism is the central characteristic of the section, since it not only embellishes less fundamental structural levels or relationships between them, but eats down to the very core of music, the most fundamental structural progression being chromatic. And the gap between *Chromatico* and *tenore* finds its counterpart in musical syntax. While these two words are set by musical events of the first structural level, the events that separate them belong to the third and fourth levels only. In addition, as if to emphasise the *Chromatico* character of the *tenore*, Lasso embellishes the latter word by chromatic neighbor-notes.

The analysis of the first section of Lasso's prologue demonstrates, I hope, that the analytical hypothesis presented in this book deserves further testing, since it can help to illuminate structural and text-setting features of an admittedly complex sixteenth-century composition. By elucidating the function of each step (whether a central point, a point subordinated to a tonal center, or both) within the tonal hierarchy of the whole work, an analyst can effectively counter Lowinsky's thesis of "atonality," of the alleged erosion of any sense of tonal centeredness.

The validity of Lowinsky's characterization of certain chromatic works of the late Renaissance as "atonal" has been questioned by several musicologists already. In his review of *Tonality and Atonality in Sixteenth-Century Music* Claude V. Palisca took issue with Lowinsky's description of the prologue to *Prophetiae Sibyllarum*:

> . . . the basic tonality here, G, is constantly reaffirmed. The first word, "Carmina," is set to a IV-I progression in G. The end of the first line of text at mm. 8-9 is accompanied by an extended V-vi^6-V-I cadence in G with a 4-3 suspension in the soprano. The caesura in the second line is marked by a V-I feminine cadence on the fourth degree, C, mm. 16-18 (V of V-V-I$^6_4$-V-I), with a 4-3 suspension in the tenor. The third and final line returns after an excursion through g minor and E$^\flat$ to G through a Mixolydian cadence in which the bass descends stepwise from c to g. To call a composition so organized "atonal" obscures the main point of it, which is to indulge in as many juxtapositions of remotely related chords as possible within a tonally centered framework. An early description of this technique is to be found in a manuscript treatise by Vincenzo Galilei. In "Discorso intorno all'uso delle dissonanze" of 1589-91 he states: "It is possible to make a composition hard and harsh in two manners: one way, through dissonances and the sixth to the bass . . . the other way, through false relations that the parts are allowed to make among themselves as they proceed successively from one tone to another. . . ." (Florence, Bibl. Naz. Cent., Ms Gal. 1, fols.

147r-147v.). . . . Lasso's example . . . uses only root-triads, with the exception of two passing chords of the sixth and the cadential suspensions mentioned earlier . . . the most striking clashes arise from consecutive major triads whose roots are a major third apart (mm. 2-3, 7-8, 10, 18-19, 20-21), the device of choice for a harsh effect. They style that results Galilei prefers to call "senz'armonia" rather than "chromatic," using "armonia" in the horizontal Greek sense, so that "senz'armonia" describes a progression of chords in which the members are not properly related to each other. This, rather than "triadic atonality," is the essence of Lasso's experimental *Prophetiae*.[14]

Palisca argues that Lasso endowed his work with a tonally centered framework established by main structural cadences but indulged in juxtapositions of unrelated chords within this framework. My analysis further clarifies this view by demonstrating that certain adjacent triads, such as B♭ and D in mm. 7-8, may be related not immediately, since they belong to two different structural levels, but only through the mediation of another triad belonging to both levels simultaneously. Similarly, William J. Mitchell set out to demonstrate tonal relatedness of events which take place between main cadential points. The following is his analysis of mm. 1-9:

The opening presents a recurrent challenge. How are we to evaluate the solo g, the C-chord, and the succeeding chord on g, all forming a small unit? In a context such as this, the tenor's g relates persuasively to the following G-chord, thus placing the C-chord in a position of dependence. . . . Such imaginative beginnings seem insuperably difficult to the harmonic analyst, since they do not advertise their chordal components. Certainly it is not unreasonable to state, on this linear basis, that an embellished G-chord is represented in bars 1-2.

The C♯-minor chord in bar 4 must be evaluated linearly if it is to make sense, for it is not a normal member of the community of chords that comprize the harmonic elements of g. The questions to be answered are directed at the ways in which a c♯ and a g♯ must behave in order to relate to the tonal center, g. The simple answers, which provide us with a significant clue to the structure of bars 1-9 are: The c♯ should move to d; the g♯ should move to a. . . .

With the ordering of the linear details behind us, we are in a position to present an inclusive sketch of this remarkable section.

EXAMPLE 6

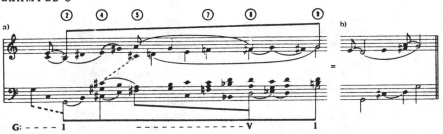

As graphed in Example 6b the main ingredients are: 1) The opening up of a G-chord by means of a harmonic support in the bass; 2) the joining of a d and g in the upper part through a stepwise motion, d-e-f♯-g; 3) The parallelism created by d, graced by e at the beginning, and g, which also has before it a gracing upper neighbor a, but much extended.[15]

A few methodological observations have to be made before an evaluation of Mitchell's interpretation is attempted. It is worth noticing certain similarities and differences between the analytical approach presented here and the Schenkerian method used by Mitchell.[16] The main similarity consists in the idea of a hierarchy of structural levels, which is common to both approaches, while the main difference involves the manner in which the events belonging to individual levels are chosen and the hierarchical relationships between levels are evaluated.

An orthodox Schenkerian analyst attempts to discover beneath the actual musical organism an underlying contrapuntal structure subject to absolute, historically unchanging rules of voice leading. In analytical practice, melodic motion by step is often given priority over all other considerations. Thus, for instance, Mitchell explains that "Lasso, in this piece, as well as elsewhere, makes frequent use of crossed parts as an immediate means of avoiding parallel fifths or octaves, and of satisfying chromatic half-step motions. Some of these are illustrated in Example 2. The usual procedure of regarding the structural top voice as a composite formed by the crossed parts will be followed here."[17]

EXAMPLE 2

The underlying assumption seems to be that beneath the actual counterpoint of the composition lies another, presumably more original one (note the word "becomes" in Mitchell's example) which may be reconstructed when we attempt to lead as many voices as possible, and in particular the top voice, stepwise, even if not only the composer's voice leading, but also such basic rules of strict counterpoint as the prohibition of parallel perfect consonances are violated in the process. Another basic assumption of the Schenkerian analytical practice is that in the presumably original counterpoint reconstructed by the above means a note is somehow retained until a note of the same or larger structural importance follows in the same voice. As a result, Mitchell is able to claim, for instance, that the chromatic c ♯ in the bass of m. 4 is resolved to d not immediately, but only in m. 8. But the very choice of what is structurally important seems often to be also governed by the principle of stepwise voice leading. Otherwise it would be difficult to explain why Mitchell chose to give relative prominence to c ♯ -triad in m. 4 of Lasso's prologue. His own explanation (that "it is not a normal member of the community of chords that comprise the harmonic elements of g") is not convincing, because already the preceding triad, B of m. 3, falls beyond any diatonic G-mode. The only justification that I can find for Mitchell's choice is that he wanted to have a stepwise progression in the top voice connecting the d′ at the beginning of the phrase (m. 2) with the g′ at its end (m. 9). This forced him to give special prominence to the top-voice e#′ and f#′in mm. 4 and 8, respectively, as well as to the chords supporting these notes.

While Mitchell's interpretation of the beginning and ending of the phrase (mm. 1-2 and 8-9) is undoubtedly correct, his attempt to explain tonal relatedness of the events connecting G- (m. 2) and D-triads (m. 8) is open to criticism. Mitchell misinterprets, in my opinion, the admittedly difficult passage, because he wants to understand it in purely tonal terms and disregards the importance of metro-rhythmic and textual considerations. I have remarked earlier that the central problem in an analysis based on the notion of structural levels (that is, also in Mitchell's Schenkerian analysis) is the correct choice of events belonging to individual levels and evaluation of the hierarchical relationships between levels. In my analysis I have attempted to demonstrate that this problem cannot be solved if the style of the analyzed composition is not considered. While Mitchell does not disregard stylistic criteria entirely (after all, he recognizes the cadences, for instance), for the most part he conducts his analysis in an historical and stylistic vacuum, subjecting Lasso's work to abstract, timeless voice-leading principles. As a result, he arbitrarily overemphasizes the importance of c#-triad (m. 4) which, in turn, obliges him to stipulate a non-existent long-range connection between c#-(m. 4) and D-triads (m. 8). The relative structural importance of E-triad (m. 5) which marks the internal division of the textual line is missed by Mitchell entirely.

Ironically, this incorrect evaluation of the relative structural inportance of events leads to serious problems in the analysis of the voice leading itself, that is, in the area with which a Schenkerian analyst is supposedly best equipped to deal. Thus, for Mitchell the most important triads in the section are G (m. 2), c# (m. 4), D (m. 8), and G (m. 9), since he wants his structural melody to ascend stepwise from d′ (m. 2), through e′ (m. 4) and f# (m. 8), to g′ (m. 9). But if, as I have suggested, E-triad in m. 5 is a more important structural event than either c#- or D-triads, the fundamental structure of the upper part is more complicated though no less logical. (For the time being I accept, at least as working hypotheses, such Schenkerian postulates as that the ''original'' counterpoint may be reconstructed beneath the actual one on the basis of the primacy of stepwise voice leading and that remote as well as immediate melodic connections exist within the so-reconstructed counterpoint.) The original upper-part d′ (m. 2) ascends chromatically through d# (m. 3) to e′ (mm. 4-5), while the tenor's g (mm. 1-2) proceeds chromatically through f# (m. 3) to g# (m. 4) and is transfered an octave higher in m. 5, where it assumes the role of the uppermost part. The remaining portion of the analyzed section involves the return of the structural melody from the chromatic to the diatonic version of the first scale step through the mediation of its upper and lower diatonic neighbor-notes, that is, the motion from g ♯'(m. 5), through a' (mm. 5-6) and f ♯' (m. 8), to g' (m. 9). The following graphs show my analysis of the voice leading of all four parts:

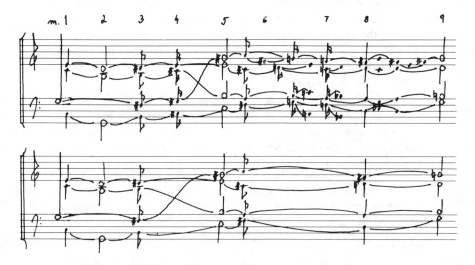

(Slurs connect notes belonging to a single "reconstructed" voice. Rhythmic values are used to indicate the relative structural importance of notes [in the order of diminishing importance: ♩, ♩, ♩, ♩, · and ○]. In any voice, a note is "retained" until a note of the same or larger value appears. The upper graph shows the complete voice leading, the lower one omits details belonging to less fundamental levels of structure.)

It must be emphasized once more that a correct analysis of voice leading depends upon the proper evaluation of the structural importance of events, and this in turn cannot be accomplished in abstraction from stylistic factors. Mitchell, on the other hand, starts with voice leading, derives the structurally important events from it and, for the most part, disregards stylistic factors.

While Lowinsky exaggerated the "atonal" incoherence of the work, Mitchell erred in the opposite direction, relegating its disturbing fundamental chromaticism to an embellishing unessential role and smoothing the chromatic structural top voice (g-g ♯'-g ♮') to the diatonic tetrachord ascending stepwise (d'-e'-f ♯'-g'). But the peculiar quality of the discussed section lies precisely in the tension between the forces of tonal coherence, on the one hand, and the constant threat to this coherence posed by the presence of chromaticism on the most fundamental structural level, on the other.

The existence of "atonality" in late Renaissance music has also been questioned by Ludwig Fincsher.[18] Taking as his point of departure one of Lowinsky's examples, Carlo Gesualdo's *Languisce al fin* from the Fifth Book of Marigals *a 5* (1611), Finscher demonstrated that the madrigal, far from being atonal, was in fact organized within the firm framework of E-mode. The connections between chords within this modally centered framework were explained by Finscher as governed by "vor allem Quintbeziehung, Terzbeziehung und Wechsel von grosser und kleiner Terz über gleichem Grundton."[19] Gesualdo's compositional technique is, according to Finscher, not "atonal" but modal, with the most important cadences of the piece indicating a single underlying mode, and with the principles of modal counterpoint governing the part-writing. Its difficulty lies in its paradoxical "mannerism" which at once affirms and breaks traditional rules.

Finscher's claim that extremely chromatic works of the late Renaissance, not only those of Gesualdo, may be understood only if their mannerist and paradoxical relationship to traditional precepts of modal centeredness and part-writing is grasped, found support in Carl Dahlhaus's study of "Gesualdos manieristische Dissonanztechnik":

> Das Verfahren, einerseits den klassischen Kontrapunkt mit Lizenzen zu durchsetzen und ihn schliesslich auszuhöhlen und anderseits auf Dissonanzfiguren des archaischen Kontrapunkts zurückzugreifen, um sie im Sinne der seconda prattica umzudeuten, teilte Gesualdo mit Komponisten wie Marenzio, Luzzaschi und Monteverdi, von denen um 1600 der "stile moderno" geprägt wurde.[20]

In his earlier study of Gesualdo's chromaticism Dahlhaus objected to Lowinsky's term "atonality," pointing out that Gesualdo's technique took its point of departure from the tradition of modal counterpoint rather than from the rudimentary tonal harmony of sixteenth-century songs and dances.[21] Dahlhaus suggested that late-Renaissance chromaticism can be illuminated by Vicentino's remark to the effect that a piece may be performed with or without accidentals:

> Vicentino verstand also den Tonsatz als abstrakten Kontrapunkt: als Gefüge von Intervallen, die als Spezies, als Terz oder Sexte ohne genauere Bestimmung, behandelt sind. Der Unterschied zwischen grosser und kleiner Terz oder Sexte ist kontrapunktisch gleichgültig. Die chromatischen und enharmonischen Alterationen, mit denen Vicentino die "meravigliosi effetti" der antiken Tongeschlechter zu restaurieren hoffte, erscheinen satztechnisch als ornamentale Zusätze. Das ästhetisch Essentielle, die Chromatik, ist kontrapunktisch akzidentell. Die Unterscheidung zwischen Gewebe und Färbung, zwischen abstraktem Kontrapunkt und kolorierenden Alterationen, ist die Voraussetzung der chromatischen Technik Gesualdos. Reguläre Dissonanzbehandlung verschränkt sich mit extremer Chromatik.[22]

This short survey of recent attempts to explain the technical principles of late-Renaissance chromaticism demonstrates clearly that almost invariably such attempts were inspired by Lowinsky's interesting and provocative study. Thus the thesis of "triadic atonality," although hardly convincing in itself, played a positive role stimulating fruitful discussions.

It remains to discuss what was learned from the sixteenth-century theorists concerning the reasons musicians used non-diatonic resources.

It has to be recalled first of all that some use of non-diatonic steps was advocated by all theorists regardless of their "progressive" or "conservative" orientation. The opinions of conservative theorists, of Zarlino in particular, are interesting precisely because they help to define the normal, commonly accepted use of non-diatonic steps and to distinguish it from extraordinary, radical, exploratory use of chromaticism. We learn from them that non-diatonic steps are normally acceptable and useful in both performance and composition. Their usefulness in performance stems from the fact that they enable instrumentalists to transpose diatonic compositions so as to accompany singers on a pitch-level which is convenient for them. It was quickly realized that only an equal division of the octave makes all transpositions possible and both the experiments with multiple equal division (such as Vicentino's and Zarlino's harpsichords) and the growing appreciation of the equal temperament were at least partly the result of this realization.

Zarlino accepts also as normal a limited use of chromatic steps in composition, because the perfection of counterpoint depends on consonances, and such steps supply consonances on those diatonic degrees where consonances are normally missing. However, chromatic steps have to be used sparingly and only temporarily in order to make clear that they are accidental. In other words, Zarlino accepts the use of chromatic steps in composition so long as they are truly chromatic, but rejects them when they introduce a local transposition or modulation combined with transposition and become locally diatonic. This indeed is as clear a distinction between the "normal" and "radical" chromaticism in the sixteenth century as can be derived from the contemporary theory.

The reason for "normal," limited chromaticism is to enrich the tonal resources in order to make smooth contrapuntal writing easier. The reasons for "radical" chromaticism, which will be presently summarized, are more complex. The non-diatonic genera were known to have been used besides the diatonic in antiquity and their revival was part of the general humanistically inspired attempt to restore the arts to their ancient excellence. Whenever the use of chromaticism was advocated, it was always in the context of the revival of ancient music. Moreover, the non-diatonic genera were often associated with less popular, more esoteric aspects of ancient culture. Taking hints from some highly regarded ancient authorities, especially Pseudo-Plutarch whose treatise on music was available in a Latin translation by Carlo Valgulio since 1532,[23] many late-Renaissance musicians believed that the non-diatonic genera were more excellent than the diatonic and that the miraculous effects that ancient musicians were supposed to have achieved were attributable to the use of these genera. Chromaticism came to be regarded as a sign of what was ancient, secret, unusual, and mysterious. This, for instance, was its function Lasso's setting of the ancient and elliptic Sibylline oracles.

The most important motive behind the interest in chromaticism was undoubtedly the association between the non-diatonic genera and the miraculous power of ancient music. Chromatic experiments were more often than not prompted by the desire to revive this power. The musical myths of ancient Greece recounting miraculous effects of music were not necessarily taken at their face value. It is doubtful that Renaissance musicians hoped literally to move stones. The power of ancient music was interpreted primarily in terms of the power to stir emotions. The ideal of music as an art able to imitate emotions and transmit them to listeners was increasingly capturing the imagination of musicians to become the dominating ideal by the end of the sixteenth century. This ideal was invariably associated with the most noble kind of ancient music, and it is only natural that some musicians sought to realize it by reviving what they thought were the technical and stylistic features of Greek practice, such as the non-diatonic genera and monody.

It has been indicated several times in this book that the second half of the sixteenth century was an era during which the earlier ideal of music as the sensual embodiment of "harmony" was challenged by the more recent ideal of music as the art of the emotional expression and impression. The most fundamental trait of the musical thought of the time was the tension between these two ideals. The tension was never completely resolved. Some theorists gave more emphasis to the ideal of "harmony," others to that of "expression," but this meant only that in any given theory one ideal dominated, not that the other one was eliminated completely.

The gradual ascendance of the newer ideal of expression was undoubtedly the result of the humanistic influence on music. Humanists' interest in ancient culture generated the growing interest in and knowledge of Greek music. Among various aspects of music discussed by ancient authors, the one that captured imagination of musicians of the Renaissance most was the ethical and emotional power of music. That music did indeed have such power in ancient times was difficult to deny, since the fact was attested by the most revered Greek authors, Plato and Aristotle.

Moreover, early Renaissance produced a coherent and influential theory which explained how powerful magical effects of music were possible. It was created by the Florentine Platonist of the second half of the fifteenth century, Marsilio Ficino.[24] Ficino was the first Renaissance writer to devote serious attention to the effects of music and to create a theory explaining how these effects were possible, how they worked. He was also the first to try to put his theory into practice.[25] It is hard to imagine that late-Renaissance music theorists were completely unaware of his ideas, especially since the ethical and emotional effects of music became an increasingly important problem in the late sixteenth-century theory. D. P. Walker summarized the relationship between Ficino's theory and later musical humanism as follows:

> There are two main resemblances between Ficino's musical theory and later musical human-
> ism. First, he is the earliest Renaissance writer I know of to treat the effects of music seriously
> and practically, and not merely as a constituent of the rhetorical topic of the *laus musicae*.
> By providing them with a rational explanation, he removes them from the status of more or
> less legendary marvels, makes them into exciting realities, and, by his astrological music,
> indicates ways of reviving them. Secondly, as I have already mentioned, Ficino's conception
> of the relative importance of music and text is the same as that of the majority of 16th
> century humanists, namely, that the text alone reaches the mind and must therefore dominate
> the music.[26]

In spite of these resemblances, Walker notes that, except for Gioseffo Zarlino, none of the late Renaissance musical humanists makes explicit reference to Ficino's theory.[27] Since none of the late sixteenth-century Italian theorists was as comprehensive as Zarlino, and since these theorists were increasingly interested in matters which had bearing on practice rather than in pure speculation, it is not surprising that they did not enter into philosophical inquisitions. It does not follow, however, that Ficino's theory was of no consequence for them. The awareness of the existence of a theory explaining the technology of musical effects was a reassuring factor for theorists and musicians trying to put such effects into practice. They knew that they were not pursuing a chimera, that musical effects were in fact obtainable. Because of their practical interests, this was all that they wanted or needed to learn from philosophers.

Besides, Zarlino was not the only one to make an explicit reference to Ficino's theory. Monteverdi's defender, L'Ottuso Accademico, in his letter published by Artusi writes:

> However, it is not necessary for this music to effect the miracle of raising the dead. It will
> certainly cause an affection, that is, a desire by the novelty of its part movement to hear rather
> often a similar type of harmony more suitable to move our mind by its novelty in this new
> practice than in that of the past, since this [new practice] strikes the sense more efficaciously.
> But how do I imagine I shall demonstrate that in music, or from this harmony, come all these
> motions . . . ? This is made clear by the authority of Marsilio Ficino in the Compendium on
> Plato's *Timaeus*, who says concerning this matter: "Concentus autem per aeream naturam in
> motu positam movet corpus." And this is the motion that appertains to body. And then: "Per
> purificatum aerem concitat spiritum animae corporisque nodum." This is the motion of one
> together with the other. "Per affectum afficit sensum simul & animum." Here is another
> similar motion. And below: "Per conformem qualitatem, mira quadam voluptate profundit."
> Here is the motion from sad to gay. And in conclusion he says: "Per naturam tam spiritualem,
> quam materialem totum simul rapit, & simul vendicat hominem." Behold in one conclusion all
> the motions and passions both of the mind and of the body.[28]

This direct reference to Ficino's theory as explaining the mechanism of musical effects by a member of Monteverdi's camp is certainly worth noticing.

It was mentioned that Ficino's conception of the relative importance of the text (influencing the mind) and music (influencing the sense and emotions) was shared by many sixteenth-century theorists. This explains why Vicentino, for instance, could in good faith claim that he favored the compromise between reason and sense. Assuming that reason is the highest faculty, and that text is the only carrier of intellectual content, Vicentino could honor reason by asserting that musical composition had to follow the text. The Monteverdian principle of "the words the mistress of the harmony" was in all probability much more than just an aesthetic slogan reflecting a change in artistic taste. Its emergence in the sixteenth century can be attributed to the recent revival of Platonism. It is not an accident that Giulio Cesare Monteverdi defends his brother's "intention to make the words the mistress of the harmony and not the servant" by invoking the authority of Plato.[29] The idea of the preeminent position of the words could be developed by the Renaissance Platonists even beyond the identification of reason with *logos*, because, being profoundly influenced by Christian doctrines, they knew that heavens and earth were created by God's word and attributed great importance to this theme.[30] As the creative Word governs the harmonic revolutions of the heavenly spheres, so in music the word is the mistress of the harmony. Giulio Cesare's slogan summarizes the result of the late sixteenth-century polemics perfectly. The fundamental opposition of musical thought of the era, the opposition between the "harmony" and the "expression of the words," is resolved not by elimination of one of the two opposed ideals, but by subordination of "harmony" to "words." It is not surprising to note that, as was pointed out by Claude V. Palisca, the same passage from Plato's *Republic* which was quoted by Giulio Cesare Monteverdi in support of his famous dictum, was also commented upon by Bishop Jacopo Sadoleto who used it in support of his appeal to give the text priority over music in his *De liberis recte instituendis* (Venice, 1533). Sadoleto was later a member of the Council of Trent, which instituted the reform of the Catholic music insuring the intelligibility of the text.[31] Vincenzo Galilei quoted Sadoleto in his counterpoint treatise in support of his critique of modern music as being devoted to the pleasure of the senses instead of trying to express the words.[32] It has been suggested that the polemic between the proponents of first and second practices had its roots in the discussions among church reformers and Papal singers in Rome of the Tridentine period (1545-63), with the humanistically inspired reformers initiating the attack on the Nederlandish polyphonic tradition represented by the Papal chapel.[33] The reform of the relationship between text and music was inspired in both the secular and religious versions by similar sources, by readings of Plato in particular.

It has to be noted, finally, that the ascendance of the ideal of the expression of the words over that of harmony, the Monteverdian subordination of the "harmony" to the "words," went hand in hand with the gradual weakening of the prestige of the concept of harmony in general, the weakening brought about by the emerging modern science.[34] For Zarlino musical harmony could be analogous to the harmony of the world, because the concord of diverse elements, the harmony, was conceived as proportion and could have been expressed in similar numerical ratios in both cases. The analogy gave music a very safe and dignified position.

But during the sixteenth century the ancient ideas of the harmony of the world and of music are being gradually undermined. We have seen the scientist Benedetti and later Vincenzo Galilei proving that the just intonation, the ratios of which provided Zarlino with mathematical basis of musical harmony, could not in fact be used in modern practice. At the same time scientists were transforming the traditional cosmology and consequently the mathematical structure of the universe changed radically.[35] Vincenzo Galilei noted this growing difficulty of establishing analogies between harmonies of various kinds quite clearly:

> Because of which I say that it is no less difficult to describe in words or demonstrate really by means of numbers or lines the [tuning] system which we use in its exact form and proportion, . . . than it is to regulate and to make proportionate among themselves the motions of celestial bodies with determinate periods and stable canons. And this is perhaps a good part of the agreement which Pythagoras judged to exist between the celestial and human harmony.[36]

The analogy between the celestial and musical harmonies became problematic, even though the early seventeenth century witnessed powerful efforts to save it in the works of Marin Mersenne and, particularly, of Johannes Kepler.[37] Consequently, the status of music became problematic too. With the gradual dissolution of the old world-view, music lost its safe place and justification as the sensuous embodiment of cosmic order and it had to find a new place and justification. This was provided by the recently revived ancient ideas of ethical and emotional power of music and by the prestigious and influential neo-Platonic philosophy proving that music could indeed operate powerful emotional effects and explaining how.

The great interest in radical chromaticism in the second half of the sixteenth century is the result of the gradual emergence of the new idea of music as an art of emotional expression. While limited use of chromatic steps, such as was allowed by Zarlino, is not incompatible with the ideal of harmony, extreme chromaticism certainly is, not only because it may reflect the desire to arouse passions, but also because it often implies equal temperament, the "irrational" intervals of which cannot supply the mathematical criterion for distinguishing harmonious and inharmonious relationships between sounds. The subordination of the traditional musical philosophy based on the concept of harmony to the new ideal of expression may well be closely correlated to the profound mutation of European thought which transformed the closed Aristotelian cosmos into the modern infinite universe, the process which John Hollander (paraphrasing Dryden) called "the untuning of the sky."[38]

Notes

INTRODUCTION

1. Leipzig: Breitkopf & Härtel, 1902.

2. See especially Edward E. Lowinsky, *Tonality and Atonality in Sixteenth-Century Music* (Berkeley and Los Angeles: University of California Press, 1961); the review of the above by Claude V. Palisca, *Journal of the American Musicological Society*, XVI (1963), 82-86; Carl Dahlhaus, "Zur chromatischen Technik Carlo Gesualdos," *Analecta Musicologica*, IV (1967), 77-96; Lowinsky, "The Musical Avant-Garde of the Renaissance or: The Peril and Profit of Foresight," in Charles S. Singleton, ed., *Art, Science, and History in the Renaissance* (Baltimore: The Johns Hopkins Press, 1967), pp. 111-162; William J. Mitchell, "The Prologue to Orlando di Lasso's *Prophetiae Sibyllarum*," *The Music Forum*, II (1970), 264-273; Ludwig Finscher, "Gesualdos 'Atonalität' und das Problem des musikalischen Manierismus," *Archiv für Musikwissenschaft*, XXIX (1972), 1-16.

3. See especially Arthur Mendel, "Pitch in Western Music Since 1500—A Re-examination," *Acta Musicologica*, L (1978), 1-93, 328.

I. NICOLA VICENTINO AND GHISELIN DANCKERTS

1. The biographical sketch below is based on Henry William Kaufmann, *The Life and Works of Nicola Vicentino (1511-c. 1576)*, Musicological Studies and Documents 11 (n.p.: American Institute of Musicology, 1966), pp. 15-48.

2. Walter Gerstenberg, "Willaert," in Friedrich Blume, ed., *Die Musik in Geschichte und Gegenwart*, Vol. 14 (Kassel and Basel: Bärenreiter, 1968), col. 663.

3. See Joseph S. Levitan, "Adrian Willaert's Famous Duo *Quidnam ebrietas*. A Composition which Closes Apparently with the Interval of a Seventh," *Tijdschrift van de Vereniging voor Nederlandsche Muziekgeschiedenis*, XV (1939), 166-233; Edward E. Lowinsky, "Willaert's Chromatic 'Duo' Re-Examined," *Tijdschrift van de Vereniging voor Nederlandsche Muziekgeschiedenis*, XVIII (1956), 1-36; Lowinsky, "Echoes of Adrian Willaert's Chromatic 'Duo' in Sixteenth- and Seventeenth-Century Compositions," in Harold Powers, ed., *Studies in Music History. Essays for Oliver Strunk* (Princeton: Princeton University Press, 1968), pp. 183-238.

4. Ghiselin Danckerts, *Trattato sopra una differentia musicale*, Rome, Biblioteca Vallicelliana, Ms. R. 56, fol. 382r.

5. *Ibid.*

6. The debate is documented in Danckerts, *op. cit.*, Part I and Nicola Vicentino, *L'antica musica ridotta alla moderna prattica* (Rome: Antonio Barre, 1555), fols. 95ʳ-98v.

7. See Robert Stevenson, "Vicente Lusitano: New Light on His Career," *Journal of the American Musicological Society*, XV (1962), 72-77.

8. *Introduttione facilissima et novissima di canto fermo, figurato, contraponto semplice et in concerto* (Rome: Antonio Blado, 1553). Two later editions appeared in Venice, published by Francesco Marcolini, 1558 and by Francesco Rampazzetto, 1561.

9. The most complete study of Danckerts and his treatise is J. de Bruyn, "Ghisilinus Danckerts, kapelaanzanger van de Pauselijke kapel van 1538, tot 1565," *Tijdschrift der Vereeniging voor nederlandsche Muziekgeschiedenis*, XVI (1946), 217-252; XVII (1949), 128-157.

10. See p. 73 below.

11. [*Descrizione dell'arciorgano*] (Venice: Nicolo Bevil'acqua, 1561). See Henry W. Kaufmann, "Vicentino's Arciorgano; an Annotated Translation," *Journal of Music Theory*, V (1961), 32-53.

12. *Il Desiderio overo de' concerti di varii strumenti musicali*, 2nd ed. (Bologna: Gioambattista Bellagamba, 1599), p. 41.

13. The most important discussions of Vicentino's theory are: Theodor Kroyer, *Die Anfänge der Chromatik im italienischen Madrigal des XVI Jahrhunderts* (Leipzig: Breitkopf & Härtel, 1902), pp. 99-121; Oscar Chilesotti, "Di Nicola Vicentino e dei generi greci secondo Vincentio Galilei," *Rivista Musicale Italiana*, XIX (1912), 546-565; Hugo Riemann, *History of Music Theory* (Lincoln: University of Nebraska Press, 1962, trans. from 2nd German ed., Berlin, 1920), pp. 311-320; Hermann Zenck, "Nicola Vicentinos 'L'antica musica' (1555)," in Hermann Zenck, Helmuth Schultz, and Walter Gerstenberg, eds., *Theodor Kroyer-Festschrift* (Regensburg: Gustav Bosse, 1933), pp. 86-101; D. P. Walker, "Musical Humanism in the 16th and Early 17th Centuries," *The Music Review*, II (1941), 1-13, 111-121, 220-227, 288-308; III (1942), 55-71; J. Murray Barbour, *Tuning and Temperament, a Historical Survey* (2nd ed.; East Lansing: Michigan State College Press, 1953), pp. 117-120; Claude V. Palisca, *The Beginnings of Baroque Music; Its Roots in Sixteenth-Century Theory and Polemics*, unpublished Ph.D. diss., Harvard University, 1953, pp. 30-34, 101-123; Walter Dürr, review of Vicentino, *L'antica musica*, facsimile ed. by Edward E. Lowinsky, in *Die Musikforschung*, XIV (1955), 446-448; Henry W. Kaufmann, "Vicentino's Arciorgano; an Annotated Translation," *Journal of Music Theory*, V (1961), 32-53; Kaufmann, *The Life and Works of Nicola Vicentino (1511-c. 1576)*, Musicological Studies and Documents 11 (n.p.: American Institute of Musicology, 1966); Paul Robert Brink, *The Archicembalo of Nicola Vicentino*, unpublished Ph.D. diss., The Ohio State University, 1966; Edward E. Lowinsky, "The Musical Avant-garde of the Renaissance or: the Peril and Profit of Foresight," in Charles S. Singleton, ed., *Art, Science, and History in the Renaissance* (Baltimore: The Johns Hopkins Press, 1967), pp. 111-162; Henry W. Kaufmann, "More on the Tuning of the *Archicembalo*," *Journal of the American Musicological Society*, XXIII (1970), 84-94; Edward E. Lowinsky, "The Problem of

Mannerism in Music: An Attempt at a Definition,'' *Studi Musicali,* III (1974), 131-218; Maria Rika Maniates, ''Vicentino's *'Incerta et ccculta scientia'* Reexamined,'' *Journal of the American Musicological Society,* XXVIII (1975), 335-51; Giulio Cattin, ''Nel quarto centenario di Nicola Vicentino teorico e compositore,'' *Studi Musicali,* V (1976), 29-57.

14. Vicentino, *L'antica musica,* fols. 17v-26v.

15. Vicentino, never a pedantic author, omits in his enumeration the intervals of less than fourth, less than minor sixth, less than minor seventh, and less than octave. Their presence in his gamut, however, is evidenced by the fact that they are available on his *archicembalo,* the instrument by means of which he wanted to introduce his gamut into musical practice. I have given them names on the basis of Vicentino's analogous interval of ''less than minor third.''

16. *Ibid.,* fol. 17v.

17. *Ibid.,* fols. 13v-15r.

18. ''. . . no more than three natural fourths, four natural fifths, and seven natural octaves will be found among the orders of the whole diatonic music.'' *Ibid.,* fol. 44r (''. . . ne gl'ordini di tutta la Musica Diatonica, non si ritroverà altro che tre quarte, & quattro quinte, & sette ottave, tutte naturali.''). Unless otherwise noted, all translations are mine. In Vicentino's vocabulary, as in ours, ''natural'' and ''diatonic'' are synonymous. The numbers of the chromatic and enharmonic species of fourths, fifths, and octaves have to be the same, since—as we shall see—Vicentino conceives of the chromatic and enharmonic series as one to one transformations of the diatonic ones.

19. *Ibid.,* fols. 43r-43v, 58v-59v, 62v-63r.

20. *Ibid.,* fols. 14r-14v.

21. Note that it is the relative, not the absolute, position of the semitones I have in mind here.

22. ''Comparing one fourth with the other, the student will see how the succession of the intervals is different [in both]: where in the diatonic fourth is the lesser interval, there in the chromatic fourth the greater interval will begin; and thus all are ordered by the opposition between the two. . . .'' *Ibid.,* fol. 59r. (''Lo studente con il Paragone di una, & de l'altra quarta, vedrà come il procedere de i gradi sarà differente, & ove sarà il minore grado in la Diatonica, ivi darà principio il grado maggiore nella Cromatica; & cosi tutti si comporranno con la oppositione di uno, & di l'altro . . .''). And later: ''. . . I shall start with the formation of the three enharmonic fourths which are formed in the same order that was followed in the chromatic fourths: the long interval is put in place of the short diatonic interval, and the short intervals—instead of the long diatonic ones . . .'' *Ibid.,* fol. 62v. (''. . . darò principio alla formatione delle tre quarte Enarmoniche, le quali si formeranno con l'ordine medesimo che s'hà tenuto nelle quarte Cromatiche; di porre il grado lungo, nel luogo del grado corto Diatonico, & i gradi corti, in cambio de i lunghi Diatonici . . .'').

23. ''Poi il genere Enarmonico, ch'io uso non è diviso, come è quello di Boetio, perche esso divide il semitono minore solamente, & io divido il maggiore, & il minore, secondo che occorre nelle compositioni per il commodo di usare varii gradi & consonanze.'' *Ibid.*, fol. 15r.

24. *Ibid.*, fols. 43v, 59v, 63r-64r.

25. *Ibid.*, fols. 43v-44r, 59v-60r, 64r-64v.

26. ''. . . cosi la natura della divisione del genere Cromatico comporta che si rompi l'ordine del Diatonico, & che si facci d'un tono due semitoni, & poi che si facci il grado del triemitono incomposto; che tutti questi gradi non vanno secondo il naturale Diatonico; & la natura dell'Enarmonico genere rompe l'ordine del genere Diatonico, & del Cromatico . . .'' *Ibid.*, fol. 66v.

27. ''E Boetio dice, che Cromatico non significa altro, si non quando ritroverai l'ordine Diatonico esser mosso, & tramutato; onde prima la Quarta che conteneva esso Genere, & caminava per tono, tono, & semitono, hora si muove per due semitoni, & un grado di terza minore, & non lo dice Cromatico solamente per le differenze delle proportioni, ma anchora per cagione delli gradi tramutati d'un'ordine di gradi, tramutati in altro ordine . . .'' *Ibid.*, fol. 14v.

28. Danckerts, *op. cit.*, Part II, Ch. 1, fol. 395r.

29. *Ibid.*, Part II, Chs. 1-3, fols. 396r-397r.

30. *Ibid.*, Part II, Ch. 6, fol. 398r.

31. *Ibid.*, Part II, Chs. 4-5, fols. 397r-398r.

32. *L'antica musica*, fols. 11r-13v.

33. The example of ''Mano Diatonica'' on fol. 11v compresses two diatonic series into one by juxtaposing B ♮ of the *hexachordum durum* with B ♭ of the *hexachordum molle*.

34. In the example of ''mano Cromatica, ascendente, con li Semitoni minori'' on fol. 11v the diatonic semitones B-c and e-f are divided. Such a division must be considered a mistake, since it introduces enharmonic dieses into the chromatic series.

35. We shall not bother the reader with the enumeration of many mistakes in the examples of ''enharmonic hands'' on fols. 12v-13r.

36. The positions are numbered in the table on p. 15 above.

37. Vicentino, following the mistake made by Boethius (*De institutione musica*, Book IV, Ch. 17), claims that the eighth mode was added by Ptolemy. See *ibid.*, fol. 46r. Actually, Ptolemy rejected the eighth mode, since it had the same octave-species as the first (*Harmonics*, Book II, Ch. 9).

38. In Ch. 23, fol. 51r Vicentino mentions, without accepting them into his system, four more modes proposed by contemporary musicians. He describes only two of them but since both are authentic it is fair to guess that the other two are plagal:

> 9th mode (authentic) starts at the 1st position
> [10th mode (plagal) starts at the 5th position]
> 11th mode (authentic) starts at the 3rd position
> [12th mode (plagal) starts at the 7th position]

39. *Ibid.*, fol. 64v.

40. The idea of the pre-compositionally determined material was made current by twelve-tone theory, but it can be useful outside the realm of serial music too. However, when the concept, which in the case of serial music indicates the set of decisions preceding a single composition, is applied to the older music, it might refer to the decisions preceding the whole compositional practice of a musical era.

41. When the accidental is put somewhat below the note to its left (or right) it applies only to the first (or second) half of the note. To avoid possible misunderstandings, Vicentino recommends that a flat written after and below the note should be reverted (◖). See *ibid.*, Book I, Ch. 12, fols. 16v-17r.

42. Vicentino follows his example of purely chromatic composition with a note which we see so often in twentieth-century scores: ". . . the accidental applies only to this note by which it is put; the rest of the notes written without accidentals will be sung according to their ordinary clef . . ." *Ibid.*, fol. 62v. (". . . quelle note che saranno signate con alcun segno, quelle solamente si canteranno per quello, & il resto senza segno si canteranno per il segno della sua chiave ordinaria . . ."). The fact that he was compelled to write such a warning testifies that this might not have been the usual practice of his contemporaries. He was particularly annoyed by the fact that composers did not indicate expressly whether they wanted the penultimate note of a cadence sharpened or not. See *ibid.*, fol. 53r.

43. When the dot is put above the note somewhat to its left (or right) it applies only to the first (or second) half of the note. See Book I, Ch. 13, fols. 17r-17v.

44. "& vedendo qui sotto scritto le sopra dette Quarte e Quinte, & Ottave per b. molle, non sarà però tramutatione alcuna à gl'orecchi differente da ♮ . quadro à b. rotondo, non occorrendo nel procedere altre mutationi de i gradi, ma solamente à gl'occhi il cantare sarà tramutato, & abbassato da ♮ . quadro à b. rotondo un semitono minore più basso, & à tal compositione non si potrà dire Cromatica Musica, perche dal suo principio, fin al fine non havrà tramutatione alcuna; ma veramente si potrà chiamare transcrittione Cromatica, cioè da b. quadro à b. rotondo . . ." *Ibid.*, fols. 46r-46v.

45. "& non si dè dire musica finta, ma più presto transcrittione finta, perche la Musica è notata con Quattro b. molli, che alla vista, pare tutta tramutata per lo notare, & à gl'orecchi nissuna differenza si sentirà dalla Musica scritta con b. molli, à quella scritta senza come di sopra hò detto, & accio che alcuno non dica Musica Cromatica à quella compositione, che sarà notata con quattro b. molli, noi già nel primo Libro haviamo dichiarato che cosa sia Musica Cromatica, laquale sarà la tramutatione che si sentirà quando prima serà tono, poi che si tramuterà in semitono, & di semitono in tono, con le spetie Cromatiche & con la

privatione del caminare per i gradi naturali . . ." *Ibid.*, fol. 47v. Translation by Kaufmann, *The Life and Works of Nicola Vicentino*, p. 130.

46.   See examples in Vicentino, *op. cit.*, Book III, Chs. 15-23, fols. 47v-51r.

47.   "The reader will notice that the chromatic modes notated above may be composed with a natural sign, with a flat, and as feigned music . . ." *Ibid.*, fol. 61r. ("Il Lettore avvertirà, che i sopra notati modi Cromatici si possono comporre per ♮ . & per b. & per musica finta . . .").

48.   *Ibid.*, Book V, Chs. 44-47, fols. 122r-123v; Ch. 59, fols. 133v-143r.

49.   Danckerts, *op. cit.*, Part III, Chs. 1-2, fols. 405r-407v. The anecdote is discussed in Lewis Lockwood, "A Dispute on Accidentals in Sixteenth-Century Rome," *Analecta Musicologica*, II (1965), 24-40. Lockwood dates the dispute in the period between 1538 and 1544.

50.   *Op. cit.*, Part II, Ch. 4, fol. 397v.

51.   "Alcuni potrebbono dire, che non essendo detto Genere, composto di due toni sesquiottavi, & un semitono minore, veramente non si potrà chiamare Diatonico; Si risponde che la Ethimologia del nome è detta dal Genere Diatonico, quando esso Genere camina per due gradi continui di toni con lo semitono, senza intervallo alcuno; & non è detto dalle proportioni, & Boetio istesso nel primo libro, à cap. XXI, narra della significatione di tutti tre li Generi, dice il Genere Diatonico si domanda Diatonico, perche camina per tono, & tono & semitono minore nella sua quarta, & non dice perche li due toni, che esso contiene, sono sesqui ottavi: Ma dice Diatonico, perche si muove per due gradi di toni continui & lo semitono: & ogni volta che si vedrà una quarta composta di due toni sesqui ottavi. overo d'un tono sesqui ottavo, & sesquinono, & semitono maggiore, overo di due toni & semitono, di quali proportioni esser si vogliano, movendosi per gradi continui di due toni, & semitono. Allhora essa quarta si domanderà Diatonico, detto dalli gradi delli toni & del semitono, & non dalle proportioni: & le sue spetie saranno li due toni, & semitono naturali . . ." *L'antica musica*, fol. 14r.

52.   ". . . questa poca differenza di uno, & dell'altro non si può sentire cantando ne sonando . . ." *Ibid.*, fol. 143v.

53.   I follow here the interpretation of Barbour, *Tuning and Temperament*, pp. 117-121. For more details see Brink, *The Archicembalo of Nicola Vicentino*, pp. 85-154; Kaufmann, "More on the Tuning of the *Archicembalo*," 84-94; Maniates, "Vicentino's '*Incerta et occulta scientia*' Reexamined," 335-51. See also Mark Lindley, "Early 16th-Century Keyboard Temperaments," *Musica Disciplina*, XXVIII (1974), 150.

54.   According to Barbour, *op. cit.*, p. 118, this fact was established by Christian Huyghens, "Novus cyclus harmonicus," *Opera varia* (Leyden, 1724), pp. 747-754.

55.   ". . . first the practitioner in tuning the common instruments such as organs, monochords, harpsichords, and other similar instruments should tune or temper diligently the keyboard of the first and second row so that it is well tuned and as perfectly as he knows and is

able to. Having tuned the first and second keyboards according to the usage of the other instruments with the fifths and fourths somewhat tempered, as is done by good masters . . .'' Vicentino, *op. cit.*, fol. 103v. (''. . . prima il prattico d'accordare gli stromenti communi come sono Organi, Monocordi, Clavicembali, Arpicordi, & altri simili stromenti dè accordare, ò temperare la tastatura del primo & secondo ordine, con diligenza, che sia bene accordata, & piu perfettamente, che egli sa, & che puo, accordata poi che haura la prima & seconda tastatur secondo l'uso de gl'altri stromenti con le quinte & quarte alquanto spontate, secondo che fanno li buoni Maestri . . .''). The expressions ''the keyboard of the first and second row'' and the equivalent ''first and second keyboard'' refer to that part of the Vicentinian keyboard which is identical with the normal sixteenth-century one. See p. 24 below.

56. Barbour, *op. cit.*, pp. 117f.

57. ''. . . inequalità di toni, fa nascere la commodità di poter usare le consonanze delle Terze, & delle Seste, così maggiori come minori.'' Vicentino, *op. cit.*, fol. 13v.

58. ''. . . le Quarte & le Quinte di Boetio sono perfette, & quelle che noi usiamo, sono un poco spontate & scarse nel acordare li stormenti.'' *Loc. cit.*

59. ''. . . che li Musici antichi usavano nella sua prattica i Generi appartati uno da l'altro, . . . noi usiamo li Generi & le spetie d'essi insieme, con consonanze di più di loro, cioè le Terze & le Seste, & per poter havere molte consonanze, come per pratticare molti gradi, non Habbiamo per inconveniente spontar una quinta, & allungare una quarta . . .'' *Loc. cit.*

60. *Ibid.*, Book V, Ch. 66, fol. 146v.

61. See p. 37 below.

62. ''. . . the *archicembalo*, . . . first and perfect, because on each key it does not lack any consonance . . .'' *Ibid.*, fol. 99r. (''. . . l'Archicembalo, . . . primo & perfetto, perche in ogni tasto non li manca consonanza alcuna . . .'').

63. [*Descrizione dell' arciorgano*] (Venice: Nicolo Bevil'acqua, 1561). The text was reprinted and translated into English by Henry W. Kaufmann, ''Vicentino's Arciorgano; an Annotated Translation,'' *Journal of Music Theory*, V (1961), 32-53.

64. *Ibid.*, p. 39.

65. *Ibid.*, p. 37.

66. Vicentino, *L'antica musica*, fol. 146v.

67. ''Questa regola non potrà seruire alla compositione fatta con parole, perche quelle daranno la regola da sè medesime, come di sopra s'ha inteso, nel trattato della imitatione, della natura delle parole, accompagnate con i gradi, & salti & con le consonanze.'' *Ibid.*, fol. 91v.

68. ''Et il Compositore, dè hauere il suo giuditio limato, & comporre le sue compositioni secondo il suggetto, & il proposito, delle parole.'' *Ibid.*, fol. 84v.

69. ''. . . il Compositore . . . sarà solamente obligato à dar l'anima, à quelle parole, & con l'Armonia di mostrare le sue passioni, quando aspre, & quando dolci, & quando allegre, & quando meste, & secondo il loro suggietto.'' *Ibid.*, fol. 48r.

70. ''. . . la musica fatta sopra parole, non è fatta per altro se non per esprimere il concetto & le passioni & gli effetti di quelle con l'armonia; & se le parole parleranno di modestia, nella compositione si procederà modestamente, & non infuriato; & d'alegrezza, non si facci la musica mesta; & se di mestitia, non si componga allegra; & quando saranno d'asprezza, non si farà dolce; & quando soaue, non s'accompagni in altro modo, perche pareranno difformi dal suo concetto . . .'' *Ibid.*, fol. 86r.

71. ''& tutti potranno porre in musica il suo modo di cantare con i gradi della diuisione del nostro stromento, che con la musica che hora s'usa, non si può scriuere alcuna canzone Franzese, ne Tedesca, ne Spagnuola, ne Vngara, ne Turca, ne Hebrea, ne d'altre nationi, perche i gradi & salti di tutte le nationi del mondo, secondo la sua pronuntia materna, non procedeno solamente per gradi di tono, & di semitoni naturali, & accidentali, ma per Diesis, & semitoni, & toni, & per salti Enarmonici; si che con questa nostra diuisione hauremo accommodato tutte le nationi del mondo, che potranno scriuer i loro accenti & comporli à quante uoci à loro parerà.'' *Ibid.*, fol. 85v.

72. ''A me pare, che tutto il continente d'una soaue & armoniosa compositione consista nell'ordire detta compositione, con ordine di tre modi principali: & inanzi ch'il Compositore compogna alcuna compositione, dè auertire sopra che uuole fabricare detta compositione: Il Primo modo sarà che deue applicare i gradi, & i salti, incitati & molli, al suggietto delle parole, ouero ad altre fantasie. Il Secondo modo non è di poca importantia, che quando detto Compositore haurà disposto i gradi, & i salti, che gl'accompagni con le consonanze, & dissonanze, incitate & molli, secondo che haurà primo disposto i gradi, acciò siano simili di natura, i gradi & salti, con le consonanze incitate & molli. Il Terzo & ultimo modo sarà, che quando il Compositore haurà contesto i gradi & i salti, & le consonanze & dissonanze insieme: allhora si darà il moto conueniente sopra à quel suggietto, che sia in proposito delle parole, ouero sopra altri pensieri.'' *Ibid.*, fol. 27r.

73. *Ibid.*, fols. 17v-26r.

74. *Ibid.*, fol. 46r.

75. ''. . . ogni uolta, che alcuni segni si porranno nelle compositioni accidentalmente muoueranno la natura di quel procedere, & il b. darà malenconia, & il ♮ . incitato, farà allegra la compositione, & il Diesis Cromatico, come si metterà ancho egli accidentalmente farà tramutar natura alla compositione . . .'' *Ibid.*, fol. 81r.

76. ''. . . the ascending motion will give always liveliness and the descending motion will give always sadness.'' *Ibid.*, fol. 146v. (''. . . sempre l'ascendere darà uiuacità, & il discendere darà mestitia.'').

77. *Ibid.*, fol. 33v.

78. *Ibid.*, fol. 34r.

79. *Ibid.*, fol. 27v.

80. See, e.g., *ibid.*, fol. 86r.

81. See, e.g., *ibid.*, fols. 81v-82r.

82. "Tutto il continente della Musica, stà nel sapere dare il moto, & gradi, & consonanze, in proposito del suggietto, sopra di che s'habbi da comporre & prima si dè auuertire che le consonanze, sono le principali, fra questi tre ordini: & la ragione è questa; che sè il Compositore considererà che gl'orecchi si notricano di consonanze; & che sè gl'orecchi udiranno i gradi senza consonanze con il Moto come fà uno, quando canta solo; & che quello possiede i gradi & il Moto, ma non le consonanze quello non satisfarà à gl'orecchi de gli oditori . . . & se gl'orecchi si pascono più di consonanze, che di sentir una uoce semplice, composta con i gradi, & con il moto; adunque le consonanze saranno le principali. perche faranno Armonia senza subalternatione alcuna, di grado, ne di moto. Ma quando le consonanze saranno accompagnate, con gradi, & con il moto in proposito del suggietto. allhora quella compositione sarà buona." *Ibid.*, fol. 81v.

83. *Ibid.*, fol. 30r.

84. *Ibid.*, fols. 31v-32r.

85. *Ibid.*, fol. 53r.

86. *Ibid.*, fol. 62v.

87. ". . . i gradi più corti daranno sempre più dolce armonia . . ." *Ibid.*, fol. 28v.

88. See, e.g., *ibid.*, fol. 4v.

89. "una asprezza grande." *Ibid.*, fol. 52r.

90. *Ibid.*, fol. 61v.

91. *Ibid.*, fols. 61v, 63v.

92. *Ibid.*, fols. 44v-46r, 47v-50v.

93. *Ibid.*, fol. 48r.

94. *Ibid.*, fol. 60v.

95. In the original the same term—mode (*modo*)—is used for both the architectural orders and for the musical modes, thus strengthening the analogy.

96. "Il maggior fondamento che dè hauere il Compositore sarà questo, che riguarderà sopra di che uorra fabricare la sua compositione. secondo le parole, ò Ecclesiastiche. ò d'altro suggetto, et il fondamento di detta fabrica sarà che eleggerà un tono, o un modo, che sarà in proposito, delle parole, o sia d'altra fantasia, & sopra quel fondamento misurerà bene con il suo giuditio, & tirerà le linee delle Quarte & delle quinte d'esso tono, sopra il buono fondamento, lequali saranno le colonne che terranno in piedi la fabrica della compositione; & de suoi termini, quantunque fra queste Quarte & quinte si riponesse le quarte & le quinte d'altri Modi. Queste non faranno danno à essa fabrica quando quelle saranno, in alcuni luoghi disposte, & con bel modo accompagnate nel mezzo di detta compositione, che con la uarietà di quella Architettura, ornerà la fabrica della compositione, come fanno i buoni Architetti, che con bel modo di procedere con le linee del Triangulo fanno abbagliar la uista à gli huomini, & con quelle fanno parere, una facciata di qualche bel Palazzo, che sarà dipinta molto appresso alla uista, di colui che guarderà tal pittura & à quello, essa li parerà molto lontana & non sarà. Questa apparentia auuiene da il modo di sapere accompagnare i colori, con le linee, & anchora molte uolte, gli Architetti accompagnano diuerse maniere, de i modi del fabricare in una fabrica come si uede nel celebrato Vitruuio, che il modo Dorico, sarà accompagnato con l'Attico, & il Corintio, con il Ionico & sono talmente bene colligati, & uniti, anchora che le maniere siano diuerse, nondimeno, il prattico artefice, con il suo giuditio, compone la fabrica con uarij ornamenti proportionata, cosi auuiene al compositore di Musica, che con l'arte puo far uarie commissioni, di Quarte, & di quinte d'altri Modi, et con uarij gradi adornare la compositione proportionata secondo gli effetti delle consonanze applicati alle parole, & dè molto osseruare il tono, ò il modo." *Ibid.*, fols. 47v-48r.

97. Comparisons between music and architecture were frequently made by Renaissance writers on the basis of numerical ratios being common to both musical consonances and to architectural proportions. See Rudolf Wittkower, *Architectural Principles in the Age of Humanism* (London: The Warburg Institute, 1949); Robert Klein, *La forme et l'intelligible. Écrits sur la Renaissance et l'art moderne* (Paris: Gallimard, 1970), pp. 151-173; Jean-Marc Bonhôte, "Resonance musicale d'une Villa de Palladio," *Musica Disciplina*, XXV (1971), 171-178. Pythagorean speculations of this kind were, however, thoroughly distasteful to Vicentino who, with his usual originality, managed to make his comparison on a different ground.

98. See, e.g., *ibid.*, fol. 79r.

99. *Ibid.*, fol. 66r.

100. *Ibid.*, fol. 55r.

101. *Ibid.*, Book III, Ch. 48, fols. 64v-65v.

102. *Ibid.*, fol. 67v. Kaufmann correctly observed that "if these remarks are a reflection of contemporary practice, they help to bolster Lowinsky's thesis of a 'secret chromatic art.' " *The Life and Works of Nicola Vicentino*, p. 144. See also Carl Dahlhaus, "Zur chromatischen Technik Carlo Gesualdos," *Analecta Musicologica*, IV (1967), 77-96.

103. "Non lasciarò di dire della abusione che a tempi nostri da pochi anni in qua è nata nel comporre i canti figurati, da certi compositori novelli; i quali disprezzando tutte le buone

leggi: ordini: e regole antiche (persuadendosi con le lor nove leggi e regole, di togliere la fama a gli altri compositori) dimostrano non sapere gli ordini delli tuoni autentici e plagali, che sono necessarii di osservarsi nelli canti diatonici, per non entrare nelli disordini, per li quali ogni cosa va in rovina; ò se gli sanno mostrano non volerli osservare, facendo professione solamente, di alzare et abbazzare le note fuor della lor ordinaria intonatione, per ridurre non solamente l'intervallo del semitonio minore à tuono intiero cosi ⊟○✻○ overo cosi ⊟○♭○ ma ancho l'intervallo del tuono a semiton minore cosi ⊟○♭○ ò cosi ⊟○✻○ overo (qualche e peggio) a semiditono cosi 𝄢○✻○ & cio senza assegnare raggion veruna se non che compongono di questa sorte alla nuova maniera, et piace cosi à loro di farlo vedendo che anchora altri lo fanno. e cosi l'un cieco guidando l'altro, tutti cascano nel fosso.'' Danckerts, *op. cit.*, Part III, Ch. 3, fol. 407v.

104.   *Ibid.*, Part III, Chs. 3-4, fols. 408r-410r. See also pp. 21f above.

105.   Many scholars identify the tendency to depart from previously established classical norms in order to express the text as one of the chief stylistic traits of musical mannerism. Vicentino was certainly one of the most eloquent early exponents of mannerist tendencies. See Claude V. Palisca, ''A Clarification of 'Musica Reservata' in Jean Taisnier's 'Astrologiae,' 1559,'' *Acta Musicologica*, XXI (1959), 133-161; Kaufmann, *The Life and Works of Nicola Vicentino*, Ch. 4: ''*Reservata*—A Problem of Musical Mannerism,'' pp. 175-224.

106.   ''. . . ogni mal grado, con cattiva consonanza, sopra le parole si potrà usare, secondo i loro effetti. . . .'' Vicentino, *L'antica musica*, fol. 48r.

107.   See, e.g., *ibid.*, fol. 27v.

108.   See, e.g., *ibid.*, fol. 35r.

109.   *Ibid.*, fol. 27v.

110.   *Ibid.*, Book V, Ch. 65, fols. 146r-146v.

111.   *Ibid.*, fols. 61v, 146r.

112.   *Ibid.*, fol. 83v.

113.   *Ibid.*, fol. 36v.

114.   *Ibid.*, fols. 80v-81r.

115.   *Ibid.*, fols. 64v-65r.

116.   *Ibid.*, fol. 29v.

117.   See p. 27 above.

118.   Vicentino, *L'antica musica*, fols. 81v-82r, 86r.

119. *Ibid.*, fols. 27r-27v, 42r.

120. *Ibid.*, fol. 67r.

121. *Ibid.*, fol. 94v.

122. *Ibid.*

123. "... nelle camere, & con bassa uoce. ..." *Ibid.*, fol. 65v.

124. *Ibid.*, fol. 37r.

125. "... un Motettino allegro tutto Cromatico, il quale noi cantiamo in chiesa il giorno della resurrettione del nostro signore, acciò che ogniuno uegga che la musica Cromatica si può cantare nelle chiese ad alta uoce." *Ibid.*, fol. 61v.

126. See, e.g., *ibid.*, fol. 37r.

127. *Ibid.*, fol. 16v.

128. *Ibid.*, fol. 128r.

129. See, e.g., *ibid.*, Book III, Ch. 14, fols. 46v-47v.

130. "Differenti sono le compositioni, secondo che sono i suggetti, sopra che sono fatte, & alcuni cantanti molte uolte non auuertiscano, cantando sopra che sia fatta la compositione, & cantano senza alcuna consideratione, & sempre à un certo suo modo, seconda la sua natura & il suo uso, & le compositioni che sono fatte sopra uarij suggetti, & uarie fantasie; portano seco differenti maniere di comporre, & cosi il cantante dè considerare la mente del Poeta Musico, & cosi del Poeta uolgare, ò Latino, & imitare con la uoce la compositione, & usare diuersi modi di cantare come sono diuerse le maniere delle compositioni." *Ibid.*, fol. 94r.

131. "& la esperienza, dell'Oratore l'insegna, che si uede il modo che tiene nell'Oratione, che hora dice forte, & hora piano, & più tardo, & più presto, & con questo muoue assai gl'oditori, & questo modo di muouere la misura, fà effetto assai nell'animo, & per tal ragione si canterà la Musica alla mente per imitar gli accenti, & effetti delle parti dell'oratione, & che effetto faria l'Oratore che recitasse una bella oratione senza l'ordine de i suoi accenti, & pronuntie, & moti ueloci, & tardi, & con il dir piano et forte quello non muoueria gl'oditori. Il simile de essere nella Musica. perche se l'Oratore muoue gli oditori con gl'ordini sopradetti, quanto maggiormente la Musica recitata con i medesimi ordini accompagnati dall'Armonia, ben unita, farà molto piu effetto." *Ibid.*, fol. 94v.

132. "& secondo il Filosofo, tutti quelli che fanno; fanno per il fine. adunque il fine della Musica è di satisfare à gl'orecchi. ..." *Ibid.*, fol. 93v. "Il Filosofo" is, of course, Aristotle.

133. *Ibid.*, fols. 3r, 7r.

134. See p. 23 above. Note that Vicentino's approach to problems of tuning is "Aristoxenian" but his tuning system is not. Sixteenth-century theorists believed that Aristoxenus invented equal temperament, a system criticized by Vicentino. See Barbour, *op. cit.*, p. 2.

135. Vicentino, *L'antica musica*, fol. 66v.

136. *Ibid.*, fol. 7r. It seems to me that Vicentino's awareness of cultural variety reflects his Venetian background. In this great center of international trade he might have had many occasions to acquaint himself with foreign and even with exotic musical practices. He himself attested to this, reporting that he had heard from some Venetian merchants about an archaic musical notation used in certain parts of contemporary Hungary. See *ibid.*, fol. 8v.

137. See, e.g., the quotations on pp. 26 and 38 above.

138. See Walker, "Musical Humanism in the 16th and Early 17th Centuries."

139. ". . . quelli effetti che scriuono gli Authori anticamente farsi. . . ." *L'antica musica*, fol. 6v.

140. *Ibid.*

141. *Ibid.*, fols. 10r, 33v.

142. See. e.g., *ibid.*, fols. 13v, 15r, 34r.

143. *Ibid.*, fol. 34r.

144. *Ibid.*, fol. 6v.

145. ". . . comprendono che (come li scrittori antichi dimostrano) era meritamente ad altro uso la Cromatica & Enarmonica Musica riserbata che la Diatonica, perche questa in feste publiche in luoghi communi à uso delle uulgari orecchie si cantaua: quelle fra li priuati sollazzi de Signori e Principi, ad uso delle purgate orecchie in lode di gran personaggi et Heroi s'adoperauano." *Ibid.*, fol. 10v. This passage has been much discussed in connection with the *musica reservata* problem. For a convincing summary see Palisca, "A Clarification of 'Musica Reservata' in Jean Taisnier's 'Astrologiae,' 1559," pp. 151f.

146. *L'antica musica*, fol. 99v.

147. "Ne l'harmonia del ordine Enharmonico ò Chromatico fa maggior miracolo che quella del Diatonico. Anchora che il detto Don Nicola volentieri daria ad intendere alla gente grossa che con la sua Musica Enharmonica e Chromatica fa fermare i fiumi e le fiere indomite piu che con la Diatonica (come fingono li poeti che facea Orpheo le Bestie nelle sijlve: Arion li Delphini; e che Amphion facea saglire e scendere le pietre et altre materie da per loro edificando le mura de Thebe, e che altri faceanno altri effetti con la Harmonia de i lor dolci concenti) se esso trovasse qualche goffo che ce lo credesse. E cosi concludo

che se debbia seguitare il giudicio de i philosophi e Musici antichi i quali . . . hanno dismessi e lasciati i due generi inusitati Chromatico et Enharmonico, e sonosi attenuti al Diatonico solo per il migliore: più facile: più pratticabile: piu naturale: e piu grato all'orecche. . . ." Danckerts, *op cit.*, Part II, Ch. 9, fol. 401v.

148.   For the discussion of the sense in which the term is used here see Paul Oskar Kristeller's essay "Humanism and Scholasticism in the Italian Renaissance" in his *Renaissance Thought: The Classic, Scholastic, and Humanist Strains* (New York: Harper and Row [Harper Torchbook], 1961), pp. 92-119.

149.   Vicentino, *L'antica musica*, fol. 10r.

II. GIOSEFFO ZARLINO AND VINCENZO GALILEI

1.   For Zarlino's biography and literature see Claude V. Palisca, "Zarlino," in Friedrich Blume, ed., *Die Musik in Geschichte und Gegenwart*, Vol. 14 (Kassel and Basel: Bärenreiter, 1968), cols. 1017-22. The most important studies of Zarlino's theories are: Hugo Riemann, *History of Music Theory* (Lincoln: University of Nebraska Press, 1962, tr. from the 2nd German ed., Berlin, 1920), pp. 280-328; Fritz Högler, "Bemerkungen zu Zarlinos Theorie," *Zeitschrift für Musikwissenschaft*, IX (1926-27), 518-27; Salvino Chiereghin, "Zarlino," *Rivista Musicale Italiana*, XXXVII (1930), 21-37, 204-18; Hermann Zenck, "Zarlinos 'Istitutioni harmoniche' als Quelle zur Musikanschauung der italienischen Renaissance," *Zeitschrift für Musikwissenschaft*, XII (1930), 540-78; D. P. Walker, "Musical Humanism in the 16th and Early 17th Centuries," *The Music Review*, II (1941), 1-13, 111-121, 220-27, 288-308; III (1942), 55-71; J. Murray Barbour, *Tuning and Temperament. A Historical Survey*, 2nd ed. (East Lansing: Michigan State College Press, 1953); Palisca, *The Beginnings of Baroque Music. Its Roots in 16th-Century Theory and Polemics*, unpublished Ph.D. diss., Harvard University, 1954; Carl Dahlhaus, "War Zarlino Dualist?," *Die Musikforschung*, X (1957), 286-90; Robert W. Wienpahl, "Zarlino, the Senario, and Tonality," *Journal of the American Musicological Society*, XII (1959), 27-41; Palisca, "Scientific Empiricism in Musical Thought," in Hedley H. Rhys, ed., *Seventeenth-Century Science and Arts* (Princeton: Princeton University Press, 1961), pp. 91-137; Raffaello Monterosso, "L'estetica di Gioseffo Zarlino," *Chigiana*, Nuova serie, IV (1967), 13-28; Richard L. Crocker, "Perché Zarlino diede una nuova numerazione ai Modi?," *Rivista Italiana di Musicologia*, III (1968), 48-58; Palisca, "Introduction," to Zarlino, *The Art of Counterpoint. Part Three of 'Le Istitutioni harmoniche,' 1558*, tr. by Guy A. Marco and Palisca (New Haven and London: Yale University Press, 1968), pp. xiii-xxvi.

2.   They are discussed in Roman Flury, *Gioseffo Zarlino als Komponist* (Winterthur: P. G. Keller, 1962).

3.   ". . . il Musico vuole. . . , che [il Genere] sia la divisione del Tetrachordo. . . . Ma il Tetrachordo è un'ordine di suoni contenuto tra quattro chorde, le cui estreme si ritrovano l'una distante dall'altra in Sesquiterza proportione. . . . Però è da notare, che appresso gli Antichi musici tre furono i generi della Melodia, o Cantilena; de i quali il primo chiamarono Diatonico, il secondo Chromatico, et il terzo Enharmonico." Gioseffo Zarlino, *Le Istitutioni harmoniche* (Venice: n.p., 1558), Part II, Ch. 16, p. 82 (p. 97 of the edition published in 1573 in Venice by Francesco de i Franceschi Senese. Henceforth all references

will be made to the original edition and followed by the page numbers of the 1573 edition given in brackets). See also Zarlino, *Dimostrationi harmoniche* (Venice: Francesco de i Franceschi Senese, 1571), Rag. IV, Def. 2, p. 212.

4. See, e.g., *Dimonstrationi*, Rag. IV, Def. 3, p. 213. For the time being I neglect the distinction that Zarlino makes between major and minor whole tones, since this distinction is proper to his tuning system and not to the tonal system. See pp. 55f. below.

5. See, e.g., *ibid.*, Rag. IV, Def. 4, p. 214.

6. See, e.g., *ibid.*, Rag. IV, Def. 5, p. 215. The distinction Zarlino makes between major and minor diesis can be neglected here, since it is proper to his tuning system and not to his tonal system. See p. 56 below.

7. *Le Istitutioni*, Part II, Ch. 28, pp. 97f. [114f.].

8. The most comprehensive study of Salinas's life and work is Arthur Michael Daniels, *The 'De Musica Libri VII' of Francisco de Salinas*, unpublished Ph.D. diss., University of Southern California, 1962. See also Daniels, "Microtonality and Mean-Tone Temperament in the Harmonic System of Francisco Salinas," *Journal of Music Theory*, IX (1965), 2-51, 234-80.

9. He lists the Greek sources that he studied in Italy in the Preface to *De Musica* (Salamanca: Mathias Gastius, 1577), fol. 5v, tr. in Daniels, *The 'De Musica Libri VII'. . . .*, pp. 13-15.

10. "sed fallitur, quoniam existimat, non plures chordas, quàm unam Chromaticam addendam esse Tetrachordo Diatonico, & procedendum in eo genere per Trihemitonium, vel Semiditonum. Quandoquidem vis Chromatici generis in hoc sita est, ut omnis in eo tonus reperiatur in duo Semitonia divisus." *Op. cit.*, IV, xxxiii, p. 233; tr. in Daniels, *op. cit.*, p. 436. See also *De Musica*, III, vi-vii, pp. 114-20.

11. *Ibid.*, III, vii, pp. 115-20.

12. "nihil enim aliud facit Enharmonium, quàm quòd ubi in Chromate Semitonium maius est supernè, ponit minus infernè: & contrà ubi minus, maius." *Ibid.*, III, viii, p. 121; tr. in Daniels, *op. cit.*, p. 203.

13. *De Musica*, III, viii, pp. 120-127.

14. ". . . il genere Diatonico, avanti che alcuno altro genere fusse ritrovato, . . . gli altri due generi furono ritrovati dopo, per gran spatio di tempo, e furono collocati tra'l Diatonico. Onde essendo stati per tal modo posti insieme, molti Musici Antichi, tra i quali sono Tolomeo, Briennio, e Boetio, hanno havuto parere, che altro non fussero gli due ultimi, che la Inspessatione del primo genere: conciosia che chiamavano ogni Tetrachordo inspessato, quando rendeva l'intervallo acuto maggiore in quantità de gli altri due primi gravi: et questo veramente è cosa propria di questi due ultimi generi. . . ." *Le Istitutioni*, Part II, Ch. 32, p. 108 [127].

15. *Ibid.*, pp. 108f. [127].

16. See, e.g., *ibid.*, Part II, Ch. 39, p. 121 [141].

17. *Ibid.*, Part II, Ch. 47, p. 140 [163].

18. See, e.g., *ibid.*, Part II, Ch. 39, p. 122 [142].

19. "Et se bene questi due intervalli non si trovano nel genere Diatonico incomposti in atto, sono tuttavia in potenza: . . . Onde dico, che'l passare da un genere all'altro, non si può intendere, quando si usa li Composti, i quali serveno per Elementi di un'altro genere: ma quando si usano li Semplici intervalli, che sono propij, et si adoperano particolarmente in quel genere, che non si possono ritrovare ne semplici, ne composti in un'altro." *Ibid.*, p. 283 [348f.], translated by Guy A. Marco and Claude V. Palisca in Zarlino, *The Art of Counterpoint* (New Haven and London: Yale University Press, 1968), p. 274. (Henceforth this translation will be referred to as *Art.*) The same argument is repeated in *Dimostrationi*, Rag. II, Def. 24, p. 97 and Rag. IV, Def. 3, p. 213, where chromaticists are additionally scourged for lack of consistency, since they use thirds in avowedly purely diatonic compositions as vertical intervals between parts and similarly they use vertical major thirds in what they claim are chromatic compositions and vertical minor thirds in enharmonic ones. This most probably refers to the compositions Nicola Vicentino published in his *L'antica musica ridotta alla moderna prattica* (Rome: Antonio Barre, 1555), fols. 52r-52v, 62r-62v, 67r, 69v-71r.

20. *Le Istitutioni*, pp. 283f. [348-50].

21. *Ibid.*, Part II, Ch. 32, p. 108 [127].

22. "Franchino Gaffur[i]o etiandio dice, che'l Chromatico è arteficiosamente fatto per ornamento del Diatonico, et lo Enharmonio è detto perfetto ornamento del naturale et artificiale Sistema musico Diatonico et Chromatico; et dice anco, che'l Tetrachordo diatonico è naturale." *Ibid.*, Part II, Ch. 9, p. 76 [90]. Zarlino refers to the following words of Franchino Gafori: "Constat igitur: questa generatione de extensione chromatica esser artificiosamente consyderata da la diligentia de li Antiqui Musici per ornamento de lo istrumento diatonico: Quale (aben che fosse con diligentia et arte contexto) fuy pero ordiato secundo lo istincto de la natura: . . . Et e dicto [il Genere Enarmonico] optime coniunctum et perfecto ornamento del naturale et Artificioso Sistema musico: cioe diatonico et chromatico." Franchinus Gafurius, *Angelicum ac divinum opus musice* (Milan: Gotardus, 1508), Book I, Chs. 10-11.

23. "Questo (come vuol Beotio) è detto Chromatico, quasi Colorato, o Variato, da Χρῶα parola greca, che vuol dir Colore; et prese questo nome dalla superficie di alcuna cosa, che levata, le fa variare il colore; Et dice bene: percioche mutando solamente una chorda mezana del Tetrachordo Diatonico, restando le altre communi; da tal mutatione nascono differenti intervalli, et varie proportioni; cioè variate forme et variati suoni." *Le Istitutioni*, Part II, Ch. 16, p. 85 [100]. Zarlino refers to Anicius Manlius Severinus Boethius, *De istitutione musica*, I.xxi.

24. "Praeterea scire etiam oportet, haec tria genera sic se habere, ut Bonum, Melius, Optimum: nam sicut Bonum per se solum potest existere, sed Melius sine bono neque esse, neque

intelligi potest, & utrumque in Optimo excellentiori modo consistit: sic Diatonum per se solum inveniri potest, quia reliquorum est fundamentum, atque subiectum. . . . Sed quamuis caeteris naturalius sit, est tamen durius, ut Boëtius ait, ad quam diritiem mollificandam Chromaticum inventum est quod sine Diatono reperiri non potest; nihil enim est aliud, quàm Diatonum spissatum, ut italoquar; & quoniam illud mollius ac perfectius reddit, in de nomen accepit, tanquam à perfectiori, ut iam non Diatonum, sed Chromaticum dicatur: quale est illud, quod experimur in his instrumentis, quae per alba, & nigra plectra pulsantur. Enharmonium etiam per se non potest subsistere, sed reliquis duobus adiunctum unum efficit spississimum, & perfectissimum, quod non Diatonium, neque Chromaticum, sed Enharmonium nuncupatur, quòd optimè coaptatum, & compaginatum sit.'' *De Musica*, III, ii, p. 104; tr. in Daniels, *op. cit.*, pp. 183f.

25. *Le Istitutioni*, Part II, Ch. 9, p. 76 [90]. See also Zarlino, *Sopplimenti musicali* (Venice: Francesco de' Franceschi Sanese, 1588), Book IV, Ch. 3, pp. 123-128 and Book VIII, Ch. 1, p. 278.

26. *Le Istitutioni*, Book II, Ch. 32, p. 108 [126]. Zarlino refers to Boethius, *op. cit.*, I.l. The identity of Timotheus is discussed in *Sopplimenti*, pp. 123-128. See also Vincenzo Galilei, ''Discorso intorno all'uso dell'Enharmonio et di chi fusse autore del Cromatico,'' Florence, Biblioteca Nazionale Centrale, Ms. Gal. 3, fols. 14r-15v.

27. ''Et se bene è cosa difficile il voler narrare in qual maniera Timotheo potesse ritrovare, o investigar questo genere; essendo che appresso di alcuno scrittore mai fin hora l'habbia potuto ritrovare; nondimeno si può mostrare con qualche ragione, che . . . Timotheo essercitandosi nel genere Diatonico, tentasse molte volte di passare con la modulatione per lo aggiunto Tetrachordo, toccando dopo la Mese la Trite synemennon, passando dipoi da questa alla Paramese, arrivando etiandio alla Paranete synemennon, over Trite diezeugmenon, che sono una chorda istessa; anchora che i Tetrachordi à cui serve le faccia cambiare il nome; et dipoi considerando, che'l passaggio fatto per queste chorde rendeva alcuna varietà; . . . cercasse di modulare per ogni Tetrachordo in cotal maniera. . . .'' *Le Istitutioni*, Part II, Ch. 32, p. 111 [130].

28. *Ibid.*, Part II, Ch. 28, p. 98 [115].

29. *Ibid.*, Part II, Ch. 32, p. 111 [129].

30. ''Cosi è cosa giusta, et honesta, che si preponga questo genere a gli altri due, come più nobile et più eccellente; havendo da lui l'essere gli altri: essendo che il Diatonico virtualmente contiene il Chromatico et l'Enharmonico, et al fine li produce in atto; ma non per il contrario. Fu veramente cosa giusta, che Tolomeo dessi ogni preminenza a questo genere, poi che come generante senza dubbio è molto più nobile del generato.'' *Ibid.*, Part II, Ch. 16, p. 84 [99].

31. ''Ma si debbe sempre avertire, . . . che quelle corde sono poste con qualche utilità in uno istrumento, et in alcuno ordine, le quali scno in tal maniera collocate, che verso il grave, overo verso l'acuto hanno una chorda corrispondente consonante per una Diapente, o ́per una Diatessaron overamente per un Ditono, overo per un Semiditono. . . .'' *Ibid.*, Part II, Ch. 47, p. 140 [163].

32. *Ibid.*, Part III, Ch. 78, p. 286 [352]. See also pp. 60f. below.

33. *Ibid.*, Ch. 47, p. 140 [163]. The instrument was still seen by Burney in Florence but it did not survive to our time. See Donald H. Boalch, *Makers of the Harpsichord and Clavichord 1440 to 1840* (London: George Ronald, 1956), p. 24.

34. *Le Istitutioni*, p. 141 [164].

35. *Ibid.*, Part III, Chs. 25 and 72, pp. 170f., 280f. [198f., 344ff.].

36. *Ibid.*, Part II, Ch. 16, pp. 82-86 [97-101]; *Sopplimenti*, Book IV, Chs. 1-3, pp. 111-130.

37. "Et ancorache le sue proportioni siano molto differenti da quelle, che ne dà Boetio; questo importa poco: impero che la diversità del genere non nasce se non dalla mutatione, et variatione de gli intervalli, che si può fare ottimamente modulando dal grave all'acuto per un Semituono nel primo intervallo, et per un altro poi nel secondo, ponendo ultimamente nel terzo un Trihemituono." *Le Istitutioni*, Part II, Ch. 32, p. 111 [129].

38. See, e.g., *ibid.*, Part II, Ch. 31, pp. 105ff. [123-126].

39. See, e.g., *ibid.*, Part I, Ch. 13, p. 23 [29]; Part II, Ch. 31, p. 105 [123].

40. *Ibid.*, Part I, Ch. 16, p. 27 [33].

41. *Ibid.*, Part I, Ch. 13, p. 23 [29].

42. *Ibid.*, Part II, Chs. 31, 37, pp. 106, 117 [125, 136].

43. *Ibid.*, Part II, Ch. 16, pp. 82ff. [98f.].

44. See p. 47 above.

45. See, e.g., *Le Istitutioni*, Part II, Ch. 40, p. 123 [143]. Zarlino's opinion was challenged almost immediately by Giovanni Battista Benedetti and later it became one of the main subjects in the controversy between Zarlino and Vincenzo Galilei. See Palisca, "Scientific Empiricism in Musical Thought," pp. 91-137.

46. Book IV, Ch. 11, pp. 152-157.

47. *De Musica*, III, viii, p. 127.

48. The whole Book II of *De Musica* (pp. 46-100) is devoted to the explanation of just intonation.

49. *Ibid.*, III, iv-v, pp. 108-114.

50. *Ibid.*, III, vii, pp. 115-20.

51. *Ibid.*, III, viii, pp. 120-27.

52. *Ibid.*, III, xxvii, pp. 164-66.

53. *Sopplimenti*, Book IV, Ch. 12, pp. 157f.

54. See, e.g., *Le Istitutioni*, Part II, Ch. 42, p. 127 [147].

55. *Ibid.*, pp. 126f. [146ff.].

56. *Dimostrationi*, Rag. IV, Prop. 1, p. 221.

57. *Ibid.*, Rag. V, Def. 1-6, pp. 267ff.

58. *Tuning and Temperament*, p. 33.

59. *Ibid.*

60. *De Musica*, III, xv-xxiii, pp. 143-157. See also Barbour, *op. cit.*, pp. 33ff.

61. "Quando noi ritrovaremo due parti nelli contrapunti, che saranno distanti l'una dall'altra per uno di questi intervalli, diremo, che quelle sono lontane per un Tuono maggiore, over minore; overamente diremo, che siano distanti per una Seconda maggiore: conciosia che cosi è nominato da i Prattici tale intervallo, a differenza della minore, che è il Semituono maggiore:" *Le Istitutioni*, Part III, Ch. 18, p. 164 [191], trans. in *Art*, pp. 36f.

62. *Le Istitutioni*, Part III, Ch. 73, pp. 281f [346f.].

63. "Potemo adunque concludere, che è impossibile di potere usare semplicemente, et da per se questi due generi ultimi, di maniera, che vi sia l'harmonia perfetta, senza l'uso delle chorde particolari di alcun'altro genere." *Ibid.*, p. 282 [347], trans. in *Art*, p. 271.

64. "si come alcuni si hanno sognato:" *Le Istitutioni*, p. 282 [347], trans. in *Art*, p. 271.

65. *Le Istitutioni*, Book III, Ch. 74, pp. 282f. [347f.].

66. "Videtur etiam falli, cum arbitratur, genus Chromaticum à Diatono separari posse, & aliquando separatum in usu fuisse." *De Musica*, IV, xxxiii, p. 233; tr. in Daniels, *op. cit.*, p. 435.

67. See, e.g., *Le Istitutioni*, Part II, Chs. 31, 49, pp. 107, 143 [126, 166].

68. "Ne solamente si serveno delle chorde propie di quel genere, del quale dicono, che è la compositione; ma etiandio di quelle, che sono propie, et serveno particolarmente a gli altri generi, et di alcune altre, che sono al tutto forestiere, . . . Lequali, per non contenere alcuna delle gia dette cose, non si possono chiamare composte in alcuno di questi due generi, che usavano gia li Musici antichi; ma in genere ritrovato, et fatto ad un modo loro, molto conforme a i loro capricci." *Ibid.*, Part III, Ch. 74, pp. 282f. [347f.], trans. in *Art*, p. 272. See also *ibid.*, Part II, Ch. 16, pp. 85f. [101].

69. *Ibid.*, Part III, Ch. 77, p. 286 [351].

70.   "Et non si maravigli alcuno, ch'io habbia detto, che si usino le chorde delli generi, et
      si proceda secondo li modi mostrati di sopra: Imperoche usiamo veramente le chorde di
      questi generi, ma non il genere; cioè usiamo le Parti, ma non il Tutto:" *Ibid.*, p. 286
      [351], trans. in *Art*, p. 279.

71.   "Onde l'uso delle chorde, et anche di uno Intervallo, che sia sonoro si può concedere:
      percioche fa buono effetto; et tale è l'uso delle Parti: ma quello del Tutto, cioè di tutte
      le chorde di uno genere, et di tutti li suoi intervalli non è lecito: conciosia che fa tristo
      effetto. Per la qual cosa l'uso del Genere, è usare tutte le sue chorde, et quelli
      intervalli tutti, che sono considerati dal Musico in tal genere, et non alcun'altro;
      et questo dico nelle modulationi, che fanno le parti della cantilena: Ma l'uso delle Chorde,
      non è altro, che lo accommodarsi di esse nelle modulationi delle cantilene diatoniche;
      procedendo per quelli intervalli, che si ritrovano, et anco si potessino ritrovare nel genere
      Diatonico; si come da molti sono state, et anco sono felicemente usate; lassando da un canto
      quelli, che sono proprij di quelle chorde chromatiche, et enharmoniche, che noi usiamo; cioe
      il Semituono minore, et li Diesis." *Le Istitutioni*, Part III, Ch. 78, p. 287 [352], trans.
      in *Art*, pp. 280f. See also *Le Istitutioni*, Part III, Ch. 57, p. 236 [278], where a progression
      using chromatic steps is allowed because the interval itself is diatonic.

72.   "vitio particolare di qualcheduno." *Ibid.*, Part III, Ch. 57, p. 237 [279], trans. in *Art*,
      p. 175.

73.   *Le Istitutioni*, Book IV, Chs. 18-30, pp. 320-337 [392-417].

74.   See, e.g., *Dimostrationi*, Rag. IV, Prop. 11, pp. 236f.

75.   "È ben vero, che'l levare un Tetrachordo da una cantilena, et porvene un'altro, si può
      fare in due maniere: Prima quando in una parte sola della cantilena, cioè in una particello
      del Tenore, o di altra parte (ma non per tutto) si pone la chorda ♭ , cioè la Tríte synemennon
      incidentalmente una, o due fiate, tra la Mese, et la Paramese; Et cosi potemo dire, che'l
      levare il Tetrachordo Diezeugmenon, il cui principio havemo nella Chorda ♮ , cioè in
      Paramese; et il porre il Synemennon, che hà il suo principio nella chorda a, cioè il
      porre la ♭ sopradetta, non hà forza di trasmutare un Modo nell'altro; et che tal Tetrachordo
      posto nella cantilena non sia naturale, ma accidentale; . . . Ma il secondo modo si fa,
      quando per tutta la cantilena, cioè in ciascuna parte, in luogo del Tetrachordo Diezeugmenon,
      usiamo il Synemennon; et in luogo di cantar la detta cantilena per la proprietà del ♮
      quadrato, la cantiamo per quella del ♭ molle; La onde essendo posto in cotal maniera,
      . . . questo Tetrachordo non è posto accidentalmente nella cantilena: ma è naturale; et
      il Modo si chiama Trasportato, . . . et cotale Tetrachordo hà possanza di trasmutare un Modo
      nell'altro." *Le Istitutioni*, Part IV, Ch. 16, p. 317 [389].

76.   "col mezo delle lor chorde accommode tra le chorde diatoniche, potemo passare all'uso
      delle harmonie perfette; accommodandosi di loro per l'acquisto di molte consonanze imperfette
      maggiori, o minori; le quali in molti luoghi non si possono havere nell'ordine delle chorde
      diatoniche; come è manifesto a ciascuno, che sia essercitato nell'Arte del comporre; le
      quali vengono alle volte al proposito, per fare l'harmonia, che corrispondi allegra, o mesta
      alla natura delle parole." *Ibid.*, Part III, Ch. 77, p. 286 [351], trans. in *Art*, p. 278.

77.   "sia talmente accommodata alla Oratione, cioè alle Parole, che nelle materie allegre,

l'harmonia non sia flebile; et per il contrario, nelle flebili, l'harmonia non sia allegra.'' *Le Istitutioni*, Part III, Ch. 26, p. 172 [200], trans. in *Art*, p. 52.

78.   *Le Istitutioni*, Part III, Chs. 10, 57, pp. 156, 238 [182, 280]. The general affective character of a mode also depends on imperfect consonances, namely, on whether the fifth of the mode (that is, the final and the fifth above it) is divided so that the third above the final is major (in which case the mode is cheerful), or minor (which renders the mode sad). See *ibid.*, p. 156 [182].

79.   ''con l'aiuto di una chorda chromatica potemo pervenire all'uso delle buone, et sonore harmonie, et schivare nel genere Diatonico alcune discommode relationi di Tritoni, Semidiapenti, et di altri simili intervalli, che fanno le parti cantando insieme; come altrove hò mostrato; senza l'aiuto della quale, molte volte si potrebbe udire non solamente assai durezze; ma anco alcune disconze modulationi. Et quantunque tutti questi inconvenienti si potessero schivare, usando solamente le chorde diatoniche, tutta via ciò si farebbe alquanto più difficilmente; massimamente volendo (come porta il dovere) cercare di variar l'harmonia; La onde aviene, che per l'uso di tal chorda li Modi si fanno più dolci, et più soavi.'' *Ibid.*, Part III, Ch. 78, p. 287 [353], trans. in *Art*, p. 281.

80.   See the quotation above and *Le Istitutioni*, Part III, Ch. 57, p. 237 [279f.]. See *ibid.*, Book III, Chs. 30 and 61, for situations in which tritone and diminished fifth may exceptionally be used.

81.   See *ibid.*, Book III, Ch. 29, for the rule and possible exceptions.

82.   ''massimamente tra le modulationi, che fanno due parti ascendendo, over discendendo insieme col movimento della Terza;'' *Ibid.*, Part III, Ch. 25, p. 170 [198], trans. in *Art*, p. 48.

83.   ''. . . partendosi il Compositore da una consonanza Imperfetta, et volendo andare alla Perfetta; debbe fare, che quella Imperfetta, che precede, le sia veramente la più vicina;'' *Le Istitutioni*, Part III, Ch. 38, p. 188 [217], trans. in *Art*, p. 79.

84.   ''Ma ciò sia detto per sempre, che l'obligo sta nelle cose possibili, et non nelle impossibili; al quale niuno è obligato.'' *Le Istitutioni*, Part III, Ch. 61, p. 249 [294], trans. in *Art*, pp. 199f. It is true that if the rule was to be consistently applied by an editor, it would lead to an unusually extensive use of *ficta* accidentals. The over-zealous application of this rule by some modern composers was severely criticized by Ghiselin Danckerts, since it introduced too many accidentals and destroyed modal purity. See *Trattato sopra una differentia musicale*, MS Rome, Biblioteca Vallicelliana, R 56, Part III, Ch. 3, fol. 408r.

85.   *De Musica*, III, vi, pp. 114f.

86.   ''Potemo dipoi col mezo delle chorde di questi generi fare le Transportationi delli Modi verso l'acuto, overamente verso il grave; le quali Transportationi sono molto necessarie a gli organisti, che serveno alle Capelle: conciosia che fa dibisogno, che alle volte trasportino il Modo, hora dall'acuto nel grave, et tallora dal grave nell'acuto; secondo che la natura delle Voci, che si trovano in quelle, lo ricerca; che senza il loro aiuto sarebbe imposibile di poterlo fare. Et quantunque tali chorde si usino spesse fiate in simili occasioni; tuttavia

non si procede per esse se non diatonicamente." *Le Istitutioni*, Part III, Ch. 77, p. 286 [351], trans. in *Art*, pp. 278f. See also *Le Istitutioni*, Part IV, Ch. 17, p. 319 [390].

87.   "per vedere, in qual maniera potessero riuscire le harmonie Chromatice, et le Enharmonice." *Ibid.*, Part II, Ch. 47, p. 140 [163].

88.   "questo è un'Istrumento, sopra il quale si potrà essercitare ogni ottimo Sonatore, non solamente nelle harmonie diatonice: ma etiandio nelle chromatice, et nelle Enharmonice: quando potrà ridurle alli Modi antichi: overamente quando a i nostri tempi potranno riuscire megliori, et più soavi di quello, che si odeno [nelle Compositioni di alcuni compositori moderni]." *Ibid.*, Part II, Ch. 47, p. 141 [164f.]. The end of the sentence, given here in square brackets, was added in the edition of 1573.

89.   See p. 35 above.

90.   ". . . Adrianum Vilartium inducit loquentem in quarto Dialogo suarum dimonstrationum, & acriter invehentem in eos, qui Chromatici videri volunt in suis Musicalibus compositionibus, eò quòd procedunt per gradus generis Chromatici, qui sunt semitonia minora. In quo meritò eos reprehendit, quandoquidem non est in eo sita vis Chromatici generis, ut per ita curtos gradus procedere necesse sit:" *De Musica*, IV, xxxiii, p. 233; tr. in Daniels, *op. cit.*, pp. 435f.

91.   "Voi Messere vi siete affaticato molto insieme con molti altri buoni Musici piu Antichi di voi, nel ridurre la Musica ad una certa maniera, o forma: che havesse qualche gravità et maesta insieme ma con costoro è stato quasi vano il vostro disegno: percioche oltra che non osservano i precetti buoni dell'Arte: insegnano anco et essortano gli altri à guastare il buono et bene ordinate: et à far peggio che fanno. Et quando fanno cosa alcuna, che sia fuori del buono et bello della Musica: si coprono col scudo della ignoranza: et dicono che sono cose fatte nel Genere Chromatico: se bene non conoscono, ne fanno quello che ello sia." *Dimostrationi*, Rag. IV, Prop. 11, pp. 236f.

92.   *Le Istitutioni*, Part IV, Ch. 31, p. 337 [417].

93.   *Republic*, 398.

94.   *Le Istitutioni*, Part IV, Ch. 32, p. 339 [419].

95.   *Ibid.*, Part IV, Chs. 31-2, pp. 337-340 [417-421].

96.   See, e.g., *Le Istitutioni*, Part II, Chs. 10, 32, Part IV, Ch. 32, pp. 77, 108, 340 [91, 126, 420].

97.   ". . . potendo la Voce formare ogni intervallo; et essendo necessario di imitare il parlar famigliare nel proferir le parole, come usano gli Oratori, et vuole anco il dovere; non è inconveniente, che si possa usar tutti quelli intervalli, che fanno al proposito, per potere esprimere i concetti, che sono contenuti nelle parole, con quelli accenti, et altre cose, nel modo, che ragionando li proferimo; accioas muovino gli affetti." *Ibid.*, Part III, Ch. 80, p. 290 [357], trans. in *Art*, p. 288. Cf. the words of Nicola Vicentino, quoted on p. 38 above.

98. "Conciosia che quantunque si potesse fare il tutto commodamente in una parte della cantilena, et si udissero tali accenti fatti con proposito, et che facessero buoni effeti; tuttavia nelli accompagnamenti si udirebbeno cose tanto ladre, che sarebbe dibisogno chiudersi le orecchi." *Le Istitutioni*, p. 291 [357], trans. in *Art*, p. 288.

99. "Opinioni delli Chromatisti ributtate" is the title of *Le Istitutioni*, Book III, Ch. 80, p. 290 [357], trans. in *Art*, p. 288.

100. ". . . che mai sono per haver cosa buona, fuori del nostro genere; usando nel modo che facemmo le chorde Chromatiche, & le Enharmoniche con proposito; se non si ritornasse a congiungere insieme (come facevano gli Antichi) il Numero, l'Harmonia, & le Parole. . . ." *Le Istitutioni*, p. 291 [358], trans. in *Art*, p. 290.

101. "la natura de i Generi non consisteva semplicemente nell'Harmonia; ma ne i Piedi posti nella Oratione." *Sopplimenti*, Book VI, Ch. 9, p. 266.

102. See, e.g., *Le Istitutioni*, Part II, Ch. 4, p. 62 [73].

103. *Dimostrationi*, Rag. IV, Prop. 11, p. 237.

104. "Ma se la Musica antica (come di sopra hò mostrato) haveva in se tale imperfettione, non par credibile, che i Musici potessero produrre ne gli animi humani tanti varij effetti, si come nelle historie si racconta: . . . Et tanto meno par credibile, perche essendo ella hoggidi ridutta a quella perfettione, che quasi di meglio non si può sperare, non si vede che faccia alcuno delli sopradetti effetti;" *Le Istitutioni*, Part II, Ch. 4, p. 62 [73].

105. ". . . la Musica etiandio al presente non è priva di far cotali effetti;" *Ibid*.

106. ". . . la Musica mai cessa in diversi modi, & in diversi tempi, di operare, & di produrre varij effetti, . . . La onde vedemo etiandio a i nostri tempi, che la Musica induce in noi varie passioni, nel modo che anticamente faceva;" *Ibid*., Part II, Ch. 9, p. 75 [89].

107. *Ibid*.

108. "Onde mi muoveno a ridere alcuni, i quali senza assegnar ragione, ne autorità alcuna dicono, che questo genere si usava anticamente nelle Feste publiche all'uso delle orecchie volgari; & che gli altri due erano posti in uso tra li privati Signori: Ma penso, che costoro non habbiano mai veduto Tolomeo, & se pur l'hanno veduto, non l'hanno inteso." *Ibid*., Part II, Ch. 16, p. 84 [99].

109. Cf. *L'antica musica ridotta alla moderna prattica* (Rome: Antonio Barre, 1555), fol. 10v, quoted on p. 41 above.

110. ". . . in universale parlando . . . Musica non è altro che Harmonia; & potremo dire, che ella sia quella lite & amicitia, che poneva Empedocle, dalla quale voleva, che si generassero tutte le cose, cioè una discordante concordia come sarebbe a dire, Concordia di varie cose, le quali si possino congiungere insieme." *Le Istitutioni*, Part I, Ch. 5, p. 10 [14], trans. in *Art*, p. xviii.

111. *Le Istitutioni*, Part I, Ch. 7, pp. 16ff. [21ff.].

112. "harmonia, la quale nasce da i suoni et dalle voci." *Ibid.*, Part I, Ch. 10, p. 19 [25].

113. *Ibid.*, Part II, Ch. 12, pp. 79f [94f.].

114. For Galilei's biography see Claude V. Palisca, "Galilei," in Friedrich Blume, ed., *Die Musik in Geschichte und Gegenwart*, Vol. IV (Kassel and Basel: Bärenreiter, 1955), cols. 1265-70. The most important discussions of Galilei's theories are: Oscar Chilesotti, "Di Nicola Vicentino e dei generi greci secondo Vincentio Galilei," *Rivista musicale italiana*, XIX (1912), 546-65; Fabio Fano, *La Camerata fiorentina. Vincenzo Galilei 1520?-1591. La sua opera d'artista e di teorico come espressione di nuove idealità musicali*, Istituzioni e Monumenti dell'Arte Musicale Italiana, Vol. IV (Milan: Edizioni Ricordi, 1934); Fano, "Alcuni chiarimenti su Vincenzo Galilei," *La Rassegna musicale*, X (1937), 85-90; Walker, "Musical Humanism . . ."; Barbour, *Tuning and Temperament*; Palisca, *The Beginnings of Baroque Music*; Palisca, "Vincenzo Galilei's Counterpoint Treatise: A Code for the Seconda Pratica," *Journal of the American Musicological Society*, IX (1956), 81-96; Palisca, "Vincenzo Galilei and Some Links between 'Pseudo-Monody' and Monody," *The Musical Quarterly*, XLVI (1960), 344-60; Palisca, "Scientific Empiricism . . ."; Stillman Drake, "Renaissance Music and Experimental Science," *Journal of the History of Ideas*, XXXI (1970), 483-500; Drake, *Galileo Studies: Personality, Tradition, and Revolution* (Ann Arbor: University of Michigan Press, 1970), pp. 43-62; Drake, "Galilei, Vincenzio," in Charles Coulston Gillispie, ed., *Dictionary of Scientific Biography*, Vol. V (New York: Charles Scribner's Sons, 1972), pp. 249f; Walker, "Some Aspects of the Musical Theory of Vincenzo Galilei and Galileo Galilei," *Proceedings of the Royal Musical Association*, C (1973-1974), 33-47. See also the literature on Giovanni de' Bardi, the Camerata, and Girolamo Mei listed below.

115. For Bardi and his Camerata see: Henriette Martin, "La 'Camerata' du Comte Bardi et la musique florentine du XVIe siècle," *Revue de Musicologie*, XIII (1932), 63-74, 152-61, 227-34; XIV (1933), 92-100, 141-51; Fabio Fano, *La Camerata fiorentina*; Nino Pirrotta, "Temperaments and Tendencies in the Florentine Camerata," *The Musical Quarterly*, XL (1954), 169-89; Pirrotta, "Tragédie et comédie dans la Camerata fiorentina," in Jean Jacquot, ed., *Musique et poésie au XVIe siècle* (Paris: Èditions du Centre National de la Recherche Scientifique, 1954), pp. 287-297; Egert Pöhlmann, "Antikenverständnis und Antikenmissverständnis in der Operntheorie der Florentiner Camerata," *Die Musikforschung*, XXII (1969), 5-13; Claude V. Palisca, "The 'Camerata Fiorentina': A Reappraisal," *Studi musicali*, I (1972), 203-36.

116. *Trattato dell'Arte del Contrapunto*, Florence, Bibl. Naz. Cent., Ms. Gal. 1, fol. 58r.

117. The correspondence, together with a commentary that demonstrates the extent to which Mei influenced Galilei and Bardi is in Claude V. Palisca, *Girolamo Mei: Letters on Ancient and Modern Music to Vincenzo Galilei and Giovanni Bardi*, Musicological Studies and Documents 3 (n.p.: American Institute of Musicology, 1960). See also Palisca, "Girolamo Mei, Mentor to the Florentine Camerata," *The Musical Quarterly*, XL (1954), 1-20.

118. The *Discorso* was first published in Giovanni Battista Doni, *Lyra Barberina*, Vol. II (Florence: Stamperia imperiale, 1763), pp. 233-48. For a partial English translation see

Oliver Strunk, ed., *Source Readings in Music History. From Classical Antiquity through the Romantic Era* (New York: W. W. Norton and Company, 1950), pp. 290-301. A manuscript version was recently discovered in Biblioteca Apostolica Vaticana: Ms. Barberinianus latinus 3990, fols. 4r-13v. See Claude V. Palisca, "The 'Camerata fiorentina'. . . ," p. 215.

119.   Giorgio Marescotti, 1581. The date of publication is discussed by Fabio Fano in the preface to his facs. ed. of the *Dialogo* (Rome: Reale Accademia d'Italia, 1934).

120.   The treatises are no longer extant. Their titles and short excerpts are known from Ercole Bottrigari, *Aletelogia di Leonardo Gallucio à' benigni, e sinceri lettori. Lettera apologetica* (Bologna, 1604), Bologna, Civico museo bibliografico musicale, Ms. B-43, pp. 119f.

121.   It is preserved in Florence, Bibl. Naz. Cent., Ms. Gal. 5, fols. 1r-58r.

122.   The treatise is preserved in three versions, the final being Florence, Bibl. Naz. Cent., Ms. Gal. 1, fols. 55r-147v. There is no title in the front but the proper title can be read on fols. 59r and 75v. The treatise is divided into two parts: 1. "intorno all'uso delle Consonanze" (fols. 55r-103v; title according to fol. 104v); 2. "intorno all'uso delle Dissonanze" (fols. 104r-147v). According to remarks on fols. 75v and 99r, the following was intended as an appendix: "Discorso intorno all'uso dell 'Enharmonio et di chi fusse autore del Cromatico," Florence, Bibl. Naz. Cent., Ms. Gal. 3, fols. 3r-34v. Finally, there is an additional clarification of the appendix: "Dubbi intorno a quanto io ho detto dell'uso dell'enharmonio, con la solutione di essi," *ibid.*, fols. 62r-68r.

123.   It was first studied in Palisca, "Vincenzo Galilei's Counterpoint Treatise."

124.   *Dialogo*, pp. 107-11.

125.   *Ibid.*, pp. 48f.

126.   For Zarlino's views see p. 44 above.

127.   *Dialogo*, pp. 119ff. and p. 44 above.

128.   For Zarlino's views see p. 45 above.

129.   *Dialogo*, p. 50.

130.   *Ibid.*, p. 49.

131.   For Zarlino's views see pp. 46f. above.

132.   *Dialogo*, p. 112 and p. 47 above.

133.   "Discorso intorno all'uso dell'Enharmonio," fols. 5r-5v.

134.   ". . . il Diatonico serva al Musico non altramente di quello che serve al Pittore il disegno

. . . il qual disegno perfetto del Diatonico poi colorisce il Musico con il Cromatico; dandogli appresso con l'enharmonico (quanto a suoni et agl'accordi) l'ultima perfettione." *Ibid.*, fols. 25r-25v.

135. *Ibid.*, fol. 24v.

136. See p. 51 above.

137. For the following discussion see pp. 52-55 above.

138. See Palisca, *Girolamo Mei*, p. 67.

139. See pp. 4f., 10, 12-15, 17-23, 25-27.

140. *Dialogo*, p. 29.

141. *Ibid.*, pp. 30, 42, 49.

142. *Tuning and Temperament*, pp. 7f., 59.

143. *Sopplimenti*, Book IV, Chs. 27-28, pp. 197-203 and Book IV, Chs. 30-32, pp. 208-216. Galilei defends his approximation in *Discorso*, pp. 55f.

144. *De Musica*, III. xxxi, pp. 172-74. See also Barbour, *op. cit.*, pp. 50f.

145. *Tuning and Temperament*, p. 6.

146. *Dialogo*, p. 30.

147. *Ibid.*, p. 33.

148. *Ibid.*, p. 34.

149. *Ibid.*

150. See p. 55 above and *Sopplimenti*, Book IV, Ch. 24, pp. 189ff. and Galilei's defense in his *Discorso*, pp. 44f., 50f.

151. See p. 55 above and *Dialogo*, p. 34.

152. *Dialogo*, p. 47.

153. *Ibid.*

154. *Ibid.*, p. 42.

155. "dove per il contrario nella distribuitione delle corde da questa diversa che usa lo Strumento di tasti, ve ne mancano comunemente molti; per lo che non può il sonatore di esso quantunque prattico & perito, trasportare in questa & in quella parte per un Tuono & per un Semituono (in quelli dico che per lo piu si esercitano) ciascuna, Cantilena, come nel Liuto con tanto comodo & utile si trasporta." *Ibid.*, p. 47.

156. *Discorso*, pp. 109-113.

157. *Dialogo*, pp. 47f. This question is also discussed in Galilei, *Discorso particolare intorno all'Unisono*, Florence, Bibl. Naz. Cent., Ms. Gal. 3, fols. 55r-61v.

158. "come quella c'habbia da levare ogni difficoltà à Cantori, Sonatori, & Compositori, per poter communemente incominciare à cantare ò sonare sopra qual delle Dodici parti vorranno, secondo l'uso de Prattici, Ut. Re. Mi. Fa. Sol. La. girando per tutte le Note, facendo (come ei dice) la Musica sferica; essendoche dove incomincieranno un'ordine, potranno anco ivi finire commodamente ogni Canto, com'in ur. Moto perpetuo; perche tutti gli istrumenti potranno tener le loro accordature & unirsi; & gli Organi (com'ei dice) non faranno ne troppo alti, no troppo bassi di tuono." *Sopplimenti*, Book IV, Ch. 31, p. 212; see also Book IV, Ch. 12, pp. 158f.

159. "qual sia corda di essa, ha con il mezzo del suo Cromatico, et nell'acuto e nel grave ciascheduno Intervallo che si adoperi nel Contrapunto." ". . . non meno che il Matematico reputi il corpo sferico tra quelli di altra forma." *Trattato dell'Arte del Contrapunto*, fol. 128r.

160. *Dialogo*, p. 30.

161. *Ibid.*, pp. 30f.

162. *Ibid.*, p. 55.

163. *Diversarum speculationum mathematicarum & physicorum liber* (Turin: apud Haeredem Nicolai Bevilaquae, 1585), pp. 277-83. The letters are dated and discussed in Palisca, "Scientific Empiricism." They were reprinted in Josef Reiss, "Jo. Bapt. Benedictus, *De intervallis musicis*," *Zeitschrift für Musikwissenschaft*, VII (1924-25), 13-20.

164. *Dialogo*, pp. 26f.

165. "ò almeno sono stati per si fatto rispetto introcotti, se ben male adoperati." *Ibid.*, p. 26, trans. in Robert H. Herman, *"Dialogo della musica antica et della moderna" of Vincenzo Galilei: Translation and Commentary*, unpublished Ph.D. diss., North Texas State University, 1973 (henceforth referred to as Herman), pp. 131f.

166. "il semituono minore, considerato in se stesso, e di poco rilievo nel contrapunto . . . nulla dimeno, applicato ad altri intervalli; apporta l'uso di lui non solo comodo al contrapuntista, ma è grandemente necessario alla perfettione dell'harmonie; . . . merciè della faculta datagli da Prattici, che è di fare l'imperfette consonanze che tra le chorde Diatoniche et comuni sono per l'ordinario minori, farli dico sempre che al contrapuntista piaccia, divenire maggiori, et di maggiori minori." *Trattato dell'Arte del Contrapunto*, fol. 64v.

167.   *Dialogo*, p. 27.

168.   See fol. 75v.

169.   See fols. 4-4v; 29v.

170.   "Discorso intorno all'uso dell'Enharmonio," fol. 8v.

171.   "Don Niccola Vicentino, huomo di non poca reputatione nella musica prattica, sonava uno strumento di Tasti che oltre le due tastature ordinarie che sono la diatonica et la cromatica et ne haveva di più un'altra da potere a voglia sua secondo però la comune intelligenza, sonare l'enharmonio. haveva inoltre il medesimo don niccola alquanti suoi scolari, che in quel mentre ch'egli sonava l'enharmonio inparticolare, cantavano quella tal sorte di musica, dal medesimo composta. la qual musica fece udire per tutte le principali città d'italia, et io inparticolare l'udii in diversi tempi et luoghi, più volte; la quale s'ella sia piaciuta o no, ce ne sii segno, che ne da alcunj altrj, ne dagl'istessi suoi scolari, fu dopo la sua morte posta in atto; uno de quali rividi a Venetia l'anno 60 detto per nome jacome finetti, che oltre al sonare di Tasti più che ordinariamente cantava di contralto molto bene, e tra le altre cose mi disse, che havendo egli voluto trovare ricapito, gli era stato di mestiere lasciare da parte l'enharmonio del suo maestro, et attendere ad altro. mai adunque come io ho detto era cantata cotal musica senza lo stromento nominato, et se per mala fortuna incantando, una de cantanti usciva, era impossibile il rimetterlo, et cio vidi io a vedere in ravenna. . . . sinche adunque che quella tal sorte di musica, haveva di necessita di quel tale strumento che guidasse le voci di cantanti per gl'incogniti tragetti per non dirle balze precipitose, et non le lasciasse andare secondo la natura del canto, et per il dritto sentiero. i quali suoni particolari del enharmonio . . . ne potevano se non essere ingrati al senso. lasciò Don niccola molte di quelle sue compositioni, et alla stampa, et in penna: lasciò parimente più d'uno di quelli strumenti di tasti; et rimasero i suoi scolari, che per il lungo studio intendevano quella tal prattica non meno del loro maestro le musiche dopo la sua morte non furono piu cantate, gli strumenti non piu sonati in quella tal maniera; et i suoi scolari . . . abbandonarono in tutto et per tutto quel si fatto enharmonio per non trovare chi più udirelo volesse. stette Don niccola al servitio del cardinale di ferrara, et fece udire le sue musiche a molti signori di autorità ne per cio creda alcuno ch'egli vi fusse introdotto per fargli udire sempli-cemente l'enharmonio; ma si bene il diatonico et cromatico; ne quali due generi compose molte belle cantilene; . . . ma come si veniva all'enharmonio; . . . per non . . . essere d'ignoranza ripresi; et altri per il rispetto che gl'apportava la grandezza del suo padrone. lodavano esso enharmonio ancora. ma il tempo vero giudice delle cose, ci ha dimostrato con l'esperienza, che qualla musica cosi divisa, non piaceva, poi ch'ella fu abbandonata, et seguita quella che non cosi in parti minore è divisa." *Ibid.*, fols. 9r-10r.

172.   "in corde forestiere, incantabili fuore d'ogn'ordinario, & piene d'artifitio. non per altro, che per haver campo piu largo di predicare se stessi & le cose loro (à meno di essi intendenti) per miracoli . . ." ". . .à guisa che sogliono i periti Organisti, per comodità del coro per un Tuono, ò per una Terza, ò per altro intervallo col mezzo de segni accidentali." *Dialogo*, p. 87, trans. in Herman, pp. 519f.

173.   *Dialogo*, p. 104; see p. 57f. above. See also "Discorso intorno all'uso dell'Enharmonio," fols. 24v, 27v.

174.   *Dialogo*, p. 104.

175.   "il quale rispetto à essi antichi, è moderno in certo modo." *Ibid.*, p. 106, trans. in Herman, p. 655.

176.   "Circa quella che da vio si desiderebbe sapere se il genere chromatico de gli antichi et il loro enarmonio tanto lodato da quelli si potessero sonare ciascuno da per se, credo che per certo si potrebbe rispondere, che si, nel medesimo modo che cantarlo, intendendo pero di cantare e sonare come anticamente si usava una aria sola, e non pju insieme, et in somma in canto fermo, et non in contrapunto, et altramente no." Letter of May 8, 1572 in Palisca, *Girolamo Mei*, p. 107.

177.   See pp. 57f. above.

178.   ". . . l'uso della musica dico, fu da gli huomini introdotto per il rispetto & fine che di comun parere dicono tutti i savij; il quale non da altro principalmente nacque che dall'esprimere con efficacia maggiore i concetti dell'animo loro nel celebrare le lodi de Dei, de Genij, & degli Heroi; come da canti fermi & piani Eccelsiastici origine di questa nostra à piu voci si può in parte comprendere; & d'imprimergli secondariamente con pari forza nelle menti de mortali per utile & comodo loro." *Dialogo*, p. 81.

179.   "non solo come dilettevole alla vita, ma ancora come utile alla virtù." *Ibid.*, p. 1.

180.   "in tale cecità perseverarono, sin'à che il Gafurio prima, & appresso il Glareano, & poscia il Zarlino (Principi veramente in quest moderna prattica) cominciarono ad investigare quello che ella fusse, & à cercare di trarla dalle tenebre ove era stata sepolta. la qual parte da loro intesa, & apprezzata, hanno à poco à poco ridotta nel termine in che ella si ritrova. Ma non pare ad alcuni intelligenti, che l'habbiano resa all'antico suo stato." *Ibid.*, trans. in Herman, pp. 36ff.

181.   "Hora da quel tempo sin'ad hoggi, concorrono tutti i miglior prattici à credere & dire, che ella sia giunta à quel colmo di perfettione che l'huomo si possa imaginare; anzi che dalla morte in quà di Cipriano Rore, Musico in questa maniera di Contrapunto veramente singulare, sia piutosto andata in declinatione che in augumento." *Dialogo*, p. 80, trans. in Herman, pp. 468f.

182.   "Principe . . . de Contrapuntisti." *Trattato dell'Arte del Contrapunto*, fol. 140r. See also *ibid.*, fols. 66v, 101v.

183.   "Però componendo sopra tutto v'ingegnerete che il verso ben regolato, e la parola quanto più si possa ben intesa sia, non lasciando traviarvi dal contrapunto quasi cattivo notatore che dalla corrente transportar si lasci, ne arrivi oltre al fiume, la ove egli proposto s'haveva, tenendo per costante che così come l'anima del corpo è più nobile, altresi le parole più nobili del contrapunto sono. . . . Ben conobbe il divin Cipriano verso il fine della sua vita quanto in questi tempi ciò fosse nella musica gravissimo errore. onde si diede con tutti i nervi dell'ingegno à far ben intender il verso, e suono delle parole ne madrigali suoi . . . havendomi quel grand'huomo detto in Venetia quel esser vero modo del comporre. Et in vero se non ei fosse stato tolto dalla morte per mio avviso havrebbe ridotta la musica delle più arie à tal perfettione, onde con facilita altri à poco à poco si sarebbe potuto

ridurre alla vera e perfetta tanto da gl'antichi lodata.'' *Discorso mandato a Caccini sopra la musica antica e 'l cantar bene*, Vatican, Biblioteca Apostolica Vaticana, Ms. Barberinianus latinus 3990, fol. 10r, trans. in Strunk, *op. cit.*, p. 295.

184.   ''il che . . . pare che a' tempi nostri habbia conseguito Girolamo Mei, huomo degno, à cui tutti i Musici, & tutti gli huomini dotti devono rendere gratie & honori.'' *Dialogo*, p. 1, trans. in Herman, pp. 38f.

185.   ''. . . voi havete oppinione che la musica debba havere per suo obbjetto il dilettare l'orecchio con l'harmonia, et che per ciò il medesimo dovesse essere quel de la antica. Or se voi intendete il diletto che nasce dal aria del cantare, la quale bene accomodata esprimendo acconciamente il concetto et facendo con l'ajuto suo . . . l'affetto, non puo essere se non gioconda ad udirsi, io agevolmente ne sono con esso voi. Ma perche le parole vostre appariscono molto resolute in favore de lo schietto senso del udito, dicendo voi e replicando per pju riprese questi termini soavità e soave per mira de la musica, e massimamente intorno à le consonanze, m'é venuto pensato che voi per ventura possiate haver solamente l'occhio à quel diletto che oggi apertamente si vede proposto per fine à nostri musici, che è quella sola delicatura, per chiamarla con questo nome, la quale altro pju profondo fine non ha che il contentare schiettamente l'orecchio ne lo udirsi, . . . e che havendo voi presuposto questo lor fine per vero per ciò andiate interpretando il termine e parole harmonia, non per il filo et ordine e modo de l'aria del canto . . . ma preocupato come io stimo dal uso de la moderna per la qualità sopra tutto de le consonanze che vi si dovesser come ne la nostra sentire di molte arie diverse. Or questo io non solamente giudico che fusse in tutto e per tutto, si come di sopra ho detto alieno da la mira de l'antica, ma medesimamente insieme cosa per sua natura tutta contraria à la intenzione di lei, e conseguentemente de suoi artefici. conciosiache questa scoperchia et non punto natural cura, sviando gli animi et occupandoli seco in altra considerazione non permette che lo strumento de la voce stato conceduto con tante sue diverse qualità spezialmente al huomo per la perfetta espressione de' concetti et affetti suoi possa perdendosi in queste quasi vanità accidentali et accessorie far l'offizio suo, ne accomodatamente, ne senza impedimento. Onde io per tanto mi credo che il fine propostosi fusse imitando la natura stessa de lo strumento del quale essi si valevano, non la soavità de le consonanze per contentar l'orecchio (conciosiache del uso di queste nel lor cantare non si truova ne testimonio ne riscontro alcuno appresso gli scrittori) ma lo esprimere interamente et con efficacia tutto quello che voleva fare intendere . . . per il mezzo et ajuto de la acutezza e gravità de la voce, . . . accompagnata con la regolata temperatura del presto et adagio, pronunziare le parti de suoi termini, secondo che l'una e l'altra qualità, ciascuna da per se per propria natura è accomodata à qualche determinato affetto. . . . et che questo dovesse essere il vero fine et propria mira de gli antichi musici assai certo lo mostra . . . e indubitamente lo conferma il vedere che la loro facultà era nel principio congiuntissima con la poesia, essendo che i primi e migliori furono insieme e musici e poeti. Or che la poesia habbja per proprio fine e mira la imitazione è cosa . . . certa. . . .'' Letter of May 8, 1572 in Palisca, *Girolamo Mei*, pp. 115ff.

186.   *Dialogo*, pp. 82f.

187.   *Ibid.*, p. 85.

188.   ''se il fine de moderni prattici è (come essi dicono) il dilettare con la diversità delle consonanze il senso dell'udito,. . . lascisi questo fine del dilettare con la diversità de loro

accordi ad essi strumenti; perche sendo privi di senso, di moto, d'intelletto, di parlare, di discorso, di ragione, & d'anima; non sono di p:u oltre capaci: ma gli huomini che sono dalla natura stati dotati di tutte queste belle nobili, & eccellenti parti, cerchino col mezzo di esse non solo di dilettare, ma come imitatori de buoni antichi, di giovare insieme, poiche acciò sono atti." *Ibid.*, p. 86, trans: in Herman, pp. 517f.

189. "& quantunque i sensi conoschino il bianco e 'l nero, e l'amaro e 'l dolce; non però gli conoscano in modo che sappiano discernere l'uno essere da desiderare & l'altro da fuggire." *Dialogo*, p. 84, trans. in Herman, pp. 499ff.

190. "Privi della parte piu nobile importante & princ:pale della musica, che sono i concetti dell'animo espressi col mezzo delle parole . . . hanno la ragione fatta schiava degli appetiti loro." *Dialogo*, p. 83, trans. in Herman, pp. 490f.

191. *Dialogo*, pp. 79f.

192. *Ibid.*, p. 87.

193. "Str. Haveva virtù il semplice suono dell'artifitiale strumento d'operare alcuno effetto nell'uditore? Bar. Non ne dubitate punto, . . . che il suono dello strumento fatto dall'arte senza l'uso delle parole, haveva secondo che io vi accennai di sopra, & come vuole Aristotile, natura d'imitare il costume, & d'haverlo in se, & grandissima facultà d'operare negli animi degli uditori gran parte degli affetti che al perito sonatore piacevano." *Ibid.*, p. 90, trans. in Herman, pp. 545f. Vincenzo's son, the great Galileo, went even further, claiming that imitation of affections by means of instrumental sound only was more praiseworthy than the imitation by means of a song. He said in one of his letters:

> . . . the farther removed the means by which one imitates are from the thing to be imitated, the more worthy of wonder the imitation will be. . . . Will we not admire a musician who moves us to sympathy with a lover by representing his sorrows and passions in song much more than if he were to do it by sobs? And this we do because song is a medium not only different from but opposite to the [natural] expression of pain while tears and sobs are very similar to it. And we would admire him even much more if he were to do it silently, with an instrument only, by means of dissonances and passionate musical accents; for the inanimate strings are [of themselves] less capable of awakening the hidden passions of our soul than is the voice that narrates them.

("... quanto più i mezzi, co'quali si imita, son lontani dalle cose da imitarsi, tanto più l'imitazione è maravigliosa. . . . Non ammireremmo noi un musico, il quale cantando e rappresentandoci le querele e le passioni d'un amante ci muovesse a compassionarlo, molto più che se piangendo ciò facesse? e questo, per essere il canto un mezzo non solo diverso, ma contrario ad esprimere i dolori, è le lagrime et il pianto similissimo. E molto più l'ammireremmo, se tacendo, col solo strumento, con crudezze et accenti patetici musicali, ciò facesse, per esser le inanimate corde meno atte a risvegliare gli affetti occulti dell'anima nostra, che la voce raccontandole.") Galileo Galilei's letter to Lodovico Cigoli of June 26, 1612 reprinted and translated in Erwin Panofsky, *Galileo as a Critic of the Arts* (The Hague: Martinus Nijhoff, 1954), pp. 32-37. See also Panofsky's comment on pp. 9ff.

194. *Dialogo*, pp. 77, 81f, 102, 104ff.

195.   "intesero . . . per Harmonia gli antichi Musici Greci, il bello & gratioso procedere dell'aria della Cantilena." *Ibid.*, p. 105, trans. in Herman, p. 652.

196.   ". . . la diversità del suono circa l'acutezza & gravità, insieme con la differenza del moto, & dell'intervallo, partorisca varietà d'harmonia, & d'affetto." *Dialogo*, p. 75, trans. in Herman, p. 436.

197.   Bardi, *op.cit.*, fols. 9r-9v, trans. in Strunk, *op. cit.*, pp. 293f.

198.   See Palisca, *Girolamo Mei*, pp. 73ff.

199.   "Dubbi intorno a quanto io ho detto dell'uso dell'enharmonio," fols. 65r-66r.

200.   "il privare la Musica delle Consonanze, et viè più quelle degl'artifiziali strumenti, è il medesimo che privare la pittura della vaghezza de' colori. imperoche si come il pittore con la diversita di essi pinge del naturale la diversità delle cose dalla natura et dall'arte prodotte, ingannando di maniera la vista che per accertarsi molte volte della verita si serve del giuditio del tatto, cosi parimente il Musico, con la diversità degl'intervalli et parti-colarmente de consonanti comunica al'intelletto tutte le passione dell'animo; et vie più informati con i mezzi debiti dall'oratione. quelli adunque che furono privi dell'uso delle consonanze, furono privi insieme di tutto il diletto che puo l'udito dagl'intervalli musici desiderare . . ." "Discorso intorno all'uso dell'Enharmonio," fol. 17v.

201.   ". . . per essere non altro il fine di questa che il diletto dell'udito, & di quella il condurre altrui per quel mezzo nella medesima affettione di se stesso." *Dialogo*, p. 89, trans. in Herman, pp. 539f.

202.   *Dialogo*, pp. 86, 88f.

203.   "Hoggi è inteso per l'imitatione delle parole non l'intero concetto et il senso di esse et di lui tutta l'oratione com'appresso degl'Antichi, ma il significato del suono di una sola." *Trattato dell'Arte del Contrapunto*, fol. 57v.

204.   "con tutto il colmo d'eccellenza della musica prattica de moderni, non si ode ò pur vede hoggi un minimo segno di quelli che l'antica faceva; ne anco si legge che ella gli facesse cinquanta ò cento anni sono quando ella non era così comune & familiare à gli huomini. di maniera che ne la novità, ne l'eccellenza di essa, ha mai havuto appresso de nostri prattici, forza d'operare alcuno di quelli virtuosi effetti che l'antica operava; dalla quale se ne traeva utile & comodo infinito: la onde necessariamente si conclude, ò che la musica, ò che la humana natura si sia mutata da quel primo suo essere." *Dialogo*, p. 81, trans. in Herman, pp. 474f.

205.   ". . . che vogliano che la musica degli antichi à comparatione della loro, fusse una baia da ridersene; & lo stupore, che col suo mezzo cagionarono negli animi & menti degli huomini, non da altro nascesse, ò derivasse, che dall'essere grossi & rozzi." *Dialogo,* p. 80, trans. in Herman, p. 467.

206.   ". . . ci sono raccontati da piu degni & famosi scrittori fuor della professione de Musici, che mai habbia havuto il mondo." *Dialogo*, p. 80, trans. in Herman, p. 468.

207. *Dialogo*, p. 80.

208. ". . . da genti che per l'ordinario sono di nullo ò poco valore, non sanno per modo di dire dove & di chi nati; non hanno beni della fortuna ò pochi, ne anco sanno à leggere. . . ." *Ibid.*, trans, in Herman, pp. 469f.

209. *Dialogo*, p. 85.

210. *Trattato dell'Arte del Contrapunto*, fol. 58v.

211. *Dialogo*, pp. 102f. and "Discorso intorno all'uso dell'Enharmonio," fol. 22v.

212. *Ibid.*, fol. 24v.

213. *Ibid.*, fol. 6r.

214. *Dialogo*, pp. 89f.

215. *Sopplimenti*, Book VIII, Ch. 11, pp. 317-20.

III. ERCOLE BOTTRIGARI AND GIOVANNI MARIA ARTUSI

1. On Bottrigari see Kathi Meyer, "Einleitung" to the facs. ed. of Bottrigari's *Il Desiderio overo de' concerti di varii strumenti musicali, Venetia, 1594*, Veröffentlichungen der Musik-Bibliothek Paul Hirsch, Vol. 5 (Berlin: Martin Breslauer, 1924), pp. 5-28; Ugo Sesini, "Studi sull' Umanesimo musicale: Ercole Bottrigari," *Convivium*, XIII (1941), 1-25; D. P. Walker, "Bottrigari," in Friedrich Blume, ed., *Die Musik in Geschichte und Gegenwart* Vol. II (Kassel-Basel, Bärenreiter, 1952), cols. 154-159.

2. *Il Patricio, overo de' tetracordi armonici di Aristosseno, parere, et vera dimostratione* (Bologna: Vittorio Benacci, 1593).

3. Francesco Patrizi, *Della Poetica. Deca istoriale* (Ferrara: Vittorio Baldini, 1586). For the fragment criticized by Bottrigari see the first complete edition of the treatise prepared by Danilo Aguzzi Barbagli, Vol. I (Florence: Istituto Nazionale de Studi sul Rinascimento, 1969), pp. 344-348.

4. Milan, Biblioteca Ambrosiana, Ms. misc. I 129 Inf., fols. 292v-298r. See Remo Giazotto, *"Il Patricio di Hercole Bottrigari dimostrato praticamente da un anonimo cinquecentista,"* *Collectanea Historiae Musicae*, I (1953), 97-112.

5. Bologna, Civico museo bibliografico musicale, Ms. B-43.

6. Milan: Stampatori archiepiscopali, 1601.

7. Bologna, Biblioteca Universitaria, Ms. 326, fols. 130r-143v.

8.　See Bottrigari, *Aletelogia*, pp. 18f. and the dedicatory letter of Artusi, *Seconda parte dell'Artusi*.

9.　*Il Trimerone, de fondamenti armonici overo lo esercizio musicale. Dialoghi ne quai si ragiona, de tuoni antichi, e moderni e de caratteri diversi usitati da musici in tutti i tempi*, Bologna, Civico museo bibliografico musicale, Ms. B-44.

10.　See *Lettera di Fiderico Verdicelli*, fol. 227r and *Aletelogia*, p. 19.

11.　*Il Melone. Discorso armonico & Il Melone secondo, considerationi musicali sopra un discorso di M. Gandolfo Sigonio intorno à' madrigali, & à' libri dell'Antica musica ridutta alla moderna prattica di D. Nicola Vicentino. E nel fine esso Discorso del Sigonio* (Ferrara: Vittorio Baldini, 1602).

12.　Sigonio is also mentioned in Bottrigari's *Lettera di Fiderico Verdicelli*, fols. 134v-135r. A correspondence between Sigonio and Melone is preserved in Paris, Bibliothèque Nationale, Ms. Italien 1110. See Edward E. Lowinsky, "Willaert's Chromatic 'Duo' Re-Examined," *Tijdschrift de Vereeniging voor Nederlandsche Muziekgeschiedenis*, XVIII (1956), 6. See also Nan Cooke Carpenter, *Music in the Medieval and Renaissance Universities* (Norman: University of Oklahoma Press, 1958), p. 355 and Henry William Kaufmann, *The Life and Works of Nicola Vicentino (1511-c.1576)*, Musicological Studies and Documents 11 (n.p.: American Institute of Musicology, 1966), pp. 97ff.

13.　The Artusi-Monteverdi controversy was studied by Denis Arnold, "Seconda Pratica: A Background to Monteverdi's Madrigals," *Music and Letters*, XXXVIII (1957), 341-352; Giuseppe Massera, "Dalle 'imperfezioni' alle 'perfezioni' della moderna musica," in Raffaello Monterosso, ed., *Congresso internazionale sul tema Claudio Monteverdi e il suo tempo. Relazioni e communicazioni. Venezia-Mantova-Cremona, 3-7 maggio 1968* (Verona: Stamperia Valdonega, 1969), pp. 397-408; Claude V. Palisca, "The Artusi-Monteverdi Controversy," in Denis Arnold and Nigel Fortune, eds., *The Monteverdi Companion* (New York: W. W. Norton and Company, Inc., 1968), pp. 133-166.

14.　L'Ottuso's identity is discussed by Palisca, "The Artusi-Monteverdi Controversy," pp. 142-45; by Stuart Reiner in his review of *The Monteverdi Companion* in *Journal of the American Musicological Society*, XXIII (1970), 344f.; and by Anthony Newcomb, "Alfonso Fontanelli and the Ancestry of the Seconda Pratica Madrigal," in Robert L. Marshall, ed., *Studies in Renaissance and Baroque Music in Honor of Arthur Mendel* (Kassel: Bärenreiter, 1974), pp. 67f.

15.　The letter is reprinted in Claudio Monteverdi, *Lettere, dediche e prefazioni*, ed. Domenico de' Paoli (Roma: Edizioni De Santis, 1973), pp. 391f.

16.　The "Dichiarattione" which contains the information about Artusi's *Discorso* is reprinted in Moteverdi, *op.cit.*, pp. 394-404 and trans. in Oliver Strunk, *Source Readings in Music History* (New York: W. W. Norton and Company, Inc., 1950), pp. 405-412.

17.　*Il Melone*, pp. 3f.

18.　*Ibid.*, pp. 16-25.

19. *Ibid.*, p. 38.

20. *Il Desiderio*, pp. 19ff. and 28. All references are to the second edition of 1599.

21. *Ibid.*, p. 6.

22. *Ibid.*, pp. 6f.

23. *Ibid.*, pp. 10ff. and 5.

24. *Ibid.*, p. 8.

25. ". . . sopranominato l'Arcimusico, per haver egli rinovata la consideratione di questi tre Generi, di due de' quali non era homai piu memoria alcuna appresso, non sò s'io mi debba dire de gli huomini, ò solamente de' Musici pratici; percioche de' Musici Teorici, ò specolativi, de' quali hoggidì se ne trovano pochissimi, eglino sono, & sempre saranno;" *Ibid.*, p. 40, tr. by Carol MacClintock in Hercole Bottrigari, *Il Desiderio or Concerning the Playing Together of Various Musical Instruments*, Musicological Studies and Documents 9 (n.p.: American Institute of Musicology, 1962), pp. 50f. Hereafter the translation will be referred to as MacClintock.

26. ". . . egli non viene, se non di rado usato per la gran difficoltà, che è parte nell'accordarlo, & accordato nel mantenerlo, parte nel sonarlo;" *Il Desiderio*, p. 41, trans. by MacClintock, p. 51.

27. ". . . all'hora che il Luzzasco Organista principale di sua Altezza, lo maneggia molto delicatamente, con alcune compositioni di Musica fatte da lui à questo proposito solo." *Il Desiderio*, p. 41, trans. by MacClintock, p. 51.

28. ". . . da Pratico Aristossenico piu tosto, che da vero, & buono Teorico Tolomaico." *Il Desiderio*, p. 41, trans. by MacClintock, p. 51.

29. ". . . oltra questo, non sono se non dui tali Arciorgani cosi anco questi nominati da lui, uno in Roma fatto già fabricare dal Cardinale di Ferrara Fel. memoria Zio di sua Altezza, & di esso Don Nicola benefattore, & patrone sotto la cura di lui: & un'altro similmente fabricato, pur sotto la cura di Don Nicola in Milano, dov'egli poi morì l'anno seguente, doppo quello atrocissimo contaggio. . . ." *Il Desiderio*, p. 41, trans. by MacClintock, pp. 51f.

30. *Il Patricio*, p. 35.

31. *Il Melone secondo*, pp. 3f.

32. "dallo universal consenso stimato non solamente il più artificioso: ma il più leggiadro, & polito Componitore in Musica de' nostri tempi." *Ibid.*, pp. 4f.

33. "A questo avertimento importantissimo stimo, che ottima cosa sia ch'io soggiunga, che non si debba far giamai concerto alcuno di strumenti Musicali senza dargli accompagnamento

di una voce humana, & quella ben conforme sempre alla materia della cantilena: & ciò per fuggire, che tale Armonia; & concento non possa da sapiuti & intelligenti esser detta muta, ò come Aristotele, & Platone lo chiama. ciò è nudo suono di Citara, ò di Aulo, con soggiungervi tosto simigliante alle voci delle bestie, & ciò per la manchezza della espressione de gli affetti & della pronuntia delle parole; delle quali, & massimamente essendo bene imitate dall'Eccellente Musico nella sua cantilena, veramente deriva il maggiore de tutti i commovimenti de gli animi delle persone ascoltratrici." *Il Desiderio*, p. 12, trans. by MacClintock, p. 23.

34.   *Il Melone*, pp. 28-33.

35.   *L'Artusi*, fols. 16r-16v.

36.   *Ibid.*, fol. 20r.

37.   *Ibid.*, fols, 15v-16r.

38.   *Ibid.*, fol. 16r.

39.   "Et è da avertire, che non si deve considerare la Constitutione delli tre generi, nella divisione della Diatessaron, come di già facevano; ma solamente quella del genere Diatonico; & la Constitutione del genere Cromatico, nella divisione del Tuono; & quello dell'Enarmonico, nella divisione del Semituono: che l'uno bisogna dividere in dui Semituoni, & l'altro in un Semituono minore, & un Diesis, se bene sono ambidui col nome di Diesis nominati." *Ibid.*, fol. 18v.

40.   *Ibid.*, fols. 18v-19r.

41.   *Ibid.*, fols. 37v-38r.

42.   Kaufmann, *The Life and Works of Nicola Vicentino*, pp. 173f.

43.   *L'Artusi*, fols. 20r-20v, 37r.

44.   "Voglio concludervi che Don Nicola havea ragione, à tenere questa Conclusione; Che la Musica, che si canta & suona sia una mescolanza, di diversi generi insieme; ma il non saperla dire per le sue cause propinque, le fecero ben perdere la scomessa fatta col Lusitanio." *Ibid.*, fol. 38r.

45.   *Ibid.*, fol. 32v. Artusi refers to Francisco Salinas, *De Musica* (Salamanca: Mathias Gastius, 1577), III.xii, pp. 135-139.

46.   "Mentre che io vado considerando, che li pratici più Moderni non conoscono differenza alcuna de Tuoni, nè di Semituoni; ma tutti dividono con ✻, & ♭ bolli, . . . vado anco pensando, che loro stessi non conoscano qual sia quella spetie d'Harmonia, che si Canti, e Suoni; se bene si può iudicare, che habbino opinione di seguitare Aristosseno, che dividea il Tuono apunto in due parti eguali: Argomento certissimo ve ne darà quella Cantilena fatta à due voci di M. Adriano . . . nè sarà molto lontano da questo molti Madrigali del

Porta, di Cipriano, del Gabrielli, & altri tanti e tanti. . . ." *L'Artusi* fol. 20v.

47. Artusi prints and discusses the piece in *ibid.*, fols. 20v-25v. For modern discussions see Joseph S. Levitan, "Adrian Willaert's Famous Duo *Quidnam ebrietas.* A Composition which Closes Apparently with the Interval of a Seventh," *Tijdschrift van de Vereniging voor Nederlandsche Muziekgeschiedenis*, XV (1939), 166-233; Edward E. Lowinsky, "Willaert's Chromatic 'Duo' Re-Examined," *Tijdschrift van de Vereniging voor Nederlandsche Muziekgeschiedenis*, XVIII (1956), 1-36; Lowinsky, "Echoes of Adrian Willaert's Chromatic 'Duo' in Sixteenth- and Seventeenth-Century Compositions," in Harold Powers, ed., *Studies in Music History. Essays for Oliver Strunk* (Princeton: Princeton University Press, 1968), pp. 183-238.

48. It was accepted by Lowinsky in the articles referred to in the preceding footnote.

49. *L'Artusi*, fols. 25v, 27v.

50. *Ibid.*, fols. 26r-27v.

51. "se bene essi non la conoscono, nè sanno esplicarla." *Ibid.*, fol. 37r. See also *ibid.*, fols. 30r-31v, 34r-34v, 36v-37r.

52. *Ibid.*, fols. 7r, 10v-11r.

53. *Ibid.*, fol. 15v. See also Bottrigari's remark of 1602: ". . . the *archicembalo* of the arch-musician Nicola Vicentino that, one reads, is now in hands of Sig. Goretto in Ferrara. . . ." (". . . lo archicembalo dello arcimusico Nicola Vincentino, che ora si legge essere in mano del Sig. Goretto in Ferrara. . . .") *Lettera di Fiderico Verdicelli*, fols. 138r-138v.

54. "Ma se si potesse ridure il Clavacembalo alla temperatura de gli Tuoni eguali, & li Semituoni similmente eguali; sentiresti una insolita Harmonia: ma mi raccordo d'haver temperato per una ottava intiera, in quella maggior essatezza che sia stato possibile, un Clavacembalo con un Liuto; ma Sonato per esser fuori della sua natural temperatura, offendeva oltramodo l'udito." *L'Artusi*, fols. 27r-27v.

55. *Seconda parte dell'Artusi*, "Nona Consideratione," pp. 29-34.

56. ". . . se bene può [la voce] piegarsi dove le piace; non può giustamente dividere il tuono in due parti eguali, e quelle modulare in maniera che faccino quello effetto, che ne gl'instromenti si sentono; però mi pare errore che quelle cose, che dalla natura non possono essere adoprate senza sua offesa, gl'inventori di cosi fatte confusioni, ne voglino empire le carte, solo per fare il bell'ingegno; non considerando, che altre sono le cose naturali, & altre le accidentali." *Ibid.*, p. 31.

57. *Ibid.*, pp. 32-34.

58. *L'Artusi*, fols. 16r, 17r.

59. *Ibid.*, fols. 16v-17r and Bottrigari, *Il Desiderio*, pp. 22f.

60.   *L'Artusi*, fols. 27v-29r.

61.   See p. 49 above.

62.   "Oltra di questo voglio che sappiate, che questi generi hanno tra di loro quella convenienza, & rispetto che ha l'ottimo al migliore; & questo al buono; può stare il buono da se solo, & può haver l'essere senza che vi sia il migliore, e l'ottimo; ma il migliore, non può esser migliore se non rispetto al buono; ne l'ottimo può da se stesso haver l'essere senza il migliore e il buono: E sta il buono adunque come principio, e fondamento del migliore, & dell'ottimo; e 'l buono, & il migliore hanno perfettione nell'ottimo. Cosi diciamo al proposito nostro, che il Diatonico può stare, & hà l'essere da se solo; perche egli è creato dalla natura, & per molto tempo è stato essercitato nell'esser suo naturale. . . . Questo [genere Cromatico] si vede che non può stare in modo alcuno per se solo, senza il Diatonico; non essendo lui altro che il Diatonico inspessato: & perche mollifica la duritie di quello, di qui è, che s'acquisto il nome di migliore & più perfetto. L'Enarmonico similmente, non può per se stesso haver l'essere; perche questo et quello sono fabricati sopra il Diatonico, ma questo è più spesso del Cromatico." *L'Artusi*, fol. 19r. Cf. also *ibid.*, fols. 37r-37v.

63.   "Chi lascia la via vecchia per la nova, spesso ingannato si ritrova. Il che intravenne à D. Nicola Vicentino, che si provò di volere introdurre, che tutti tre li generi si cantassero, la qual cosa per la difficoltà sua; e per il poco piacere, che ne riceveva il senso dell'udito, non hebbe quel felice successo, che si pensava. . . ." *Seconda parte dell'Artusi*, p. 4.

64.   *L'Artusi*, fol. 16r.

65.   See, e.g., *ibid.*, fols. 15r-16r, 20v.

66.   *Ibid.*, fols. 37v and 16r.

67.   *Ibid.*, fols. 48r-48v.

68.   *Sopplimenti musicali* (Venice: Francesco de' Franceschi, Sanese, 1588), Book VI, Ch. 9, p. 265.

69.   *L'Artusi*, fol. 16r. See also *ibid.*, fol. 20v.

70.   ". . . chi'io non faccio le mie cose a caso. . . ." Claudio Monteverdi, Letter prefacing his *Il quinto libro de madrigali a cinque voci* (Venice: Ricciardo Amadino, 1605), reprinted in Monteverdi, *Lettere, dediche e prefazioni* p. 391, trans. in Strunk, *op.cit.*, p. 406.

71.   ". . . fabrica sopra li fondamenti della verità." Monteverdi, *op.cit.*, p. 392, trans. in Strunk, *op.cit.*, pp. 411f.

72.   ". . . è stato il primo rinovatore ne nostri caratteri il Divino Cipriano Rore, . . . seguitata, e ampliata, non solamente da li Signori detti, ma dal Ingegneri, dal Marenzo, da Giaches Wert, dal Luzzasco, e parimente da Giaccopo Peri, da Giulio Caccini e finalmente da li spiriti più elevati, e intendenti de la vera arte, . . ." ". . . perfettionata ultimamente da

Messer Adriano con l'atto prattico, e dal Eccellentissimo Zarlino con regole giudiciosissime;'' Giulio Cesare Monteverdi, ''Dichiaratione della lettera stampata nel quinto libro de suoi madrigali,'' in Claudio Monteverdi, *Scherzi musicali a tre voci* (Venice: Ricciardo Amadino, 1607), reprinted in Claudio Monteverdi, *Lettere, dediche e prefazioni*, p. 399, trans. in Strunk, *op.cit.*, p. 408.

73. ''prima prattica intende che sia quella che versa intorno alla perfettione del armonia; cioè che considera l'armonia non comandata, ma comandante, e non serva ma signora del oratione, . . . Seconda prattica, . . . intende che sia quella che versa intorno alla perfettione della melodia, cioè che considera l'armonia comandata, e non comandante, e per signora dell'armonia pone l'oratione, . . .'' Giulio Cesare Monteverdi, *op.cit.*, pp. 398f., trans. in Strunk, *op.cit.*, pp. 408f.

74. ''. . . del che parlando Platone, dice queste parole, Melodiam ex tribus constare, oratione, harmonia, Rithmo e poco più a basso Quin etiam consonum ipsum et dissonum eodem modo, quando-quidem Rithmus et Harmonia orationem sequitur non ipsa oratio Rithum et Harmoniam sequitur.'' Giulio Cesare Monteverdi, *op.cit.*, p. 396, trans. in Strunk, *op.cit.*, pp. 406f.

75. ''Il fine del Musico, e quello del Poeta tutto è uno. . . . Il fine del Poeta è di giovare, & dilettare; adunque quello del Cantore, ò Sonatore sarà di giovare, & dilettare.'' *L'Artusi*, fols. 4r-4v.

76. *Le Istitutioni harmoniche* (Venice: n.p., 1558), Part I, Chs. 3-4, pp. 8ff.

77. *Seconda parte dell'Artusi*, p. 10.

78. ''Non è pero necessario, che questa Musica facci il miracolo di suscitar morti; cagionerà affetto, cioè desiderio con la novità della sua modulatione. . . .'' *Ibid.*, p. 17.

79. *Ibid.*, p. 19.

IV. CONCLUSION

1. This is attested primarily by the fact that intervals distant by an octave are used similarly in sixteenth-century counterpoint. The existence of octave equivalence is implied by many theorists, both ''conservative'' and ''progressive.'' See e.g. Ghiselin Danckerts, *Trattato sopra una differentia musicale*, Rome, Biblioteca Vallicelliana, Ms. R. 56, Part III, Ch. 3, fol. 408r; Vincenzo Galilei, *Trattato dell' Arte del Contrapunto*, Florence, Bibl. Naz. Cent., Ms. Gal. 1, fols. 65v-66r. See also p. 3 above.

2. Quoted from the modern edition in Luca Marenzio, *Sämtliche Werke*, ed. Alfred Einstein, Vol. I (Leipzig: Breitkopf & Härtel, 1929), pp. 69f. The madrigal originally appeared in Marenzio, *Il secondo libro de madrigali a cinque voci* (Venice: Angelo Gardano, 1581).

3. Some examples of enharmonically equivalent notation in music of Gesualdo and his contemporaries are discussed in Carl Dahlhaus, ''Domenico Belli und der chromatische Kontrapunkt um 1600,'' *Die Musikforschung*, XV (1962), 315-340.

4. See J. Murray Barbour, *Timing and Temperament. A Historical Survey*, 2nd ed. (East Lansing: Michigan State College Press, 1953), p. 8.

5. Note, however, that the distinction between the authentic and plagal is often observed in the titles of polyphonic works of the sixteenth century, since such features of the traditional plainchant modal theory as, for instance, the reciting pitches (which are different in corresponding authentic and plagal modes) may account for certain aspects of polyphonic works as well, for example, for the choice of pitches on which to place structurally important internal cadences. See e.g., Leeman L. Perkins, "Mode and Structure in the Masses of Josquin," *Journal of the American Musicological Society*, XXVI (1973), 189-239 and Bernhard Meier, *Die Tonarten der klassischen Vokalpolyphonie* (Utrecht: Oosthoek, Scheltema & Holkema, 1974).

6. *Le Istitutioni harmoniche* (Venice: n.p., 1558), Part IV, Chs. 18-29, pp. 320-335 [392-415].

7. Vicentino's discussion of "modal architecture" is quoted at length on pp. 32f. above.

8. Transcribed from the unique sixteenth-century source of ca. 1560, possibly Lasso's autograph, Vienna, Österreichische Nationalbibliothek, Ms. mus. 18744, fol. 23r. (Cantus, Tenor), 25r. (Altus), 22r. (Bassus). For a modern edition, see Orlando Lasso, *Prophetiae Sibyllarum*, ed. Joachim Therstappen, Das Chorwerk 48 (Wolfenbüttel: Möseler Verlag, 1937), p. 5. The piece originally appeared in Orlando de Lasso, *Prophetiae Sibyllarum* (Munich: Nicolaus Henricus, 1600). It is discussed in Wolfgang Boetticher, *Orlando di Lasso und seine Zeit 1532-1594*, Vol. I (Kassel and Basel: Bärenreiter-Verlag, 1958), pp. 71-79 and in Horst Leuchtmann, *Orlando di Lasso*, Vol. I (Wiesbaden: Breitkopf & Härtel, 1976), pp. 124-34. For other discussions see nn. 9, 14-15 below.

9. *Tonality and Atonality in Sixteenth-Century Music* (Berkeley and Los Angeles: The University of California Press, 1961), p. 39.

10. See Joel Lester, "Root-Position and Inverted Triads in Theory around 1600," *Journal of the American Musicological Society*, XXVII (1974), 110-19.

11. For a particularly persuasive warning against the anachronistic use of the concept of "triad" see Carl Dahlhaus, *Untersuchungen über die Entstehung der harmonischen Tonalität*, Saarbrücker Studien zur Musikwissenschaft 2 (Kassel: Bärenreiter, 1967), pp. 57-140.

12. See Joel Lester, "Major-Minor Concepts and Modal Theory in Germany, 1592-1680," *Journal of the American Musicological Society*, XXX (1977), 208-53.

13. Cf. William J. Mitchell's remarks quoted on p. 112 below. Mitchell's remarks might be amplified by an observation that the tenor's g's are the only notes in these first two measures which are heard in metrically strong position.

14. *Journal of the American Musicological Society*, XVI (1963), 84f.

15. "The Prologue to Orlando di Lasso's *Prophetiae Sibyllarum*," *The Music Forum*, II (1970), 267ff.

16. For a general introduction to the method see especially Heinrich Schenker, *Der freie Satz*, 2nd ed. (Vienna: Universal Edition, 1956) and Felix Salzer, *Structural Hearing: Tonal Coherence in Music*, 2nd ed. (New York: Dover Publications, Inc., 1962). Salzer's version of the theory is particularly relevant here, since it represents the most influential attempt to apply Schenker's ideas to pre-eighteenth-century music.

17. Mitchell, *op. cit.*, pp. 266f.

18. "Gesualdos 'Atonalität' und das Problem des musikalischen Manierismus," *Archiv für Musikwissenschaft*, XXIX (1972), 1-16.

19. *Ibid.*, pp. 7f.

20. In Henrich Hüschen and Dietz-Rüdiger Moser, eds., *Convivium musicorum: Festschrift Wolfgang Boetticher zum sechzigsten Geburtstag am 19. August 1974* (Berlin: Merseburger, 1974), p. 39.

21. "Zur chromatischen Technik Carlo Gesualdos," *Analecta Musicologica*, IV (1967), 77.

22. *Ibid.*, pp. 80f. See also Dahlhaus, "Relationes harmonicae," *Archiv für Musikwissenschaft*, XXXII (1975), 208-27.

23. Carlo Valgulio, *Plutarchi Chaeronei philosophi historicique clarissimi opuscula (quae quidem extant) omnia, undequaque collecta, et diligentissime jam pridem recognita* (Venice: Jo. Ant. et Fratres de Sabio, 1532).

24. See especially D. P. Walker, *Spiritual and Demonic Magic from Ficino to Campanella* (London: The Warburg Institute, 1958) and Frances A. Yates, *Giordano Bruno and the Hermetic Tradition* (Chicago: The University of Chicago Press, 1964).

25. Walker, *op.cit.*, pp. 12-24.

26. *Ibid.*, pp. 25f.

27. *Ibid.*, pp. 28f.

28. "Non è però necessario, che questa Musica facci il miracolo di suscitar morti; cagionerà bene affetto; cioè desiderio con la novità della sua modulatione d'udir bene spesso simil sorte di concento, più atto à mover l'animo nostro con la novità sua in questa nova pratica, che nella passata come quella che con più efficacia ferisce il senso. Ma dove vo io vagando à dimostrare, che nella Musica, ò da questo concento, ne venghino tutti questi . . . moti, ciò facci chiaro la autorità di Marsilio Ficino nel Compendio sopra il Timeo di Platone, il quale in questo proposito dice. *Concentus autem per aeream naturam in motu positam movet corpus. Et ecco il moto, che s'appartiene al corpo, & poscia. Per purificatum aerem concitat spiritum* [aereum] *animi* [sic! should be: animae] *corporisque modum* [sic! should be: nodum]. Ecco il moto dell'uno, e l'altro insieme. *Per affectum afficit sensum simul & animum.* Eccone un'altro moto simile; & più sotto. *Per conformem*

qualitatem, mira quadam voluptate profundit. Ecco il moto di mesto in allegro; & nel concludere dice. *Per naturam tam spiritualem, quam materialem totum simul rapit, & simul vendicat hominem.* Et ecco in uno concluso tutti gli moti, & le passioni si dell'animo, come del corpo.'' Giovanni Maria Artusi, *Seconda parte dell'Artusi overo delle imperfettioni della moderna musica* (Venice: Giacomo Vincenti, 1603), pp. 17f. Ficino's text is emended in square brackets according to Marsilio Ficino, *Opera omnia* (Basel: ex officina Henricpetrina, 1576), p. 1453. It is translated in Walker, *op. cit.*, p. 9: ''. . . musical sound by the movement of the air moves the body: by purified air it excites the aerial spirit which is the bond of body and soul: by emotion it affects the senses and at the same time the soul: . . . by the conformity of its quality it floods us with a wonderful pleasure: by its nature, both spiritual and material, it at once seizes, and claims as its own, man in his entirety.''

29.   ''Dichiaratione della lettera stampata nel quinto libro de suoi madrigali,'' in Claudio Monteverdi, *Scherzi musicali a tre voci* (Venice: Ricciardo Amadino, 1607), trans. in Oliver Strunk, *Source Readings in Music History* (New York: W. W. Norton and Company, Inc., 1950), pp. 405-12. Strunk notes that ''Monteverdi quotes Plato in the Latin translation of Marsilio Ficino.'' *Ibid.*, p. 407, n. 3. Monteverdi's use of Plato is discussed by Claude V. Palisca, ''The Artusi-Monteverdi Controversy,'' in Denis Arnold and Nigel Fortune, eds., *The Monteverdi Companion* (New York: W. W. Norton and Company, Inc., 1968), pp. 160-63.

30.   See Yates, *op. cit.*, pp. 85f.

31.   Palisca, ''The Artusi-Monteverdi Controversy,'' pp. 161f.

32.   *Trattato dell'Arte del Contrapunto*, fols. 146r-147r.

33.   Palisca, *The Beginnings of Baroque Music. Its Roots in 16th-Century Theory and Polemics*, unpublished Ph.D. diss., Harvard University, 1954, pp. 92-101. The author discusses a letter of Bishop Cirillo Franco of Loreto dating from 1549 who attacks the contrapuntal church music for its failure to inspire the proper attitude of devotion and advocates the imitation of ancient Greek practices. Franco considers his critique to be aimed also at secular music and wants music to experience the same rebirth that letters and arts have. He also advocates the restoration of the non-diatonic genera. The aim is to create harmonies that move affections of listeners. Franco's letter is also discussed in K.G. Fellerer, ''Church Music at the Council of Trent,'' *The Musical Quarterly*, XXXIX (1953), 576-94. The letter was published in Aldo Manuzio, ed., *Lettere volgari di diversi nobilissimi huomini, et eccellentissimi ingegni, scritte in diverse materie*, Vol. III (Venice: Aldus, 1564), fols. 114r-118v. This was the first edition of this volume according to Antoine-Augustine Renouard, *Annales de l'imprimerie des Aldes, ou Histoire des trois Manuces et de leurs Éditions*, Vol. I (Paris: Renouard, 1803), pp. 343f. The letter was recently published in Pierluigi da Palestrina, *Pope Marcellus Mass*, ed. Lewis Lockwood (New York: Norton, 1975), pp. 10-16.

34.   For the history of the concept of world harmony see Leo Spitzer, *Classical and Christian Ideas of World Harmony. Prolegomena to an Interpretation of the Word ''Stimmung''* (Baltimore: The Johns Hopkins Press, 1963). That the divorce of value and fact, the discarding of all considerations based on value-concepts, such as the harmony, is implied

by modern science, was stressed in Alexandre Koyré, *From the Closed World to the Infinite Universe* (Baltimore: The Johns Hopkins Press, 1957). See also Marius Schneider, "Die musikalischen Grundlagen der Sphärenharmonie," *Acta Musicologica*, XXXII (1960), 136-51.

35. Cf. Koyré, *op. cit., passim.*

36. "Per lo che vengo a dire, esser non men difficile a descriver con parole, o dimostrare realmente per via di numeri, o di linee il Sistema che noi usiamo nell'esatta sua forma & proportione; . . . quanto è difficile con terminati periodi, e stabili canoni regolare & proportionare tra di loro i moti de corpi celesti. & questa è forse buona parte della convenienza che Pitagora giudicò esser tra la celeste & l'umana Armonia." *Discorso intorno all'opere di messer Gioseffo Zarlino da Chioggia, et altri importanti particolari attenenti alla musica* (Florence: Giorgio Marescotti, 1589), p. 118.

37. Cf. Marin Mersenne, *Harmonie universelle* (Paris: S. Cramoisy, 1636-37) and Johannes Kepler, *Harmonices mundi* (Linz: Joannes Plancus, 1619).

38. John Hollander, *The Untuning of the Sky. Ideas of Music in English Poetry, 1500-1700* (New York: W. W. Norton and Company, Inc., 1970).

Bibliography

Aldrich, Putnam. "An Approach to the Analysis of Renaissance Music." *The Music Review*, XXX (1969), 1-21.

Allaire, Gaston G. *The Theory of Hexachords, Solmization and the Modal System: A Practical Application*. N.p.: American Institute of Musicology, 1972.

Anfuso, Nella and Gianuario, Annibale. *Preparatione alla Interpretatione della 'Poìesis' Monteverdiana*. Florence: OTOS, 1971.

Anonymous. "Del libro chiamato il Patricio overo de' Tetracordi d'Hercole Butrigario." Milan, Biblioteca Ambrosiana, Ms. misc. I 129 Inf., fols. 292v-298r.

Arnold, Denis. "Seconda Pratica: A Background to Monteverdi's Madrigals." *Music and Letters*, XXXVIII (1957), 341-352.

———— and Fortune, Nigel, eds. *The Monteverdi Companion*. New York: W. W. Norton and Company, 1968.

Artusi, Giovanni Maria. *L'Artusi, overo delle imperfettioni della moderna musica*. Venice: Giacomo Vincenti, 1600.

————. *Seconda parte dell'Artusi overo delle imperfettioni della moderna musica*. Venice: Giacomo Vincenti, 1603.

————. *Discorso secondo musicale di Antonio Braccino da Todi per la dichiaratione della lettera posta ne' Scherzi musicali del Sig. Claudio Monteverde*. Venice: Giacomo Vincenti, 1608.

Barbour, J. Murray. *Tuning and Temperament. A Historical Survey*. 2nd ed.; East Lansing: Michigan State College Press, 1953.

Bardi, Giovanni de'. *Discorso mandato a Caccini sopra la musica antica e 'l cantar bene*. Vatican, Biblioteca Apostolica Vaticana, Ms. Barberinianus latinus 3990, fols. 4r-13v and in Giovanni Battista Doni, *Lyra Barberina*, Vol. II (Florence: Stamperia imperiale, 1763), pp. 233-48.

Benedetti, Giovanni Battista. *Diversarum speculationum mathematicarum & physiocorum liber*. Turin: apud Haeredem Nicolai Bevilaquae, 1585.

Bergquist, Peter. "Mode and Polyphony around 1500: Theory and Practice." *The Music Forum*, I (1967), 99-161.

Boalch, Donald H. *Makers of the Harpsichord and Clavichord, 1440 to 1840*. London: George Ronald, 1956.

Boetticher, Wolfgang. *Orlando di Lasso und seine Zeit 1532-1594*, Vol. I. Kassel and Basel: Bärenreiter-Verlag, 1958.

Bonhôte, Jean-Marc. "Resonance musicale d'une villa de Palladio." *Musica Disciplina*, XXV (1971), 171-78.

Bottrigari, Ercole. *Il Patricio, overo de' tetracordi armonici di Aristosseno, parere, et vera dimostratione*. Bologna: Vittorio Benacci, 1593.

————. *Il Desiderio overo de' concerti di varii strumenti musicali*. Venice: Ricciardo Amadino, 1594.

————. *Il Desiderio or Concerning the Playing Together of Various Musical Instruments*. Musicological Studies and Documents 9. N.p.: American Institute of Musicology, 1962.

————. *Il Trimerone, de fondamenti armonici overo lo esercizio musicale dialoghi ne quai si ragiona, de tuoni antichi, e moderni e de caratteri diversi usitati da musici in tutti i tempi* (Bologna, 1599). Bologna, Civico museo bibliografico musicale, Ms. B-44.

————. *Il Melone. Discorso armonico & Il Melone secondo, considerationi musicali sopra un discorso di M. Gandolfo Sigonio intorno à' madrigali, & à' libri dell'Antica musica ridutta alla moderna prattica di D. Nicola Vicentino. E nel fine esso Discorso del Sigonio*. Ferrara: Vittorio Baldini, 1602.

————. *Lettera di Federico Verdicelli a' benigni, e sinceri lettori in difesa del Sig.e Caval:e Hercole Bottrigaro contra quanto in pregiudicio della rifutazione di lui ha scritto un certo Artusi in due sue lettere una per dedicatoria all 'Ill.mo Senato di Bologna l'altra à cortesi lettori sotto la data di Milano à 12 di luglio 1601 & stampate in Milano appresso gli stampatori archiepis* (Bologna, 1602). Bologna, Biblioteca Universitaria, Ms. 326, fols. 130r-143v.

————. *Aletelogia di Leonardo Gallucio à' benigni, e sinceri lettori. Lettera apologetica* (Bologna, 1604). Bologna, Civico museo bibliografico musicale, Ms. B-43.

Boyd, Malcolm. "Structural Cadences in the Sixteenth-Century Mass." *The Music Review*, XXXIII (1972), 1-13.

Brandes, Heinz. *Studien zur musikalischen Figurenlehre im 16. Jahrhundert*. Ph.D. dissertation. Friedrich-Wilhelms-Universität, Berlin. Berlin: Triltsch und Hunther, 1935.

Brink, Paul Robert. *The Archicembalo of Nicola Vicentino*. Unpublished Ph.D. dissertation. The Ohio State University, 1966.

Bruyn, J. de. "Ghisilinus Danckerts, kapelaanzager van de Pauselijke kapel van 1538 tot 1565." *Tijdschrift der Vereeniging voor nederlandsche Muziekgeschiedenis*, XVI (1946), 217-252; XVII (1949), 128-157.

Bullivant, Roger. "The Nature of Chromaticism." *The Music Review*, XXIV (1963), 97-129, 279-304.

Carapetyan, Armen. "The Concept of Imitazione della Natura in the Sixteenth Century." *Journal of Renaissance and Baroque Music*, I (1946), 47-67.

Carpenter, Nan Cooke. *Music in the Medieval and Renaissance Universities*. Norman: University of Oklahoma Press, 1958.

Cattin, Giulio. "Nel quarto centenario di Nicola Vicentino teorico e compositore." *Studi Musicali*, V (1976), 29-57.

Chailley, Jacques. "Esprit et technique du chromatisme de la Renaissance," in Jean Jacquot, ed., *Musique et poésie au XVIe siècle*. Paris: Éditions du Centre National de la Recherche Scientifique, 1954, pp. 225-239.

Chiereghin, Salvino. "Zarlino." *Rivista Musicale Italiana*, XXXVII (1930), 21-37.

Chilesotti, Oscar. "Di Nicola Vicentino e dei generi greci secondo Vincentio Galilei." *Rivista Musicale Italiana*, XIX (1912), 546-65.

Clough, John. "The Leading Tone in Direct Chromaticism: From Renaissance to Baroque." *Journal of Music Theory*, I (1957), 2-21.

————. "Indirect Chromaticism in the Renaissance." *Journal of Music Theory*, III (1959), 147-150.

Crocker, Richard L. "Perchè Zarlino diede una nuova numerazione ai modi?" *Rivista Italiana di Musicologia*, III (1968), 48-58.

Dahlhaus, Carl. "War Zarlino Dualist?" *Die Musikforschung*, X (1957), 286-90.

————. "Domenico Belli und der chromatische Kontrapunkt um 1600." *Die Musikforschung*, XV (1962), 315-40.

————. "Zu Costeleys chromatischer Chanson." *Die Musikforschung*, XVI (1963), 253-65.

————. *Untersuchungen über die Entstehung der harmonischen Tonalität*. Saabrücker Studien zur Musikwissenschaft 2r. Kassel: Bärenreiter, 1967.

————. "Zur chromatischen Technik Carlo Gesualdos." *Analecta Musicologica*, IV (1967), 77-96.

————. "Gesualdos manieristische Dissonanztechnik," in Heinrich Hüschen and Dietz-Rüdiger Moser, eds., *Convivium musicorum. Festschrift Wolfgang Boetticher zum sechzigsten Geburtstag am 19. August 1974.* Berlin: Verlag Merseburger, 1974, pp. 34-43.

————. "Relationes harmonicae." *Archiv für Musikwissenschaft,* XXXII (1975), 208-27.

————. "Zur Tonartenlehre des 16. Jahrhunderts. Eine Duplik." *Die Musikforschung,* XXIX (1976), 300-303.

Danckerts, Ghiselin. *Trattato sopra una differentia musicale.* Rome: Biblioteca Vallicelliana, Ms. R. 56.

Daniels, Arthur Michael. *The 'De Musica Libri VII' of Francisco de Salinas.* Unpublished Ph.D. dissertation. University of Southern California, 1962.

————. "Microtonality and Mean-Tone Temperament in the Harmonic System of Francisco Salinas." *Journal of Music Theory,* IX (1965), 2-51, 234-80.

Drake, Stillman. "Renaissance Music and Experimental Science." *Journal of the History of Ideas,* XXXI (1970), 483-500.

————. *Galileo Studies: Personality, Tradition, and Revolution.* Ann Arbor: University of Michigan Press, 1970.

————. "Galilei, Vincenzio," in Charles Coulston Gillispie, ed., *Dictionary of Scientific Biography,* Vol. V. New York: Charles Scribner's Sons, 1972, pp. 249f.

Dürr, Walter. Review of Vicentino, *L'antica musica,* facs, ed. Edward E. Lowinsky. *Die Musikforschung,* XIV (1955), 446-48.

————. "Zur mehrstimmigen Behandlung des chromatischen Schrittes in der Polyphonie des 16. Jahrhunderts." *Kongress-Bericht, Kassel, 1962.* Kassel: Bärenreiter, 1963, pp. 136-38.

Einstein, Alfred. *The Italian Madrigal,* 3 vols. Princeton: Princeton University Press, 1949.

Elders, Willem. *Studien zur Symbolik in der Musik der alten Niederländer.* Bilthoven: A. B. Creyghton, 1968.

Engel, Hans. *Luca Marenzio.* Florence: Olschki, 1953.

Fano, Fabio. Preface to facs. ed. of Galilei's *Dialogo.* Rome: Reale Accademia d'Italia, 1934.

————. *La Camerata fiorentina. Vincenzo Galilei 1520?-1591. La sua opera d'artista e di teorico come espressione di nuove idealità musicali.* "Istituzioni e Monumenti dell'Arte Musicale Italiana," Vol. IV. Milan: Edizioni Ricordi, 1934.

————. "Alcuna chiarimenti su Vincenzo Galilei." *La Rassegna musicale,* X (1937), 85-90.

Federhofer, Hellmut. "Der Manierismus-Begriff in der Musikgeschichte." *Studi Musicali,* III (1974), 37-53.

Fellerer, K. G. "Church Music and the Council of Trent." *The Musical Quarterly,* XXXIX (1953), 576-94.

Ficino, Marsilio. *Opera Omnia.* Basel: ex officina Henricpetrina, 1576.

Ficker, Rudolf von. "Beiträge zur Chromatik des 14. bis 16. Jahrhunderts." *Studien zur Musikwissenschaft,* II (1914), 5-33.

Finscher, Ludwig. "Gesualdos 'Atonalität' und das Problem des muskialischen Manierismus." *Archiv für Musikwissenschaft,* XXIX (1972), 1-16.

————. "Zur Problematik des Manierismus-Begriffes in der Musikgeschichtsschreibung." *Studi Musicali,* III (1974), 75-83.

Flury, Roman. *Gioseffo Zarlino als Komponist.* Winterthur: P. G. Keller, 1962.

Franco, Cirillo. Letter to Ugolino Gualteruzzi, Loreto, February 16, 1549, in Aldo Manuzio, ed., *Lettere volgari di diversi nobilissimi huomini, et eccellentissimi ingegni, scritte in diverse materie,* Vol. III. Venice: Aldus, 1564, fols. 114r-118v.

Gafurius, Franchinus. *Angelicum ac divinum opus musice.* Milan: Gotardus, 1508.

Galilei, Vincenzo. *Dialogo della musica antica, et della moderna.* Florence: Giorgio Marescotti, 1581.

————. *Discorso intorno all'opere di messer Gioseffo Zarlino da Chioggia, et altri importanti particolari attenenti alla musica.* Florence: Giorgio Marescotti, 1589.

————. *Trattato dell'Arte del Contrapunto.* Florence, Biblioteca Nazionale Centrale, Ms. Galileiani 1, fols. 55r-147v.

————. "Discorso intorno all'uso dell'Enharmonio et di chi fusse autore del Cromatico." Florence, Biblioteca Nazionale Centrale, Ms. Galileiani 3, fols. 3r-34v.

————. "Dubbi intorno a quanto io ho detto dell'uso dell'enharmonio, con la solutione di essi." Florence, Biblioteca Nazionale Centrale, Ms. Galileiani 3, fols. 62r-68r.

————. *Discorso particolare intorno all'Unisono.* Florence, Biblioteca Nazionale Centrale, Ms. Galileiani 3, fols. 55r-61v.

————. *[Critica intorno ai supplementi musicali di G. Zarlino].* Florence, Biblioteca Nazionale Centrale, Ms. Galileiani 5, fols. 1r-58r.

Gerstenberg, Walter. "Willaert," in Friedrich Blume, ed. *Die Musik in Geschichte und Gegenwart,* Vol. XIV. Kassel and Basel: Bärenreiter, 1968, cols. 662-76.

Giazotto, Remo. " 'Il Patricio' di Hercole Bottrigari dimostrato particamente da un anonimo cinquecentista." *Collectanea Historiae Musicae,* I (1953), 97-112.

Haar, James. "False Relations and Chromaticism in Sixteenth-Century Music." *Journal of the American Musicological Society,* XXX (1977), 391-418.

Harrán, Don. "Vicentino and His Rules of Text Underlay." *The Musical Quarterly,* LIX (1973), 620-32.

Herman, Robert H. *"Dialogo della musica antica et della moderna" of Vincenzo Galilei: Translation and Commentary.* Unpublished Ph.D. dissertation. North Texas State University, 1973.

Hermelinck, Siegfried. *Dispositiones Modorum. Die Tonarten in der Musik Palestrinas und seines Zeitgenossen.* Tutzing: Hans Schneider, 1960.

Högler, Fritz. "Bemerkungen zu Zarlinos Theorie." *Zeitschrift für Musikwissenschaft,* IX (1926-27), 518-27.

Hollander, John. *The Untuning of the Sky. Ideas of Music in English Poetry, 1500-1700.* New York: W. W. Norton and Company, 1970.

Jackson, Roland. "On Frescobaldi's Chromaticism and Its Background." *The Musical Quarterly,* LVII (1971), 255-69.

Jeppesen, Knud. *The Style of Palestrina and the Dissonance.* New York: Dover Publications, Inc., 1970.

————. "Eine musikhistorische Korrespondenz des frühen Cinquecento." *Acta Musicologica,* XIII (1942), 3-39.

Kämper, Dietrich. *Studien zur instrumentalen Ensemblemusik des 16. Jahrhunderts in Italien.* "Analecta Musicologica," Vol. X. Cologne and Vienna: Böhlau Verlag, 1970.

Kahl, Willi. "Das Geschichtsbewusstsein in der Musikanschauung der italienischen Renaissance und des deutschen Humanismus," in Willfried Brennecke and Hans Haase, eds. *Hans Albrecht in Memoriam. Gedenkenschrift mit Beiträgen von Freuden und Schülern.* Kassel: Bärenreiter, 1962, pp. 39-47.

Kallenbach-Greller, Lotte. "Die historischen Grundlagen der Vierteltöne." *Archiv für Musikwissenschaft,* VIII (1926), 473-85.

Kaufmann, Henry W. "Vicentino's *Arciorgano:* an Annotated Translation." *Journal of Music Theory,* V (1961), 32-53.

————. *The Life and Works of Nicola Vicentino 1511-c.1576.* Musicological Studies and Documents 11. N.p.: American Institute of Musicology, 1966.

————. "More on the Tuning of the *Archicembalo.*" *Journal of the American Musicological Society,* XXIII (1970), 84-94.

Kepler, Johannes. *Harmonices mundi.* Linz: Joannes Plancus, 1619.

Klein, Robert. *La forme et l'intelligible. Écrits sur la Renaissance et l'art moderne.* Paris: Gallimard, 1970.

Koyfe, Alexandre. *From the Closed World to the Infinite Universe.* Baltimore: The Johns Hopkins Press, 1957.

Kristeller, Paul Oskar. *Renaissance Thought: The Classic, Scholastic, and Humanistic Strains.* New York: Harper and Row, 1961.

Kroyer, Theodor. *Die Anfänge der Chromatik im italienischen Madrigal des XVI. Jahrhunderts.* Leipzig: Breitkopf & Härtel, 1902.

————. "Zum Akzidenzienproblem im Ausgang des 16. Jahrhunderts." *Kongress-Bericht, Wien, 1909,* pp. 112-24.

Lasso, Orlando di. *Prophetiae Sibyllarum.* Munich: Nicolaus Henricus, 1600.

————, *Prophetiae Sibyllarum,* ed. Joachim Therstappen, Das Chorwerk 48. Wolfenbüttel: Möseler Verlag, 1937.

Lenoble, R. *Mersenne ou la naissance du méchanisme.* Paris: Librairie Philosophique J. Vrin, 1943.

Lester, Joel. "Root-Position and Inverted Triads in Theory around 1600." *Journal of the American Musicological Society,* XXVII (1974), 110-19.

————. "Major-Minor Concepts and Modal Theory in Germany, 1592-1680." *Journal of the American Musicological Society,* XXX (1977), 208-53.

————. "The Recognition of Major and Minor Keys in German Theory: 1680-1730." *Journal of Music Theory,* XXII (1978), 65-103.

Leuchtmann, Horst. *Orlando di Lasso,* 2 vols. Wiesbaden: Breitkopf & Härtel, 1976-77.

Levitan, Joseph S. "Adrian Willaert's Famous Duo *Quidnam ebrietas.* A Composition which Closes Apparently with the Interval of a Seventh." *Tijdschrift van de Vereniging voor Nederlandsche Muziekgeschiedenis,* XV (1939), 166-233.

Levy, Kenneth J. "Costeley's Chromatic Chanson." *Annales Musicologiques,* III (1955), 213-63.

Lindley, Mark. "Early 16th-Century Keyboard Temperaments." *Musica Disciplina,* XXVIII (1974), 129-51.

Lockwood, Lewis H. "Vincenzo Ruffo and Musical Reform after the Council of Trent." *The Musical Quarterly,* XLIII (1957), 342-71.

————. "A Dispute on Accidentals in Sixteenth-Century Rome." *Analecta Musicologica,* II (1965), 24-40.

————. "On 'Mannerism' and 'Renaissance' as Terms and Concepts in Music History " *Studi Musicali,* III (1974), 85-100.

Lowinsky, Edward E. *Secret Chromatic Art in the Netherland Motet.* New York: Columbia University Press, 1946.

————. "Willaert's Chromatic 'Duo' Re-Examined." *Tijdschrift van de Vereniging voor Nederlandsche Muziekgeschiedenis,* XVIII (1956), 1-36.

————. *Tonality and Atonality in Sixteenth-Century Music.* Berkeley, and Los Angeles: The University of California Press, 1961.

———— "Echoes of Adrian Willaert's Chromatic 'Duo' in Sixteenth- and Seventeenth-Century Compositions," in Harold Powers, ed. *Studies in Music History. Essays for Oliver Strunk.* Princeton: Princeton University Press, 1968, pp. 183-238.

————. "The Musical Avant-Garde of the Renaissance or: The Peril and Profit of Foresight," in Charles S. Singleton, ed. *Art, Science, and History in the Renaissance.* Baltimore: The Johns Hopkins Press, 1967, pp. 111-62.

————. "The Problem of Mannerism in Music: An Attempt at a Definition." *Studi Musicali,* III (1974), 131-218.

Ludwig, Hellmut. *Marin Mersenne und seine Musiklehre.* Berlin: Buchandung des Waisenhauses, 1935.

Lusitano, Vincentio. *Introduttione facilissima, et novissima, di canto fermo, figurato, contraponto semplice, et in concerto.* Rome: Antonio Blado, 1553.

Maniates, Maria Rika. "Vicentino's *'Incerta et occulta scientia'* Reexamined." *Journal of the American Musicological Society,* XXVIII (1975), 335-51.

Manuzio, Aldo, ed. *Lettere volgari di diversi nobilissimi huomini, et eccellentissimi ingegni, scritte in diverse materie,* Vol. III. Venice: Aldus, 1564.

Marenzio, Luca. *Il secondo libro de madrigali a cinque voci.* Venice: Angelo Gardano, 1581.

————. *Sämtliche Werke,* ed. Alfred Einstein, Vol. I. Leipzig: Breitkopf & Härtel, 1929.

Martin, Henriette. "La 'Camerata' du Comte Bardi et la musique florentine du XVIe siècle." *Revue de musicologie*, XIII (1932), 63-74, 152-61, 227-34; XIV (1933), 92-100, 141-51.

Massera, Giuseppe. "Dalle 'imperfezioni' alle 'perfezioni' della moderna musica," in Rafaello Monterosso, ed. *Congresso internazionale sul tema Claudio Monteverdi e il suo tempo. Relazioni e comunicazioni. Venezia-Mantova-Cremona, 3-7 maggio, 1968*. Verona: Stamperia Valdonega, 1969, pp. 397-408.

Meier, Bernhard. *Die Tonarten der klassischen Vokalpolyphonie*. Utrecht: Oosthoek, Scheltema & Holkema, 1974.

Mendel, Arthur. "Pitch in the 16th and Early 17th Centuries." *The Musical Quarterly*, XXXIV (1948), 28-45, 199-221, 336-357, 575-593.

———. "Devices for Transposition in the Organ before 1600." *Acta Musicologica*, XXI (1949), 24-40.

———. "Pitch in Western Music since 1500—A Re-examination." *Acta Musicologica*, L (1978), 1-93, 328.

Mersenne, Marin. *Harmonie universelle*. Paris: S. Cramoisy, 1636-37.

Meyer, Kathi. "Einleitung" to the facs. ed. of Bottrigari's *Il Desiderio*. Veröffentlichungen der Musik-Bibliothek Paul Hirsch 5. Berlin: Martin Breslauer, 1924, pp. 5-28.

Mitchell, William J. "The Study of Chromaticism." *Journal of Music Theory*, VI (1962), 2-31.

———. "The Prologue to Orlando di Lasso's *Prophetiae Sibyllarum*." *The Music Forum*, II (1970), 264-73.

Monterosso, Raffaello. "L'estetica di Gioseffo Zarlino." *Chigiana*, Nuova serie, IV (1967), 13-28.

Monteverdi, Claudio. Letter prefacing his *Il quinto libro de madrigali a cinque voci*. Venice: Ricciardo Amadino, 1605.

———. *Lettere, dediche e prefazioni*, ed. Domenico de' Paoli. Rome: Edizioni De Santis, 1973.

Monteverdi, Giulio Cesare. "Dichiaratione della lettera stampata nel quinto libro de suoi madrigali," in Claudio Monteverdi. *Scherzi musicali a tre voci*. Venice: Ricciardo Amadino, 1607.

Morey, Carl. "The Diatonic, Chromatic, and Enharmonic Dances by Martino Pesenti." *Acta Musicologica*, XXXVIII (1966), 185-89.

Newcomb, Anthony A. *Music at the Court of Ferrara, 1550-1600*. Unpublished Ph.D. dissertation. Princeton University, 1969.

———. "Alfonso Fontanelli and the Ancestry of the Seconda Pratica Madrigal," in Robert L. Marshall, ed. *Studies in Renaissance and Baroque Music in Honor of Arthur Mendel*. Kassel: Bärenreiter, 1974, pp. 74-68.

Nick, Charles U. *A Stylistic Analysis of the Music of Nicola Vicentino*. Unpublished Ph.D. dissertation. Indiana University, 1967.

Palestrina, Pierluigi da. *Pope Marcellus Mass*, ed. Lewis Lockwood. New York: Norton, 1975.

Palisca, Claude V. *The Beginnings of Baroque Music. Its Roots in 16th-Century Theory and Polemics*. Unpublished Ph.D. dissertation. Harvard University, 1954.

———. "Girolamo Mei, Mentor to the Florentine Camerata." *The Musical Quarterly*, XL (1954), 1-20.

———. "Galilei," in Friedrich Blume, ed. *Die Musik in Geschichte und Gegenwart*, Vol. IV. Kassel and Basel: Bärenreiter, 1955, cols. 1265-70.

———. "Vincenzo Galilei's Counterpoint Treatise: A Code for the Seconda Pratica." *Journal of the American Musicological Society*, IX (1956), 81-96.

———. "A Clarification of 'Musica Reservata' in Jean Taisnier's 'Astrologiae,' 1559." *Acta Musicologica*, XXXI (1959), 133-61.

———. *Girolamo Mei: Letters on Ancient and Modern Music to Vincenzo Galilei and Giovanni Bardi*. Musicological Studies and Documents 3. N.p.: American Institute of Musicology, 1960.

———. "Vincenzo Galilei and Some Links between 'Pseudo-Monody' and Monody." *The Musical Quarterly*, XLVI (1960), 344-60.

———. "Scientific Empiricism in Musical Thought," in Hedley H. Rhys, ed. *Seventeenth-Century*

Science and Arts. Princeton: Princeton University Press, 1961, pp. 91-137.

————. Review of Lowinsky's *Tonality and Atonality. Journal of the American Musicological Society*, XVI (1963), 82-86.

————. "The Alterati of Florence. Pioneers in the Theory of Dramatic Music," in William W. Austin, ed. *New Looks at Italian Opera. Essays in Honor of Donald J. Grout*. Ithaca: Cornell University Press, 1968, pp. 9-38.

———— "The Artusi-Monteverdi Controversy," in Denis Arnold and Nigel Fortune, eds. *The Monteverdi Companion*. New York: W. W. Norton and Company, Inc., 1968, pp. 133-66.

————. "Introduction" to Zarlino, *The Art of Counterpoint*. New Haven and London: Yale University Press, 1968, pp. xiii-xxvi.

————. "Zarlino," in Friedrich Blume, ed. *Die Musik in Geschichte und Gegenwart*, Vol. XIV. Kassel and Basel: Bärenreiter, 1968, cols. 1017-22.

————. "The 'Camerata Fiorentina': A Reappraisal." *Studi musicali*, I (1972), 203-36.

————. "Towards an Intrinsically Musical Definition of Mannerism in the Sixteenth Century." *Studi Musicali*, III (1974), 313-46.

Panofsky, Erwin. *Galileo as a Critic of the Arts*. The Hague: Martinus Nijhoff, 1954.

————. *Studies in Iconology*. New York: Harper and Row, 1962.

————. *Idea. A Concept in Art Theory*. New York: Harper and Row, 1968.

Patrizi, Francesco. *Della Poetica*, ed. Danilo Aguzzi Barbagli. Florence: Istituto Nazionale di Studi sul Rinascimento, 1969-71.

Perkins, Leeman L. "Mode and Structure in the Masses of Josquin." *Journal of the American Musicological Society*, XXVI (1973), 189-239.

Pirrotta, Nino. "Temperaments and Tendencies in the Florentine Camerata." *The Musical Quarterly*, XL (1954), 169-89.

————. "Tragédie et comédie dans la Camerata fiorentina," in Jean Jacquot, ed. *Musique et poésie au XVIe siècle*. Paris: Éditions du Centre National de la Recherche Scientifique, 1954, pp. 287-97.

Pöhlmann, Egert. "Antikenverständnis und Antikenmissverständnis in der Operntheorie der Florentiner Camerata." *Die Musikforschung*, XXII (1969), 5-13.

Randel, Don M. "Emerging Triadic Tonality in the Fifteenth Century." *The Musical Quarterly*, LVII (1971), 73-86.

Rayner, Clare G. "The Enigmatic Cima: Meantone Tuning and Transpositions." *The Galpin Society Journal*, XXII (1969), 23-39.

Reese, Gustave. *Music in the Renaissance*, 2nd ed. New York: W. W. Norton and Company, Inc., 1959.

Reiner, Stuart. Review of *The Monteverdi Companion. Journal of the American Musicological Society*, XXIII (1970), 343-49.

Reiss, Josef. "Jo. Bapt. Benedictus, *De intervallis musicis*." *Zeitschrift für Musikwissenschaft*, VII (1924-25), 13-20.

Renouard, Antoine-Augustin. *Annales de l'imprimerie des Aldes, ou Histoire des trois Manuces et de leurs Éditions*, Vol. I. Paris: Renouard, 1803.

Riemann, Hugo. *History of Music Theory*, tr. from 2nd German ed., Berlin, 1920. Lincoln: University of Nebraska Press, 1962.

Ruhnke, Martin. "Lassos Chromatik und die Orgelstimmung," in Heinrich Hüschen and Dietz-Rüdiger Moser, eds. *Convivium musicorum. Festschrift Wolfgang Boetticher zum Sechzigsten Geburtstag am 19. August 1974*. Berlin: Verlag Merseburger, 1974, pp. 291-308.

Russel, Raymond. *The Harpsichord and Clavichord*. London: Faber and Faber, 1959.

Salinas, Francisco. *De Musica*. Salamanca: Mathias Gastius, 1577.

Salzer, Felix. *Structural Hearing: Tonal Coherence in Music*. 2nd ed.; New York: Dover Publications, Inc., 1962.

Schenker, Heinrich. *Der freie Satz*. 2nd ed.: Vienna: Universal Edition, 1956.

Schneider, Marius. "Die musikalischen Grundlagen der Sphärenharmonie." *Acta Musicologica*, XXXII (1960), 136-51.

Sesini, Ugo. "Studi sull'Umanesimo musicale: Ercole Bottrigari." *Convivium*, XIII (1941), 1-25.

Spitzer, Leo. *Classical and Christian Ideas of World Harmony. Prologomena to an Interpretation of the Word "Stimmung"*. Baltimore: The Johns Hopkins Press, 1963.

Stevenson, Robert. "Vicente Lusitano: New Light on His Career." *Journal of the American Musicological Society*, XV (1962), 72-77.

Strunk, Oliver, ed. *Source Readings in Music History. From Classical Antiquity through the Romantic Era*. New York: W. W. Norton and Company, 1950.

Terni, Clemente. "Galileo Galilei e la musica." *Chigiana*, Nuova serie, I (1964), 249-60.

Treitler, Leo. "Tone System in the Secular Works of Guillaume Dufay." *Journal of the American Musicological Society*, XVIII (1965), 131-69.

Valgulio, Carlo. *Plutarchi Chaeronei philosophi historicique clarissimi opuscula (quae quidem extant) omnia, undequaque collecta, et diligentissime jam pridem recognita*. Venice: Jo. Ant. et Fratres de Sabio, 1532.

Vicentino, Nicola. *L'antica musica ridotta alla moderna prattica*. Rome: Antonio Barre, 1555.

―――. *[Descrizione dell'arciorgano]*. Venice: Nicolo Bevil'acqua, 1561.

Walker, D. P. "Musical Humanism in the 16th and Early 17th Centuries." *The Music Review*, II (1941), 1-13, 111-21, 220-27, 288-308; III (1942), 55-71.

―――. "Bottrigari," in Friedrich Blume, ed. *Die Musik in Geschichte und Gegenwart*, Vol. II. Kassel and Basel: Bärenreiter, 1952, cols. 154-59.

―――. *Spiritual and Demonic Magic from Ficino to Campanella*. London: The Warburg Institute, 1958.

―――. "Kepler's Celestial Music." *Journal of the Warburg and Courtauld Institutes*, XXX (1967), 228-50.

―――. *The Ancient Theology*. London: Duckworth, 1972.

―――. "Some Aspects of the Musical Theory of Vincenzo Galilei and Galileo Galilei." *Proceedings of the Royal Musical Association*, C (1973-1974), 33-47.

Watkins, Glenn. *Gesualdo, The Man and His Music*. Chapel Hill: The University of North Carolina Press, 1973.

―――. "Carlo Gesualdo and the Delimitations of Late Mannerist Style." *Studi Musicali*, III (1974), 55-74.

Werner, Eric. "The Last Pythagorean Musician: Johannes Kepler," in Jan LaRue, ed. *Aspects of Medieval and Renaissance Music. A Birthday Offering to Gustave Reese*. New York: W. W. Norton and Company, 1966, pp. 867-82.

Wienpahl, Robert W. "Zarlino, the Senario, and Tonality." *Journal of the American Musicological Society*, XII (1959), 27-41.

Wittkower, Rudolf. *Architectural Principles in the Age of Humanism*. London: The Warburg Institute, 1949.

Yates, Frances A. *Giordano Bruno and the Hermetic Tradition*. Chicago: The University of Chicago Press, 1964.

―――. "The Hermetic Tradition in Renaissance Science," in Charles S. Singleton, ed. *Art, Science, and History in the Renaissance*. Baltimore: The Johns Hopkins Press, 1967, pp. 255-74.

Zarlino, Gioseffo. *Le Istitutioni harmoniche*. Venice: n.p., 1558.

―――. *The Art of Counterpoint. Part Three of 'Le Istitutioni harmoniche,' 1558*, tr. by Guy A. Marco and Claude V. Palisca. New Haven and London: Yale University Press, 1968.

―――. *Dimostrationi harmoniche*. Venice: Francesco de i Franceschi Senese, 1571.

―――. *Sopplimenti musicali*. Venice: Francesco de' Franceschi, Sanese, 1588.

Zenck, Hermann. "Zarlinos 'Istitutioni harmoniche' als Quelle zur Musikanschauung der italienischen Renaissance." *Zeitschrift für Musikwissenschaft*, XII (1930), 540-78.

————. ''Nicola Vicentinos 'L'Antica musica' (1555),'' in Zenck, Helmuth Schultz, and Walter Gerstenberg, eds. *Theodor Kroyer-Festschrift*. Regensburg: Gustav Bosse, 1933, pp. 86-101.

Index